REAL WORLD
IMAGE
SHARPENING

with Adobe Photoshop, Camera Raw, and Lightroom, Second Edition

BRUCE FRASER
JEFF SCHEWE

PEACHPIT PRESS
BERKELEY, CALIFORNIA

REAL WORLD IMAGE SHARPENING WITH ADOBE PHOTOSHOP, CAMERA RAW, AND LIGHTROOM, SECOND EDITION

Bruce Fraser and Jeff Schewe

Peachpit Press
1249 Eighth Street
Berkeley, CA 94710
510/524-2178
510/524-2221 (fax)

Find us on the Web at: www.peachpit.com
To report errors, please send a note to: errata@peachpit.com
Peachpit Press is a division of Pearson Education.
Published in association with Adobe Press
For the latest on Adobe Press books, go to: www.adobepress.com
Copyright © 2010 by Jeff Schewe

Editor: Rebecca Gulick
Production Editor: Lisa Brazieal
Copy Editor: Emily K. Wolman
Proofreader: Elle Yoko Suzuki
Compositor: WolfsonDesign
Indexer: Valerie Haynes Perry
Cover Design: Charlene Will
Cover Illustration: John Weber
Cover Photo: Jeff Schewe

13-digit ISBN: 978-0-321-63755-0
10-digit ISBN: 0-321-63755-0

9 8 7 6 5 4 3 2 1
Printed and bound in the United States of America

TABLE OF CONTENTS

PREFACE
Real World Sharpening

For almost 20 years, ever since it first shipped in 1990, Bruce and Jeff have labored in the vineyards of Photoshop, coaxing pixels to do our bidding. In that time, we've seen huge advances in the handling of image tone and color. When Bruce started digital imaging, getting the image to look the same on two different monitors was a major breakthrough, and matching the print to the screen appearance was the stuff of science fiction. Nowadays, it tends to be the rule rather than the exception.

We've made gargantuan strides in the handling of image tone and color, but when it comes to control of image *detail*, which is what this book is really about, we're still only a little more advanced than we were in 1990. It's just about impossible to make two different displays render image sharpness exactly the same way, and predicting print sharpness from the display is an exercise fraught with pitfalls and perils. In fact, we're back in the days of, "If you want to know what it will look like when you print it, print it and then look at it."

As a result, sharpening (and the equally important other side of the coin, noise reduction and smoothing) tends to be an *ad hoc* practice. We flail around until we get something that looks decent on the display and hope that appearance will somehow be transferred to the printed piece.

Photoshop CS4, Camera Raw, and Lightroom offer many powerful features for handling image detail. But how do you know what to aim for? This book contains a plethora of different sharpening tricks and techniques, but perhaps the most important contribution it strives to make is to provide you with an analytical framework that lets you think about sharpening in a new way. When we sharpen, we have to take at least three things into account:

* The relationship between image detail and system noise that's imposed by the capture medium—we want to sharpen image details but we don't want to exaggerate film grain or digital noise.

* The requirements of the image content—the wrong kind of sharpening can exaggerate texture we'd rather downplay, or even obscure detail instead of emphasizing it.

* The needs of the print process—when we translate pixels into marks on paper (or canvas, or any other substrate on which we print) we inevitably introduce some softness for which we try to compensate by sharpening.

The huge problem is that these needs often contradict one another.

THE SHARPENING WORKFLOW

The solution is the sharpening workflow. By treating each demand separately, we can assure that all are addressed optimally. To some, this may smack of heresy: Doesn't everyone know that you can sharpen an image only once? We demonstrate that multipass sharpening is not only feasible but optimal. It's simply impossible to address all the conflicting needs of image source, image content, and output process in a single round of sharpening.

That said, multipass sharpening demands care and attention to detail. Blasting images with multiple hits of sharpening can create a hideously oversharpened mess, which is why the conventional wisdom dictates that you sharpen only once. However, the techniques described in this book allow you to sharpen images safely and optimally.

The sharpening workflow confers another benefit. By separating sharpening for output from the other sharpening processes, it creates use-neutral master images that you can easily repurpose for different output processes, at different sizes and resolutions.

Sharpening and the Display

One of the hardest sharpening lessons to learn is that what you see on your computer display can be highly misleading. But the screen is often all you have to rely on for your judgments before output.

Some display technologies render images much more sharply than others—the same image almost invariably looks sharper on an LCD display than it does on a CRT. Display resolution also has an impact. We've gone to some lengths to debunk the polite fiction that computer screens display images at 72 pixels per inch, and have even given instructions that will let you determine the real resolution of *your* display, which is the one that really matters.

The most important lesson of all, however, is that good sharpening for print can often look terrible—really, hideously, horribly bad—on screen. Learning the relationship between what you see on *your* display and what shows up on hard copy is a vital skill this book helps you acquire.

Objective Realities

Some parts of the sharpening equation are determinate. Human visual acuity—the ability to discern fine details—has limits that are rooted in the physiology of the eye. The same visual properties that we exploit to produce the illusion of continuous tone from dots of four colors of ink also have a direct bearing on sharpening.

Print sharpening is also a determinate process. Any given print process will always translate pixels into dots in the same way, regardless of image source or image content, so for any print process, there's a right answer in terms of sharpening. (Of course, there are also many wrong ones.)

Creative Capacities

Sharpening is also a creative tool. We use sharpening to emphasize important detail (and sometimes we use blurring to suppress irrelevant, distracting detail), make a point, tell a story, invoke an emotion, or provide an illusion of three dimensions in our two-dimensional photographs. The sharpening workflow has a place for creativity, too. But it's important to know when to be creative and when to go by the numbers.

Multiple-Application Workflows

The first edition of this book dealt only with sharpening in Photoshop. For many reasons, a Photoshop-only workflow is no longer practical for most people using digital cameras. As a result of the changes in the industry (some of them helped by Bruce's philosophies) we wanted to describe and facilitate the approach of using the right tool for the job. Sometimes that won't be just Photoshop but may be Camera Raw or Lightroom or all three.

WHO NEEDS THIS BOOK?

If you work with images that are destined for hard copy, and you aren't totally confident about all your sharpening decisions, our hope is that you'll find this book beneficial. No matter whether you make your own prints, send them out to an online printing service, or deliver commercial work destined for offset press, the sharpening workflow can help you get the most out of your images.

This is not a book for Photoshop beginners, but neither is it a book only for Photoshop experts. Some of the techniques described herein use fairly esoteric Photoshop features with which you may or may not be familiar. Don't let that put you off. We've yet to encounter a piece of software that was smarter than its users, and Photoshop is no exception. Almost all the techniques in this book are nondestructive—they don't touch your original pixels—so you can't do any harm to your images by trying them.

How the Book Is Organized

We've tried to present all the information you need to build your own sharpening workflow.

The first two chapters look at the technical underpinnings of sharpening. Chapter 1, *What Is Sharpening?*, explores the fundamental nature of sharpening —what it does and how it works. Chapter 2, *Why Do We Sharpen?*, discusses the need for sharpening, and all the factors we need to address when we sharpen.

Chapter 3, *Sharpening Strategies*, provides an overview of the sharpening workflow and shows how it addresses each sharpening phase. Chapter 4, *Sharpening Tools,* describes the various tools that the sharpening workflow employs.

Chapter 5, *Industrial-Strength Sharpening Techniques*, shows how to use the tools described in Chapter 4 to satisfy the goals outlined in Chapter 3 by building a sharpening workflow from initial sharpening, through creative tweaking, all the way to final output.

Chapter 6, *Putting the Tools to Work*, shows how to create actions and do batch processing in Photoshop. It also emphasizes the importance of presets in Camera Raw and Lightroom. All of this is aimed at making your sharpening workflow efficient.

A WORD TO WINDOWS USERS

This book applies to both Windows and Mac OS. Since Bruce and Jeff have been using Macs for over 20 years, all the dialog boxes, menus, and palettes are illustrated using screen shots from the Mac OS version. Similarly, when discussing the many keyboard shortcuts in the program, we cite the Mac OS versions and try to include the Windows version. In every shortcut cited in this book, the Command key translates to the Ctrl key and the Option key translates to the Alt key. We apologize to all you Windows users for the small inconvenience, but because Photoshop is so close to being identical on both platforms, we picked the one we knew and ran with it.

THIS BOOK'S ORIGINS

Much of the material in this book is an outgrowth of work that Bruce Fraser originally did in the process of developing a commercial sharpening tool, PhotoKit Sharpener, from PixelGenius, LLC. Bruce was proud of PhotoKit Sharpener and was particularly proud to have been asked by Adobe to consult on the development of the advanced capture sharpening that went into Camera Raw 4.1 and Lightroom 1.1. While Bruce didn't get the chance to finish the consult, the Camera Raw team worked with Jeff to incorporate Bruce's capture-sharpening philosophies into Camera Raw and Lightroom.

PixelGenius is also proud that Adobe chose to work with us to adapt the PhotoKit Sharpener technology for Lightroom and Camera Raw. We appreciate that the Camera Raw and Lightroom teams have exhibited such respect to what Bruce thought was his most important contribution to the industry: the development of the concept of a sharpening workflow and its components; capture, creative, and output sharpening.

IMAGE CREDITS

Most of the images in the book were shot either by Bruce Fraser or Jeff Schewe. We are indebted to Martin Evening for the use of two of his images, which are credited in-place.

THANK YOU!

We couldn't have written this book without the excellent support of our publishing team, which includes Rebecca Gulick, Editor; Lisa Brazieal, Production Editor; Emily K. Wolman, Development and Copy Editor; Elle Yoko Suzuki, Proofreader; Owen Wolfson, Compositor; Valerie Haynes Perry, Indexer; Charlene Will, Cover Designer; and John Weber, Cover Illustrator.

Thanks to our pals and partners in PixelGenius, LLC—Martin Evening, Mac Holbert, Seth Resnick, and Andrew Rodney, for being the finest bunch of people with whom it has ever been our pleasure and privilege to work. An even bigger vote of thanks goes to the late Mike Skurski, our founding engineer, without whom we would never have been able to produce a successful software product. We all miss you. And thanks to the Pixel Mafia—you know who you are!

We also owe a debt of gratitude to the Knoll brothers (John and Thomas) for having the good sense to create Photoshop in the first place, as well as longtime engineer Mark Hamburg, with whom we've had the good fortune to work for many years. Our thanks also go out to the Lightroom team for their help and support.

And as always, Bruce would have wanted to thank his lovely wife, Angela, for being his best friend and partner, for supporting him in all his activities, and for making his life such a very happy one. Jeff thanks his wife, Rebecca, and daughter, Erica, for putting up with all the late hours (and missed family time) book writing seems to require.

CHAPTER ONE

What Is Sharpening?

And How Does It Work?

An old saw in photography goes, "If you want great prints, use a tripod!" While it's usually delivered half-jokingly, the important grain of truth is that one of the ways our brains try to make sense of the world as seen through our eyes is by breaking down the scene into edges (objects) and non-edges (surfaces). If the edges in an image appear too sharp or not sharp enough, our brains tell us that there's something wrong, and in the case of a photograph, the image appears unconvincing.

Sharpening is arguably one of the most important yet least understood aspects of digital image reproduction. Examples of badly sharpened images are easy to find—you probably need look no further than your daily newspaper or favorite magazine. Good sharpening, on the other hand, is invisible.

Sharpening can't fix sloppy focus or a shaky camera. What it can and should do is to ensure that the sharpness of the original capture is carried through faithfully to the final output. Of course, sometimes we also use sharpening to improve reality—we may add some extra snap to the eyes and hair in a head shot, for example. But the primary purpose of sharpening is *not* to rescue overly soft images, but simply to counteract the inevitable softening that happens when we turn photons into pixels and pixels into marks on paper.

In Chapter 2, we'll look at the various factors that give rise to the need for sharpening. But before we examine those, let's look at how sharpening works, whether it's done in a wet darkroom using analog tools or accomplished digitally either in the camera or in Adobe Photoshop, Adobe Camera Raw, or Adobe Lightroom.

Emphasizing Edges

Sharpening works by increasing the contrast around edges. Edges in images always involve darker tonal values adjacent to lighter ones. We can emphasize the edges by making the dark tonal values darker and the light tonal values lighter.

In the analog darkroom, this was accomplished using an *unsharp mask*. (See the sidebar "Why Is It Called 'Unsharp Mask' When It's Used to Sharpen?" for details on just how this process worked.) In the digital domain, we sharpen by identifying the dark and light pixels that represent edges, and then we lower the value of the dark pixels to make them darker and raise the value of the light pixels to make them lighter.

This adjustment creates a "halo" that makes the edges, and, hence, the entire image, seem sharper. The concept is simple, but as with many things in digital imaging, the devil is in the details that we discuss throughout this book!

Figure 1-1 shows the same image before and after sharpening. (The image also illustrates the pitfalls of driving in rural Scotland—a good metaphor for the myriad things that can go wrong when we use sharpening inappropriately.)

Figure 1-1 Before and after sharpening

Unsharpened   Sharpened

The only difference between the two versions is the sharpening. Figure 1-2 shows a zoomed-in comparison with an accompanying graph of the values of a single row of pixels before and after sharpening.

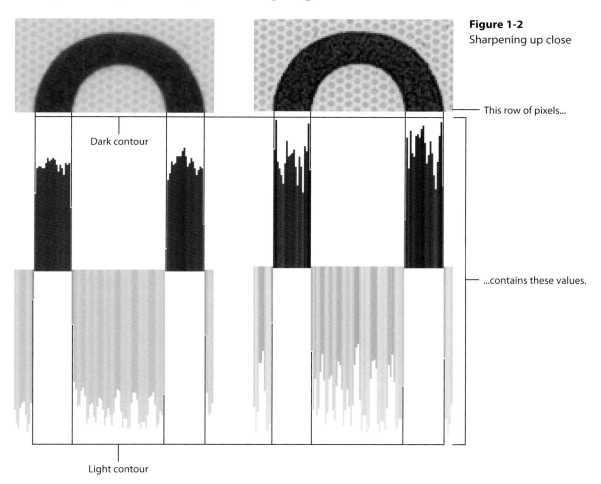

Figure 1-2
Sharpening up close

This row of pixels...

...contains these values.

Dark contour

Light contour

Notice that the tonal range—the distance between the lightest and darkest tones—of the sharpened version is wider than that of the unsharpened version. Also notice that the biggest differences occur at the edge transitions of the capital O, while smaller differences emphasize the texture of the sign's background.

Sharpening is closely related to contrast, but simply increasing the contrast over an entire image just produces an over-contrasted image. Successful sharpening demands that we localize the contrast boost to those parts of the image that actually represent edges.

Why Is It Called "Unsharp Mask" When It's Used to Sharpen?

Sharpening predates digital imaging by many decades. If you've often wondered why one of Photoshop's main sharpening tools is named the Unsharp Mask filter when it's supposed to make the image sharper, rest assured that you're not alone.

The name originated from an analog wet-darkroom technique that increases the apparent sharpness of a photographic print using a duplicate of the negative to create a mask that increases contrast along the edges. The original and the duplicate negatives are placed on either side of a piece of glass—often just plain old window glass—and the entire sandwich is placed in the enlarger's negative carrier.

When the enlarger is focused on the bottom negative, the top, out-of-focus copy creates a contrast mask that boosts the contrast along the edges in the image. Meanwhile, the out-of-focus dark contour burns the dark side of the edges and the out-of-focus light contour dodges the light side of the edges.

This technique is called "unsharp masking" because the mask—the top negative—is out of focus and, hence, isn't sharp. In short, it's an unsharp mask that has the effect of increasing the apparent sharpness in the print!

So the "unsharp" in "unsharp mask" refers to the mask, not the result, and it's this analog technique that Photoshop's Unsharp Mask filter replicates (though with much more control than its analog counterpart).

Analog Roots

As a photographic practice, sharpening has its roots in the analog world. However, the analog unsharp masking technique offered only two controls:

- The distance between the two negatives (the thickness of the glass) controlled the width of the sharpening halo.

- The exposure time controlled the strength of the contrast boost.

The tedious alignment, limited control, and uncertain results prevented unsharp masking from becoming a mainstream practice in analog photography. But it did see considerable use in sharpening analog color separations for offset printing. It was done by making a blurred duplicate of the continuous-tone separation and then printing it together with the sharp version as a contact print, after which the separation was screened for halftone lines (lines of dots per inch).

Sharpening for continuous-tone photographic prints was something of a luxury, but when the continuous-tone original was turned into cyan, magenta, yellow, and black dots of ink, some of the original sharpness was lost. So sharpening became, and remains to this day, a standard operation in prepress. When the drum scanner replaced the stat camera (stationary camera used to shoot film from camera-ready artwork), digital sharpening became the norm.

DIGITAL PROCESSING

Digital sharpening tools offer far more precision, control, and options than the analog darkroom ever did. The inevitable downside is that with greater control comes greater responsibility, and the more options on offer, the more opportunities for mistakes, as we'll demonstrate throughout this book.

Unsharp Mask Filter

Photoshop's Unsharp Mask (USM) filter is a process that is similar to the analog version of sharpening. It creates an unseen (meaning you never see it) blurred version of the image in the background and uses the difference between the original version and the blurred version to determine edges that will be sharpened. Figure 1-3 shows a graphical representation of how Photoshop's USM filter works.

Figure 1-3 shows an original unsharpened image. The original layer was duplicated and the second layer was blurred three pixels using the Gaussian Blur filter. The blurred copy layer was set to Difference mode. To show the resulting difference, we've added a strong Levels adjustment layer to emphasize the results.

In the last image, the result of placing the layers in Difference mode was loaded as a selection (where white allows an effect and black resists) and used as a layer mask for a Curves adjustment to lighten the light edges and darken the dark edges. This is essentially the same function as the USM Radius and Amount adjustments, and is the basis of most digital sharpening algorithms.

Figure 1-3 Unsharp masking as simulated in Photoshop

Original image layer

Duplicated layer blurred three pixels

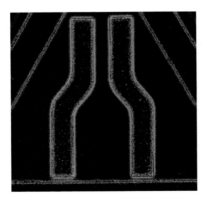

Blurred image over original image in Difference blend mode

Difference mode used as a mask to change contrast

The Threshold adjustment determines how much of a difference there must be between the blurred and unblurred copy before the sharpening process is applied. With a zero threshold, the sharpening would be applied to any difference. The higher the threshold, the less the sharpening will be applied for lower contrast edges. Figure 1-4 shows the result of increasing the threshold.

Increasing the threshold from zero to 50 means that only the higher contrast edges will be sharpened—the lower contrast edges will not.

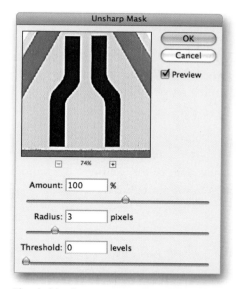

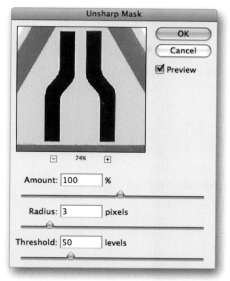

Figure 1-4 Threshold adjustment

Threshold at 0   Threshold at 50

Digital Noise Reduction

There are other digital sharpening algorithms above and beyond Photoshop's USM filter, and we cover them extensively in this book. However, there's one key difference between digital and analog sharpening with which we have to contend in varying degrees: the handling of noise. Analog sharpening rarely increased noise and often had the effect of reducing it, because the mask was made from a different piece of film than the original, so the distribution of the film grain—the main noise component in film images—was different. This had the desirable effect of making the noise in the mask cancel out the noise in the original. With digital sharpening, we aren't so lucky.

When it comes to digital sharpening, noise reduction is the flip side of the same coin. Sharpening tools such as Photoshop's USM filter evaluate one pixel at a time, determining how different it is from its neighbors. If the difference is great enough, the filter decides that this pixel represents an edge and adjusts its value accordingly.

The inherent problem is that the computer has no way of knowing whether the pixel differences represent real image information or noise, so unless we take steps to prevent it, most sharpening routines emphasize the noise as well as the edges. If you refer back to Figure 1-2, you'll see that the capital O in the sharpened version of the image is much noisier than in the unsharpened one.

However, if you refer even further back to Figure 1-1, it's unlikely that you'll see any objectionable noise in the printed reproduction at that size. The noise is confined to dark tones in small areas. Figure 1-5, on the other hand, shows what can happen if we fail to take noise into account.

Figure 1-5 Noise problems

Full image shows where the detail section came from.

This version was processed with no noise reduction and no sharpening.

This version was sharpened globally, emphasizing noise as well as detail.

This version had noise reduction applied before sharpening, and had sharpening applied through a mask.

This image is something of a "bad-case" scenario, shot at ISO 1600 on a fairly noisy digital SLR. It would have been a worst-case scenario if the shot had been unexposed, but it dramatizes the point that we must take noise into account when we sharpen if we don't want our images to appear like sandpaper.

In many cases, we can prevent the sandpaper effect simply by protecting the noisy areas from sharpening. But in extreme cases like the one shown in Figure 1-5, some more proactive noise reduction may be needed before the application of sharpening.

Digital noise reduction is essentially the opposite of sharpening. Instead of increasing localized contrast, it reduces it, thereby rendering the noise less visible or even removing it entirely. Of course, the inevitable catch is that as it reduces the noise it also de-emphasizes the edges, making the image softer.

So one of the first key skills to master in sharpening is striking the right balance between emphasizing edges and reducing noise—walking the fine line between sharpness and sandpaper. Overly aggressive noise reduction creates an irreparably soft image, so noise reduction must be used with caution, and always should be done prior to sharpening (otherwise we sharpen the noise as well as the image). Most of the time, simply making sure that we don't sharpen noise does the trick. But when images are captured on high-speed film or at high ISO settings on a digital camera, we may have to do a little more to reduce noise.

Sharpening and Pixels

All digital sharpening is carried out on pixels. Throughout this book, we'll examine images at the pixel level to see what happens to the pixels through various stages of image reproduction. But, with the exception of images destined for on-screen display on the Web or in an information kiosk, the final product is not pixels but, rather, marks on paper or some other substrate.

The physical relationship between the image pixels on a display and the marks on paper is rarely obvious. In conventional halftone printing—the kind we use on printing presses—it typically takes between two and four pixels to form a single halftone dot in grayscale printing. When we print in color, this relationship is even less obvious, since the halftone dots are spread across four different color plates.

Inkjet printers use a different type of screening, but again, the relationship between printer dots is complicated. Even in the relatively simple scenario of printing to a true continuous-tone printer, where the pixels are reproduced one-to-one, the pixels on the print are typically much smaller than the same pixels on screen.

We can't control how the pixels get turned into printer dots, yet we can control the degree of contrast boost and the size of the pixels on output. In so doing, we control, in turn, the width of the sharpening halo. The goal is to avoid haloes that our eyes pick out as discrete features, while making them strong enough and just wide enough to produce a sharpening effect.

Since we can control only the final size of the pixels, we must do our final sharpening at final output size and resolution to get the sharpening halo right. If the image is resized after sharpening, the haloes either get bigger and visually obvious, or they become too small and we lose the sharpening effect.

For some people, that means that *all* sharpening must be deferred until the image is at output size; otherwise, multiple rounds of sharpening will destroy the image. That's one of the notions this book seeks to challenge: It's certainly true that multiple rounds of sharpening *can* destroy the image, and that the final, critical round of sharpening must be tailored to the output process and applied to the final image pixels. But throughout this book, we argue that optimal sharpening simply cannot be accomplished by a single pass of sharpening at the end of the image preparation process. This is because the softening that occurs when pixels are turned into print dots is only one of several, often competing factors that must be addressed.

In the next chapter, we'll look at all of the different factors we must take into account when we sharpen.

CHAPTER TWO

Why Do We Sharpen?

And What Must We Take Into Account When We Do So?

Whenever we turn photons into pixels, we lose some degree of sharpness. No matter how high-resolution our capture devices or how expensive our lenses, they sample a fixed grid of pixels and are thus limited. So cameras (and scanners) turn the continuous gradations of tone and color that exist in the real world into discrete pixels of the digital world. When the pixels are small enough, they provide the convincing *illusion* of continuous tone, but it *is* just an illusion. Image sharpening is one of the things we simply must do to make the illusion convincing.

The reason that sharpening is such a complex topic (and the reason for this book) is that successful sharpening requires the consideration of several potentially competing factors. These factors, which we'll discuss in detail in this chapter, fall into three basic categories:

- The image source
- The image content
- The image use

For decades, the standard operating procedure has been to punt on the issue of how and when to sharpen, and just try to handle all sharpening in one single pass, usually at the end of image processing, just before output. With film scans, this worked after a fashion, though we suspect the results were rarely optimal. With most digital captures, the results are even less likely to be optimal simply due to how most digital cameras work.

Does My Image Need Sharpening?

Yes. Even if your image appears reasonably sharp when viewed at Actual Pixels (the Adobe Photoshop View menu command that displays the image at 100% zoom) on your computer display, the image will need sharpening depending on the final use. Of course, if your image appears in soft focus in Actual Pixels view, it definitely needs sharpening no matter what the final use.

One of the harshest sharpening lessons we've learned is that it's extremely difficult to make judgments about output sharpening by looking at pixels on a computer display. If your images are destined for a specific type of display—for example, a kiosk—ideally, you should look at the images on that display before making any final judgments. Barring that, use the display as a guide, as explained in the "The Display as a Guide" section, below.

Sharpening and Displays

NOTE: You'll notice that we refer to the screen that connects to your computer that allows you to see images as a "display." A computer "monitor" is something that monitors your computer, not a display. We realize this is a small distinction, but we have good friends in the computer industry who would complain if we referred to the device on which we view images as a "monitor."

Unless a TV or computer display is your final output, making images look sharp on the display almost invariably results in an under-sharpened printed output. But even displays themselves vary hugely in the way they reproduce sharpness.

Display Technologies

LCDs (liquid crystal displays) are much sharper than CRT (cathode-ray tube) displays when set to their native resolution. An image that looks sharp on an LCD device may still look soft on a CRT, and an image that looks sharp on a CRT display may look slightly crunchy on an LCD.

If your images are being prepared for the Web, realize that you have very little control over what the other billion or so Web users will see. Nowadays, many more users have LCDs than CRT displays. In fact, CRTs are no longer being made. All you can do is aim for the middle of a very large barn door, but remember that an LCD is likely to be more representative of the general Web population than is a CRT.

Display Resolution

The resolution of the display also has a major impact on how we see image sharpness. An image that looks pleasingly sharp on a display running at 1600 x 1200 shows obvious, less-pleasing sharpening haloes on the same display running at 1024 x 768. The pixels are displayed at a larger size when the display is run at 1024 x 768, so the sharpening haloes become bigger and, thus, more obvious.

Again, if you're sharpening images for the Web, you need to aim for the "average" display resolution, which is probably closer to 1024 x 768 than 1600 x 1200.

The Display as a Guide

Sharpening for use on a display is an uncertain endeavor unless you know the exact display for which you're sharpening. Yet a much bigger issue is how to use the display as a *guide* for print sharpening. The easy answer is, unfortunately, that there are no easy answers!

Luckily, the situation isn't entirely hopeless—it's just challenging. The fundamental concern that should always be foremost in your mind is the actual size of the pixels on output. But to understand the relationship between what you see on the screen and what you get on output, some additional information is useful.

First, determine the display's true resolution. Many of us tend to leave unquestioned the polite fiction that computer displays have a resolution of 72 pixels per inch (ppi). This is often not the case—in fact, it's quite unlikely that your display's resolution is exactly 72 ppi, though it may be close.

Display vendors usually specify the size of the image area as a diagonal measurement, which makes for a big number but isn't the actual resolution. Determining the display's true resolution is a simple exercise that requires no equipment more complicated than a tape measure:

1.   Using a tape measure, measure the *width,* in inches, of the image area on your display.

2.   Divide the number of horizontal pixels that your display can show by the number of inches from Step 1.

     The resulting number is the true resolution of your display in pixels per inch.

For example, the horizontal image area of both of Jeff's main LCDs (a 30" NEC 3090WXi and an Apple 30" Cinema) is 25.25 inches. The native resolution for both is 2560 x 1600 pixels, so the actual resolution is 101.4 ppi. A third LCD has a resolution of 1920 x 1200 pixels and is running at 87.8 ppi.

The image area on CRTs is more variable than on LCDs, because the geometry controls let you adjust the picture size.

Table 2-1 shows the approximate resolutions for typical display sizes and pixel dimensions.

Table 2-1 True display resolution

Display size	Pixel dimensions	Resolution (ppi)
30" LCD	2560 x 1600	101
21" LCD	1600 x 1200	95
	1280 x 1024	76
	1024 x 768	61
	800 x 600	47
21/22" CRT	1920 x 1440	122
	1600 x 1200	102
	1280 x 1024	82
	1152 x 870	74
	1024 x 768	65
	800 x 600	51
17" laptop	1920 x 1200	133
15" laptop	1440 x 900	100

Knowing your display's true resolution is the key to understanding the relationship between the pixels you see on your display and the final printed results.

If your display is around 100 ppi and you're printing at around 240 ppi, viewing the image at 50% will give you a truer picture of the final sharpening. Similarly, if your display is around 75 ppi and you're printing at 300 ppi, the 25% view will give you a closer idea of final sharpness than any of the higher zoom percentages. It still won't be perfect—Adobe Photoshop's downsampling algorithms, regardless of the version, have a different effect on sharpness than do the mechanisms by which printers or platesetters turn image pixels into dots—but it'll be a lot closer than the Actual Pixels (100%) view. See the sidebar "How Does Photoshop Display Images?" for information about changes in Photoshop CS4's display engine.

Thus the problem remains: You simply cannot reliably judge image sharpening intended for printed output on a computer display. Even if you reduce the screen zoom, you are still evaluating your higher-resolution image on a low-resolution device. Neither the image sharpening nor image noise nor grain can be displayed accurately at a reduced zoom. The effective resolution of the display will be a third to a quarter of the resolution contained in the image.

How Does Photoshop Display Images?

Photoshop CS4 takes the open image (or images) and scales it down (downsamples) from its actual resolution to a size and resolution for on-screen display. In previous versions of Photoshop, users had to avoid odd zoom percentages because Photoshop scaled images for display using a Nearest Neighbor interpolation for speed. The 50%, 25%, and conceivably the 12.5% views preserved sharpness reasonably well, but the odd zoom percentages (66.7%, 33.3%, and intermediate zoom percentages) did not, because Photoshop applied fairly strong anti-aliasing (partial filling of edge pixels to create smooth line edges) to those zoom levels. Photoshop CS4's ability to use your computer's video card's GPU (graphics processing unit) for display enhancements is a major change in how Photoshop can display images.

With the Enable OpenGL Drawing option checked, Photoshop uses high-precision modeling and smoothing by using a bilinear interpolation when scaling images for on-screen display. However, while this is a great improvement in display quality, it further complicates an already complicated situation, because not everybody has suitable video cards, or users may need to turn off the Enable OpenGL Drawing for compatibility reasons. And while it certainly can make a wide range of display percentages look good, the GPU doesn't magically add any resolution to your display. So your computer's display is still a low-resolution viewing device (even if it looks a lot better in Photoshop CS4).

The only really reliable method of actually seeing your image pixels is to evaluate the image at a screen zoom of 100%, where one image pixel will be displayed on one display pixel. Only at this 1:1 ratio can you see what image detail is contained in the image. The problem with this is that at 1:1, the image will be two to four times larger than the printed dimensions. At that size, the relationship of image detail to printed detail is inaccurate. Thus there are no good solutions short of making a print and evaluating it.

The key point to all this is that when we look at sharpening on a display, we're viewing it "through a glass, darkly" (though the Apostle Paul doubtless had something else in mind when he coined the phrase). At some fairly far-off future date, we may benefit from some technology that compensates for the large variation in the ways different displays show the same pixels' sharpness, just as color management currently lets us compensate for the way different displays show the same pixels' colors.

But that day won't come soon. Until then, you'll have to learn to make that compensation in your head. This is not trivial, but is it not impossible. First, you need to understand the size relationship between your pixels on screen and your pixels on output. Then it's a matter of learning the behavior of your display, and making constant comparisons between what it shows you and what ends up in print, so that you gain experience as to what will work. Throughout the remainder of this book, we'll provide pointers as to the kinds of things to look for.

SHARPENING ISSUES

As photographers and digital imaging artists, we are confronted by a variety of sharpening issues. Most prominent is the inevitable softening that occurs whenever we digitize, or turn a continuous stream of photons into discrete square pixels. No matter how good our lenses, no matter how high-resolution our digital cameras or scanners, the digitization process always loses some apparent sharpness.

In addition, there are the normal photographic aspects that impact sharpness, such as camera or subject blur, lens diffraction, optical defects, and issues of film grain or sensor noise.

Further softening occurs on output, when we translate image pixels to printer dots. Each output process has its own requirements for sharpening—we must apply very different sharpening to the same pixels printed at 300 ppi on a continuous-tone printer than at 300 ppi on a 150-line screen halftone printer.

Last but not least are the issues presented by the image content itself. A forest of trees needs different sharpening treatment than a model's headshot. Sharpening that emphasizes the fine detail in the trees turns the model's skin into a moonscape, while sharpening that emphasizes the model's eyes and lips may obscure the detail in the forest. Somehow, we have to reconcile the various and often contradictory needs of the image source, the image content, and the output process.

We'll spend the rest of this chapter looking at these disparate demands in detail, because until they're understood and addressed, sharpening won't do justice to the image—and may actually do more harm than good.

IMAGE SOURCES

The image source imposes its own signature and its own limitations on the image. The signature is the relationship between the noise that we want to de-emphasize and the detail that we want to emphasize. The limitations are the degree to which the image can be enlarged and the smallest details that can be captured.

In part, enlargement is limited by the gross pixel count, especially with digital captures. But the noise signature also plays a role—we typically scan film to obtain a significantly higher pixel count than digital captures offer, yet film scans cannot withstand as much enlargement as a digital capture of equivalent pixel dimensions. This is because digital captures generally have less noise than scanned film: The interaction between the film grain and the scanner's pixel grid exaggerates the grain to produce a noise signature that's stronger than noise from digital cameras.

NOTE: Much more heat than light has been generated in discussions of the equivalent information content of digital and film captures. Without adding too much fuel to the fire, our experience tells us that 35mm film scanned at 6300 ppi (creating a file approximately 8900 x 5700 pixels) has about the same potential for enlargement as a digital capture in the 6 to 8 megapixel range (approximately 3000-3500 x 2000-2350 pixels). This is a very approximate rule of thumb.

Detail, Film Grain, and Scanner Noise

A primary sharpening challenge lies in emphasizing detail without emphasizing noise. We can often accomplish this by simply protecting the noisy areas from sharpening. In more extreme cases, we may need to apply some noise reduction prior to sharpening. (We'll discuss specific techniques for doing both in Chapter 4, "Sharpening Tools.")

Many of the techniques you'll need to deploy depend on the final use of the image. Downsampling can hide a great deal of noise, making the image easier to sharpen, so for one-off uses at sizes that are small enough to allow downsampling by 50% or more, noise may be less of a concern. But as we approach the practical size limitations of the capture, the noise becomes ever more obvious and may need special handling.

Scanned transparencies, scanned negatives, and digital captures all have their own noise characteristics. They share the property that noise increases with higher ISO (International Standards Organization) ratings, but they differ in important ways too. First, let's look at scanned film.

Transparency Film Grain

The grain in scanned film becomes visually obvious at scanning resolutions far below that required to resolve individual grains. (Resolving individual grains would require scanning at ridiculously high resolutions of around 11,000 ppi, providing no more usable image information than a lower-resolution scan.)

Grain is most obvious in small formats like 35mm, and much less obvious in medium or large-format transparencies. However, much of the image noise comes not from the grain itself, but from the interaction of the grain, the scanner's sampling grid, and any digital noise introduced by the scanner.

The grain in color transparencies tends to be monochromatic, but the scanner noise is typically strongest in the blue channel, since the blue filter is the least efficient in terms of allowing light to pass through. As a result, transparency grain often shows up at its strongest in clear blue skies, though close examination of the pixels shows that the grain is present in the other channels, albeit to a lesser extent.

Figure 2-1 shows three views of typical scanned 35mm transparency noise:

- The first view is an attempt to show the actual image pixels, printed at 72 ppi. Note, however, that the grain viewed on screen actually looks worse than the grain in print due to the softening effect of the halftone process.

- The second view is a "contact print" that reproduces the actual scanned pixels at 300 ppi, the optimal resolution for the 150-line screen with which this book is printed. This view represents the optimal enlargement one can reasonably attempt from this capture. (On many images, we can drop the resolution to 225 ppi, and hence make a bigger print, but fine diagonal features will usually suffer.)

- The third view shows the entire image, still unsharpened, but downsampled to 300 ppi. The image appears reasonably sharp and more or less grain-free, due to the massive downsampling—the image is now only 16% of the original captured size.

Figure 2-2 shows noise reduction and sharpening for the image at the contact print resolution. The sharpened version was created by applying noise reduction and preliminary sharpening, and selectively using layer masks to isolate the edges on the full-resolution 6300-ppi capture. The image was resized (but not resampled) to 300-ppi, and then sharpening was applied, which was tuned to the halftone printing process.

For the downsampled image, the preliminary sharpening and noise reduction for the optimally sharpened version were performed on the full-resolution 6300-ppi capture. Then the image was downsampled to 300 ppi using Photoshop's Bicubic Sharper algorithm and sharpened for the halftone process.

The differences between Figures 2-1 and 2-2 are much more subtle on the downsampled version than they are in the contact print, reinforcing the point that final output size makes a big difference. Also, note how crunchy and oversharpened the zoomed-in view appears. If one were sharpening by eye, it's unlikely that one would be willing to take the sharpening and noise reduction this far.

Figure 2-1 Noise in scanned transparency

This zoomed-in view shows the unsharpened pixels from a 35mm transparency scanned at 6300 ppi, printed at 72 ppi.

This view shows a larger section of the unsharpened image printed at 300 ppi to produce the maximum size the capture can support optimally. (The full-sized image would be approximately 20" x 30".)

This view shows the entire image downsampled to 300 ppi, with the zoomed area above outlined in black. The image is still unsharpened, but the noise is largely rendered invisible due to the downsampling.

Figure 2-2 Scanned transparency with noise reduction and sharpening

This zoomed-in view shows the pixel crop from the scan printed at 72 ppi. This has undergone noise reduction, selective sharpening, and final output sharpening. At this zoomed-in view, the image appears over sharpened.

This view shows a larger section of the reduced noise and sharpened image printed at 300 ppi. This is the output size for which the noise reduction and sharpening was intended.

This view shows the entire image downsampled to 300 ppi with noise reduction and sharpening applied. Note that the output sharpening was applied after downsampling using Photoshop's Bicubic Sharper interpolation algorithm.

Figure 2-3 shows the individual color channels of the unsharpened scan in the same Actual Pixels view as the first illustration in Figure 2-1, and how dramatically noisier the blue channel is than the red or green. This is more a function of scanner noise than film grain. The blue tricolor separation filters in most scanners are terribly inefficient and absorb a lot of light, so less light is gathered in the blue channel of the film scan. The purpose of the figure is to convey an impression of typical grain in a transparency scan, and to show its diminishing influence as we reduce the image size.

Figure 2-3 Noise in scanned transparencies by channel

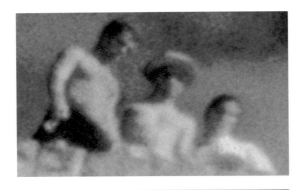

This zoomed-in view shows the unsharpened pixels from the red channel.

This zoomed-in view shows the unsharpened pixels from the green channel.

This zoomed-in view shows the unsharpened pixels from the blue channel. Notice how much more obvious the noise in the blue channel is compared to the red or green.

Color Negative Film Grain

Grain is typically much more obvious in scanned color negatives than in scanned transparencies. It's not that color negative material is inherently grainier than transparencies, but color negatives record a wide dynamic range from the scene and compress it into a narrow dynamic range on film. When we scan the less contrasty negative film, we expand that narrow dynamic range recorded on the negative film using tone curves. In so doing, we exaggerate the grain more than we do with color transparencies.

As with a color transparency, noise is a product of the film grain, the scanner's sampling grid, and the noise introduced by the scanner. However, the color negative's noise signature is noticeably different from that of transparency film. Noise in color negatives manifests itself as color noise rather than monochromatic noise, and thus demands a different treatment.

Moreover, while the degree to which we have to address grain separately from sharpening depends on the enlargement factor needed, just as it does with transparency film, color negative requires more aggressive treatment, and requires it at lower enlargement factors, than transparency film.

Figure 2-4 shows the typical noise before sharpening from a 35mm color negative scanned at 6300 ppi, using the same view sizing as Figure 2-1:

- The first image is an Actual Pixels view printed at 72 ppi. Again, remember that the on-screen appearance is a little worse than the print you see here due to the softening effect of the halftone process.

- The second image is a contact print view showing a snippet of the image made by printing the captured pixels at 300 ppi—the full-sized image would be around 20" x 30".

- The third image is the full image downsampled to 300 ppi.

The extreme downsampling to 300 ppi in the bottom image mitigates the grain by downsampling the grain almost out of existence. But the contact print view shows that grain in color negative scans is stronger and a bigger problem than that in transparency scans, and hence requires special handling at lower magnification factors than color transparencies.

As a result, traditional prepress has generally shunned color negatives in favor of transparencies, no matter the film format. Reproducing images from 35mm color negative is certainly challenging, but it's by no means impossible to produce good results. Shooting larger-format film reduces the grain problem by reducing the enlargement factor, which is why prepress has generally preferred the larger formats.

Figure 2-4 Noise in scanned color negative

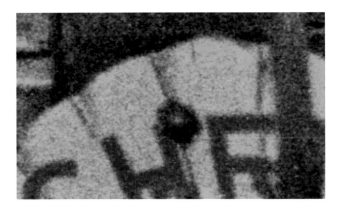

This zoomed-in view shows the unsharpened pixels from a 35mm color negative scanned at 6300 ppi, printed at 72 ppi.

This view shows a larger section of the unsharpened image printed at 300 ppi to produce the maximum size the capture can support optimally. (The full-sized image would be approximately 20" x 30".)

This view shows the entire image downsampled to 300 ppi, with the zoomed area above outlined in white. The image is still unsharpened, but the noise is largely rendered invisible due to the downsampling.

Figure 2-5 shows noise reduction and sharpening for the image at the contact print resolution. The sharpened version was created by applying noise reduction and preliminary sharpening, and selectively using layer masks to

Figure 2-5 Scanned color negative with noise reduction and sharpening

This zoomed-in view shows the pixel crop from the scan printed at 72 ppi. This has undergone noise reduction, selective sharpening, and final output sharpening. At this zoomed-in view, the image looks oversharpened but the noise (grain) has been reduced.

This view shows a larger section of the reduced noise and sharpened image printed at 300 ppi. This is the output size for which the noise reduction and sharpening was intended.

This view shows the entire image downsampled to 300 ppi with noise reduction and sharpening applied. Note that the output sharpening was applied after downsampling using Photoshop's Bicubic Sharper interpolation algorithm.

isolate the edges on the full-resolution 6300-ppi capture. The image was resized (but not resampled) to 300 ppi, and then sharpening was applied, which was tuned to the halftone printing process.

For the downsampled image, the preliminary sharpening and noise reduction for the sharpened version were performed on the full-resolution 6300-ppi capture. Then the image was downsampled to 300 ppi using Photoshop's Bicubic Sharper algorithm and sharpened for the halftone process.

Figure 2-6 Channel noise in scanned color negatives

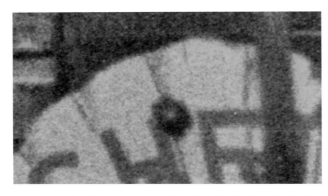

This zoomed-in view shows the unsharpened pixels from the red channel.

This zoomed-in view shows the unsharpened pixels from the green channel.

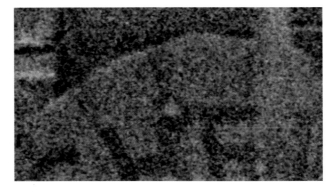

This zoomed-in view shows the unsharpened pixels from the blue channel. Notice that for the color negative scan, all three channels are showing considerable noise.

Figure 2-6 shows the actual pixels from the individual channels. Again, the blue channel is the noisiest of the three due to the physics of the scanner, but the color negative shows more noise in the green and blue channels than the transparency shows. This increased noise (or grain) is a function of the increase of the contrast of lower contrast color negative material with a final tone curve applied.

With the color negative, the difference between the two versions is more obvious than with the transparency example, even in the downsampled version. So clearly, grain is a more pressing concern with color negative than with transparency, though it varies with enlargement factor.

DETAIL, NOISE, AND DIGITAL CAPTURE

Noise in digital captures differs from the noise in scanned film in several important ways. But before examining the differences in detail, we should point out that several different technologies, each with its own properties, get lumped into the "digital camera" general category. There are Bayer array cameras used in DSLR and medium-format cameras and scanning-back cameras. The primary type we'll be discussing is the Bayer array type, as shown later in Figure 2-7.

Sensor Types

Depending on whom you talk to, there will always be a debate on the relative merits of CCD (charge-coupled device) sensors versus CMOS (complimentary metal-oxide semiconductor) camera sensors. Their fundamental difference lies in the manner of manufacturing. CMOS sensors are made just like any other integrated circuit and can be produced for less cost than the more exotic (and expensive) manner of manufacturing CCDs.

CCD and CMOS sensors also operate slightly differently:

- A CCD captures photons on the capacitor array (the photoactive photo site region, or the photosensitive part of the sensor), causing each capacitor to accumulate an electric charge in proportion to the amount of light falling in that region. Once the capacitor array captures the charge, a control circuit causes each capacitor to transfer the charge to the coupled transmission region. The controlling circuit converts the entire semiconductor contents of the array to a sequence of voltages, which is recorded to memory (or disk).

- A CMOS is a broader class of integrated circuit that is used in a variety of microprocessors, static RAM, and other digital logic circuits. CMOS circuits use a combination of P-type and N-type metal-oxide-semiconductor field-effect transistors (MOSFETs) to implement logic gates in signal-processing equipment such as camera sensors. The MOSFET is used to amplify or switch electronic signals. When on but static, CMOS sensors generate less heat and consume and dissipate less power than CCD sensors.

Which Is Better, CCD or CMOS?

Neither sensor type is perfect. Both are generally Bayer filter mosaics in digital camera use. However, the Foveon X3 sensor uses three stacked active pixel sensors, utilizing the sensor's silicon itself as the color filter, based on the wave-length-dependent absorption of light in silicon. Large-format digital camera backs, such as the BetterLight (www.betterlight.com), use a scanning trilinear array instead of a Bayer pattern (explained in Figure 2-7). The downside is that the array must travel the width of the capture area, which takes time, but the upside is that no demosaicing is required.

The vast majority of digital cameras, whether point-and-shoot or digital SLRs, are color filter array (CFA) cameras. In a CFA camera, each photo site, or sensel, on the sensor is covered by a color filter and contributes a single pixel to one color channel. The "missing" color information is then interpolated from the neighboring pixels in a process known as demosaicing.

Figure 2-7 shows a typical Bayer pattern CFA, in which each photosensor is filtered so that it captures only a single color of light: red, green, or blue. Twice as many green filters are used as red or blue, because our eyes are most sensitive to green light.

When you shoot JPEG (Joint Photographic Experts Group, which was the name of the committee that created it) or TIFF (Tagged Image File Format), the demosaicing is performed in the camera using the camera vendor's proprietary routines. When you shoot in the raw image format, the demosaicing is done by the raw converter, which typically offers more control.

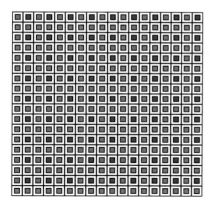

Figure 2-7 A typical Bayer pattern color filter array

Demosaicing is a complex process that inevitably involves a trade-off between localized contrast (which looks a lot like sharpening) and anti-aliasing (which looks like blurring), to prevent artifacts that arise when a detail in the image falls on only one color of pixel. Many cameras include an optical low-pass filter to reduce artifacts, but the raw converter, whether in the camera or in post-capture software, performs a significant role, so one raw converter's output with "no sharpening" may appear sharper than another raw converter also set to no sharpening. Similarly, while most raw converters offer some noise reduction, the actual results may differ.

NOTE: Most all DSLR cameras contain a piece of glass called an anti-aliasing (AA), or optical low-pass blur, filter to prevent Moiré patterns. Moiré patterns are repeating light and dark bands (that often introduce colors) that may occur when photographing a repeating pattern or texture. Moiré patterns can appear when the sampling resolution (the sensor) approaches the frequency of the captured signal. To reduce or eliminate this digital artifact, camera manufacturers add AA filters to soften or blur the high-frequency image data. Removal of the AA filter can increase the apparent sharpness of the sensor, yet at the risk of having a lot of potential Moiré patterns in your captures. While not suggested for most common uses, companies such as LPD (www.maxmax.com) can remove one or more of the AA filters and increase the sensors' sharpness. LPD can also remove a camera's infrared filter, thus giving a false-color infrared camera whose color rendering is unnatural and unique. Note that removing filters voids a camera's warranty, so you may end up with a limited-purpose digital camera.

Figure 2-8 shows an array of digital captures from a variety of Bayer array cameras. The cameras include a Canon EOS-1Ds Mark III, a Canon EOS Digital Rebel XTi, a Fuji FinePix A820, a Phase One P65+ 6x4.5 camera back, and an Apple iPhone. The captures were all brought into Adobe Photoshop Camera Raw 5.3 for processing and slight cropping (to hide which image came from which camera). The figures were then resampled using Bicubic Sharper to match the same width, and then output sharpening was applied. When looking at the images reproduced in the book, try to determine which camera produced which image.

Figure 2-8 Capture comparison from five different cameras. The scene was set up outside under natural daylight, because the iPhone can't be connected to an electronic flash.

Capture A

Capture B

Capture C

Capture D

Capture E

As long as the size of the image capture provides resolution that is above the threshold needed for reproduction, even an Apple iPhone can produce a reasonable image. However, the size will be severely restricted due to limited resolution. In Figure 2-9, we reveal which capture came from which camera by reproducing a "contact print" of a 2.5" x 2" section of the capture at 300 ppi. This will show how a 60MP P65+ medium-format capture compares to a 1.9MP iPhone.

As you can see, the capture from a P65+ back has a lot more resolution than the iPhone. Though it must be said: Properly handled, the iPhone does a decent job of capturing an image, as long as you don't have unreasonable expectations from a 1.9MP camera phone.

To better understand the relative usable image sizes, here are the reproduction sizes, uncropped, that each of the cameras can produce without upsampling:

- iPhone: 4" x 5.3"

- Fuji FinePix A820: 8.2" x 11"

- Canon EOS Digital Rebel XTi: 10.8" x 16.2"

- Canon EOS-1Ds Mark III: 15.6" x 23.4"

- Phase One P65+ camera back: 28" x 37.4"

Clearly, one doesn't expect a capture from a $199 Apple iPhone to equal a capture from a $39,990 digital back, particularly when evaluating the maximum reproduction size of a capture. Figure 2-10 shows a small section of each capture at a Photoshop screen zoom of 400% to illustrate the real difference in the captures' effective resolutions.

Figure 2-9 Capture comparison from five different cameras decoded and reproduced at 300 ppi.

Capture A from Apple iPhone, 1.9MP

Capture B from Fuji FinePix A820, 8.1MP

Capture C from Canon EOS Digital Rebel XTi, 10.1MP

Capture D from Canon EOS-1Ds Mark III, 21MP

Capture E from Phase One P65+, 60MP

 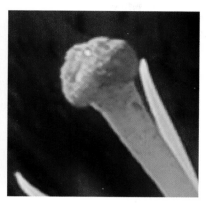

Figure 2-10 Comparison of the iPhone to the P65+ capture at a Photoshop screen zoom of 400%

iPhone   P65+

The other difference in this camera comparison is that of the five cameras, only the iPhone and the Fuji FinePix can capture only JPEG file formats. The other cameras can capture raw files that allow substantially more post-processing, including image sharpening and noise reduction. Both of the JPEG-only cameras apply a dose of sharpening and probably some noise reduction in the analog to digital conversion.

Cameras that shoot JPEG present an additional issue: The nature of JPEG compression creates 8-by-8-pixel blocks that can become visually obvious after editing or, at high ISO ratings, before editing.

Sensor Noise

Sensor noise is present in every digital capture because it's an unavoidable phenomenon of the way digital sensors capture light. If you have enough light for an optimal exposure, the ratio of signal (real image data) to noise may be so good that the noise is not perceptible. As you push the limits of your camera to capture a scene with low light levels, long exposures, and/or higher ISO amplification (or gain), the ratio of signal to noise will decrease, and you will experience visible noise in the image. Many technological factors (usually proportional to the cost) have an effect on the amount of noise created by a particular sensor, but you cannot eliminate it.

There are two main types of sensor noise: random noise (or pseudo-random noise following a Poisson distribution) and pattern noise. Pattern noise can often be substantially reduced by computational methods. Random noise really can't be eliminated, although low-level blurring can reduce it.

ISO and Sensor Noise

Increasing a camera's ISO setting increases the amplification applied to the sensor's captured signal, thereby increasing perceptible shot noise, early-stage electronic read noise, and thermal noise. The amplifiers themselves may also contribute some noise of their own, thus adding to the total read noise present in the final image. Consequently, increasing the ISO results in noisier-looking images, particularly in the shadow areas where the SNR ratio is lowest. Ironically, while the noise is amplified (and images appear noisier), the actual noise signature in a high-ISO capture is essentially the same as at a lower ISO—it's just made more visible by the amplification and thus considered objectionable.

The better the sensor design and light gathering efficiency, the better the noise signature of a given camera will be. There have been great strides in recent years in the substantial improvement of light gathering efficiency by reducing the wasted space surrounding sensor photo sites, as well as developing light-gathering microlenses. Recent cameras such as the Nikon D3 have even claimed to offer up to ISO 25,600. However, these extended ISO settings are not implemented through true analog hardware amplification as described above, but instead through digital gains (equivalent to pushing the Exposure control in post-processing by +1 or +2 stops). Even so, the highest real ISO of the D3 (using hardware amplification) is 6400, which is remarkable and very usable in practice. Recent Canon cameras such as the 5D Mark II have increased the highest available real ISO to 3200, just a stop behind Nikon.

If this discussion of sensor noise made your eyes glaze over, here's the main takeaway: To a certain degree, sensor noise will always be there. The higher the ISO setting on the camera, the more the noise will become perceptible. With a given camera, the noise may become objectionable at some higher ISO settings and lead you toward wanting to do something to reduce the apparent noise. The manner of dealing with the various sensor noises usually breaks down into color noise and luminance noise reduction, and will depend entirely on what application you are using. Camera Raw and Adobe Lightroom have separate noise controls for color and luminance. Photoshop's Reduce Noise filter also has separate controls as well as adjustments for detail preservation. Reduce Noise also enables you to use different levels of noise reduction on a per-channel basis.

To show these two noise types in Figure 2-11, captures were made with the Canon 10D at ISO 100 and processed in Camera Raw. To make the noise more visible, a levels adjustment was made.

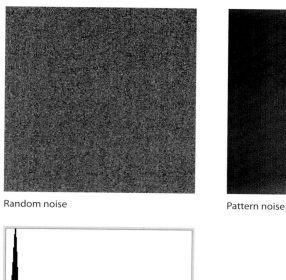

Figure 2-11 Sensor noise type examples

Random noise

Pattern noise

Levels adjustment to make noise visible

There are three common causes of sensor noise, and it's useful to make the distinction between the noise type and its cause:

- *Shot noise* (or photon noise) is a quantum effect of light and time. An image sensor photo site, the photosensitive part of the sensor, counts the stream photons that strike it over a particular period of time, but the light from a scene does not arrive at the sensor in an even regular stream. When you expose the sensor for a short period of time (in ratio to the total number of photons), the lack of regularity in the stream will create fluctuations in the photon count, causing random noise. The more photons that strike a sensor during exposure, the higher the signal-to-noise (SNR) ratio, and the less the amount of perceived noise. Sensors with larger pixels, like those found on full-frame DSLRs or medium-format digital camera backs, gather more photons per pixel (in other words, each pixel is more efficient) and hence produce images with less perceived shot noise. Since shot noise is a fundamental property of light, even images captured by a theoretically perfect sensor would still have some shot noise.

- *Read noise* (or readout noise) is a combination of noise components inherent in the sensor electronics that convert the stored sensor charge into digital data (zeros and ones). Read noise often contains fixed-pattern and random components. Fixed-pattern read noise is the more visually objectionable of the two, often showing up in images as horizontal or vertical lines, or other easily seen patterns. Fortunately, most of the fixed-pattern noise can be eliminated through so-called "black subtraction" or "black frame subtraction" methods. Some cameras actually perform this step in hardware prior to writing the raw file to the memory card.

- *Dark noise* (or thermal noise) is caused primarily by the heat energy in the sensor itself being converted into a digitized signal. Like read noise, dark noise also tends to have random and fixed-pattern components. In some cases, the fixed pattern is related to the position of various electronics around the sensor and can lead to one part of the image being considerably noisier than other areas; this unpleasant effect can be reduced by the same dark exposure subtraction methods used for patterned readout noise. Very high-end astronomical cameras and some medium-format backs use cooling systems to reduce or eliminate thermal noise, though this is very expensive and can be quite bulky.

Noise Reduction

We'll cover noise-reduction strategies and techniques in later chapters, but it's useful to note that most noise reduction in raw or post-processing is dealt with by separating chroma or color noise separately from luminance noise.

Color Noise

All CFA cameras suffer from color noise to a greater or lesser degree. Color noise can appear in highlights, shadows, or midtones, though it is usually more visible in the shadows and at higher ISO settings. The visual characteristics of the color noise vary from camera to camera, depending on the sensor's color filters and analog-to-digital hardware.

Color noise in JPEGs, discussed below, can be more problematic. The in-camera conversion doesn't always do a good job of eliminating color noise, and the JPEG compression process tends to accentuate any color noise that isn't eliminated in the in-camera conversion.

Figure 2-12 shows color noise from a digital raw capture made at ISO 3200. The capture is from an older camera, a Canon EOS 10D, to better show the color noise. Recent cameras exhibit better color noise reduction as part of the analog to digital conversion.

Figure 2-12 Color noise in a digital raw capture

The ISO 3200 image processed with no color noise reduction

The same image with color noise reduction set to 50 in Camera Raw

Luminance Noise

Like color noise, luminance noise varies with both ISO speed and exposure. Underexposed digital captures are much more prone to noise, particularly in the shadows, than underexposed film captures. It's quite possible (and rather likely) that a well-exposed ISO 1600 digital capture may be less noisy than a very underexposed ISO 100 digital capture. Figure 2-13 shows examples of the noise signature of the same poor old Canon EOS 10D. We tend to use this camera a lot for demos needing really bad noise (because the camera is so good at producing noise). Recent Canon cameras, however, have improved their noise signatures tremendously, and that's what we shoot real images with!

Figure 2-13
Luminance noise in a series of digital captures, all at a 400% zoom level.

ISO 100

ISO 200

ISO 400

ISO 800

ISO 1600

ISO 3200

Each of the raw files in Figure 2-13 were processed in Camera Raw 5.3 with the default Detail panel settings of zero luminance noise reduction and 25 color noise reduction. The noise, when viewed at a 400% zoom, is obvious and objectionable at ISO 800 and above. But what exactly are you seeing when zoomed into 400% in Photoshop? It's visual science fiction. Remember that a computer display is a low-resolution device that shows views of an image that are either greatly exaggerated in size or substantially lowered in resolution. What you see on the display is not going to be what you get in final reproduction unless the display is the final destination. Even then, an image would likely have to be downsampled substantially, which acts as its own noise-reduction agent.

Figure 2-14 shows that noise is size sensitive. The first image shows the same 400% zoom after both color and noise reduction have been applied, and the second image shows the reduced noise image when at contact print size.

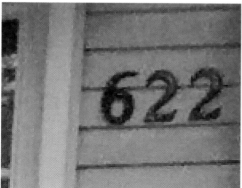 

Figure 2-14
Size sensitivity of noise

ISO 3200 after noise reduction at 400% zoom

ISO 3200 after noise reducion at contact print size

While the contact print in Figure 2-14 still shows evidence of higher ISO noise, the noise reduction certainly mitigates how objectionable the noise would be if the overall image were reproduced at the capture's native size, which would be 10.2" x 6.8" at 300 ppi. If the image were downsampled, the noise would become virtually invisible. Figure 2-15 shows both the ISO 100 and the ISO 3200 reduced to 50% of the original size, as well as the full crop of the ISO 3200 at about 30% of the original size.

Figure 2-15
Noise reduction as a result
of downsampling

ISO 100 downsampled to 50%

ISO 3200 noise reduced and downsampled
to 50%

ISO 3200 noise reduced and downsampled to 30%

The main point to be made when considering high-ISO noise and noise-reduction techniques is at what point is noise relevant or irrelevant? Looking at an image at 100-400% zoom in Photoshop does not give you a realistic (nor particularly useful) view of your image's noise signature for print. Zooming out to 25-50% can give you a more realistic representation, albeit in much lower resolution than your printer can print.

Some raw converters, particularly those from camera vendors, have a tendency to bury shadow noise by simply clipping shadows to black, but it's usually worthwhile addressing luminance noise in the raw converter when you shoot raw. At very high ISO speeds, however, a dedicated third-party noise removal tool may be needed to get the best rendering.

Luminance noise in high-ISO JPEGs should always be addressed before sharpening, and any remaining noise should be protected from sharpening, otherwise it will simply become more obvious. We'll discuss specific techniques for doing so in Chapter 5.

Noise, Exposure, and ETTR

There are photographic exposure techniques that can help reduce noise and improve the signal even before doing the image processing. The concept of "expose to the right" (ETTR) has received considerable discussion and debate. One of the first people to have written about ETTR was Michael Reichmann, who manages and writes for the Luminous Landscape website (www.luminous-landscape.com). A lot of people tend to misunderstand the instructions or misconstrue the reasoning behind the ETTR concept. While in practice the intent is to increase the overall exposure in a digital capture, the increase is not designed to be an overexposure, but rather a correct exposure for the scene.

The first tenet of ETTR is that in order to even engage in the practice, you must understand the implications of the scene contrast range and how it fits into the dynamic range of your sensor. If you are shooting on a bright sunny day with lots of light and deep shadows, don't even think about ETTR. However, if you are shooting a scene that has low contrast and all of the tonality you want to capture falls within the 10 to 12 stops (or more) that today's sensor can capture, you will get a better signal-to-noise ratio if you move the histogram to the right by increasing the exposure. You can do this either manually by opening up the aperture or using a slower shutter speed, or by setting the exposure compensation in your camera to increase the exposure. How much you may want to increase the exposure (expose to move the histogram to the right) depends entirely on the scene contrast range and your dynamic range of the sensor. But if the contrast range is only six to seven stops, you can probably increase the exposure compensation one to two stops without fear of actual tone clipping (driving tones to saturation).

You should also take your camera's overexposure warning with a degree of skepticism. Most of these warnings will be at least one full stop conservative, which will tend to induce you to ETTL (expose to the left, resulting in wasted signal).

Figure 2-16 shows three exposures and their Camera Raw histograms before and after normalizing the image adjustment settings in Camera Raw. The images were shot with a Canon EOS-1Ds Mark III at ISO 400. The camera was set to auto-bracket exposure by the camera for normal, under 1.33, and over 1.33 stops. The F-stop was F/11 and the shutter speed was used to vary the exposures from 1/320, 1/125, and 1/50 of a second.

There are several points to note about the before and after in the image adjustments. First, it can be argued that even the "normal" exposure was actually a slight underexposure by the camera meter. In Camera Raw, the normal needed a .20 Exposure increase. Also, the normal and under-exposure had shadow clipping before adjustment that was eliminated by increasing or moving the levels to the right. The overexposure is indicating potential highlight clipping, which is eliminated in the after adjustments by moving the levels to the left.

All three of the post-adjustment histograms are very similar, as might be expected since care was given to make the image adjustments so all three exposures ended up alike. There was no noise reduction applied in Camera Raw, but the capture sharpening was optimized and the color noise reduction was at default. The images were output sharpened after downsampling with Photoshop's Bicubic Sharper.

While the original scene contrast wasn't measured, the estimated range was eight to nine stops. Considering the 1Ds Mark III has arguably 10-11 stops of dynamic range, a +1.33 exposure compensation really wasn't putting highlight texture at much risk of being clipped.

So, this shows that three different exposures can be normalized by an experienced Camera Raw user, which is all well and good, but what about the SNR ratio? Does this prove that ETTR is useful in producing a better signal (image) with less noise? Yes. Figure 2-17 shows the ETTR results up close.

Images and histograms before image adjustments

1.33 stop underexposure   Normal exposure   1.33 stop overexposure

Figure 2-16
Expose to the right (ETTR) example images and histograms

Images and histograms after image adjustments

1.33 stop underexposure   Normal exposure   1.33 stop overexposure

Figure 2-17 ETTR results at a 300% in Photoshop

1.33 stop underexposure after a +1.5 Exposure adjustment in Camera Raw

Normal exposure after a +.20 Exposure adjustment

1.33 overexposure after Camera Raw Basic adjustments of -0.5 Exposure and +29 Recovery, and Parametric Curve adjustments of -11 Highlights, -10 Lights, -3 Darks, and -9 Shadows

As you can see, the underexposed image suffered from a substantial increase in perceptible noise after the required image adjustments were applied. This is a typical result of trying to substantially lighten digital captures and a very good reason not to underexpose if at all possible. Even the normal exposure has a slight noise that might be expected with an ISO of 400 and a small increase in exposure. What is notable is that the +1.33 image, the ETTR one, has a superior signal to noise ratio. Why?

Some people may think that due to the linear nature of raw digital captures, that more levels are contained in the brightest portions of the exposure. For a 12-bit capture, the brightest stop of data contains 2048 levels of data. Each step down reduces the data levels by half. When you end up in the lower exposure areas, you end up with very few levels of data.

However, if you understand what noise is and what causes it, you'll realize that simply increasing the number of photons your sensor captures will increase the SNR ratio (and reduce the noise in the capture). Opening the aperture or using a slower shutter speed allows the sensor to gather more light, and that's why there's less noise. As long as the increased exposure doesn't lead to highlight texture clipping, you improve the image quality by increasing the exposure.

You'll note that we don't say to increase your ISO when trying to deploy ETTR. Increasing the ISO does indeed increase the amplification of the analog to digital converter, but it doesn't magically add a bunch of photons to the capture. Whether you shoot at ISO 100 or ISO 3200, the amount of light available in a given set of exposure parameters remains constant. It is the amount of light—the number of photons—that dictates the actual noise. If you increase the photon count, you increase the SNR ratio.

In practice, there may indeed be situations where increasing your ISO is useful and more than compensates for the increase in noise. If you are locked into a certain aperture and shutter speed, increasing the ISO will have the effect of moving at least the shadow regions of the image to the right and improving the shadow's SNR ratio. However, the increase in the SNR in the shadows yields less and less benefit as you increase the ISO. Going from ISO 100 to 200 will improve the shadow SNR, while going from ISO 1600 to 3200 probably won't return much value. You should test your own camera to determine where the sweet spot is for increasing shadow SNR via ISO boosts. The odds are that going much past ISO 400 will offer diminishing returns or add additional problems in other regions of the image.

Noise, Detail, and Enlargement

We've seen that the influence of the image source decreases with down-sampling, particularly the issue of noise. The converse is also true. When we enlarge digital captures past their native resolution, noise reduction and localized sharpening become increasingly more important as the enlarge-ment factor increases.

The degree to which we can enlarge digital captures depends in part on the image quality and content. Images with soft detail can generally withstand more enlargement than those with lots of fine detail. (We'll look at image content issues in greater detail later in this chapter.) Images that have excel-lent image quality, such as lower noise, no camera shake, and proper expo-sure, can still be successfully enlarged.

The images shown in Figure 2-15 contain fine detail. But if the demands of the reproduction require it, they can, with care, easily be enlarged by 200%.

However, the lower the noise, the better the upsampled result will be, because upsampling noise just makes bigger noise. The key is first to apply appropriate noise reduction. The ISO 100 image is relatively clean, but the ISO 400 image needs noise reduction prior to upsampling.

Figure 2-18 shows the ISO 100 and ISO 400 images before and after upsampling 200% using Photoshop's Bicubic Smoother interpolation. What you are seeing is the native resolution images shown at an 800% zoom while the upsampled images are shown at 400% zoom. This is to compare the before and after upsampled images at the same dimensions.

Figure 2-18 Impact of noise in upsampling

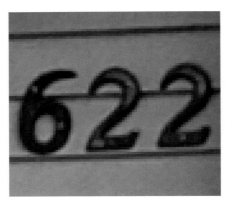
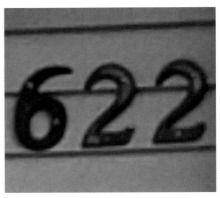

800% zoom of ISO 100 before upsampling   400% zoom of ISO 100 after 2x upsampling

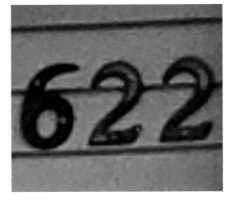

800% zoom of ISO 400 before upsampling   400% zoom of ISO 400 after 2x upsampling

Neither the ISO 100 nor ISO 400 images had substantial noise reduction applied (except the default color noise reduction) prior to upsampling. You can see that Bicubic Smoother did a good job of creating pixels and eliminating the pixilated look of the 800% zoom. However, the ISO 400 image's noise did not interpolate well. It would have been optimal to apply noise reduction prior to upsampling to help keep the noise from being factored into the algorithm. Even the ISO 100 image should have had some level of noise reduction applied prior to upsampling.

Figure 2-19 shows the result of having already applied a round of noise reduction to the ISO 400 image prior to upsampling in Photoshop.

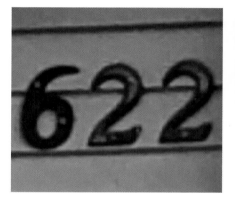

Figure 2-19
Noise reduction prior to upsampling

400% zoom of ISO 400 with noise reduction prior to upsampling and 2x upsampling

Contact print size of noise reduced and 2x upsampled ISO 400 image

As you can see, there is a substantial improvement in the post upsampling if the noise reduction is applied prior to resampling. Noise reduction will be covered in more detail later, but it's pretty clear that noise can cause image problems and must be addressed as far upstream in the image-processing pipeline as possible.

JPEG and Noise

When we shoot raw, the raw converter offers a good deal of control over sharpening and noise reduction. When we shoot JPEG, however, we simply have to work with what the camera gives us. Most cameras offer settings for JPEG quality, size, and sharpness, but few, if any, offer control over noise reduction.

It's much easier to deal with noise that hasn't been sharpened in the camera than it is to de-emphasize it after the fact, so we generally recommend leaving any in-camera sharpening turned off (see the sidebar, "Why Camera Vendors Offer In-Camera Sharpening").

Why Camera Vendors Offer In-Camera Sharpening

Camera vendors offer in-camera sharpening to play to two very different audiences: consumers who use point-and-shoot cameras and pros who are compelled to shoot JPEG for speed reasons.

Most consumers don't have access to sophisticated sharpening tools and techniques like the ones we discuss in this book, and would be dismayed to find that all of their images looked softer than those from a point-and-shoot film camera, which their current digital point-and-shoot probably replaced (and were designed to emulate).

Pros who shoot JPEG typically do so because time pressures (both in shooting and in processing) prevent them from shooting raw. Many photojournalists and wedding photographers fall into this category. In-camera sharpening produces reasonable (though hardly ever optimal) results with no substantial user intervention, and thus allows them to deliver their images in a timely fashion.

But in-camera sharpening is a global, one-size-fits-all process. If the final use is a small-size reproduction, it may be good enough, but if you want optimal sharpening using the techniques described in this book, and you have to shoot JPEG, we recommend that you turn off in-camera sharpening and do the sharpening in post-processing.

JPEG presents special challenges, not just because of the relative lack of control it offers over raw, but also due to the nature of JPEG compression. JPEG attempts to produce "visually lossless" compression, and at low compression settings (such as the typical JPEG Fine that's offered by most digital cameras) you may be hard-pressed to tell the difference between a JPEG and a raw capture simply by looking at them side by side. Figure 2-20 shows just such a comparison.

The JPEG is the left image in Figure 2-20, the raw is on the right. Both were sharpened identically and printed at 300 ppi. The two versions have small differences in tonality and color balance, but they're extremely similar in terms of sharpness and detail.

Figure 2-20
Raw and JPEG compared

One of these images was shot as a Large Fine JPEG from a Canon EOS 10D. The other was shot as raw from the same camera. Can you tell which is which?

However, Figure 2-20 represents something of a best-case scenario. Both images were well exposed and shot at ISO 100. At higher speeds or with underexposed images, the relative inflexibility of JPEG becomes more apparent, with increased noise and, at higher ISO speeds, some magenta-green color artifacts.

Figure 2-21 shows what JPEG compression does to colors when the JPEG compression is encoded. JPEG compression tries to preserve the luminance information of the image while compressing the heck out of the color information. Not all JPEG compression is lossy, resulting in some degree of image degradation, but the JPEG compression used in cameras to produce JPEGs is. The compression uses blocks (called Minimum Coded Units, or MCUs), usually 16 x 16 pixels, and does substantial chroma subsampling (compression). The end result: Color gradients and noise are the components of an image that suffer the most with JPEG encoding.

The example shown in Figure 2-21 is done specifically to highlight what JPEG encoding compression does to colors and gradients. Obviously this is a radical example designed to show very bad results. But it's useful to show this so you understand, at the camera level, what's going on when you capture JPEG. Obviously the camera JPEG won't have this dramatic degradation, but there is some, and the color space conversion and gamma encoding prior to JPEG compression mean that the resulting file has substantially less editing headroom than the raw file would.

Figure 2-21 Effects of JPEG compression on color

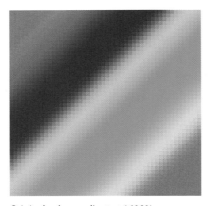

Original color gradient at 1600% zoom

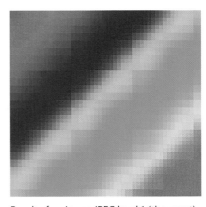

Result of saving as JPEG level 1 (the worst)

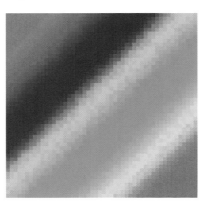

Original color gradient with noise to simulate higher ISO

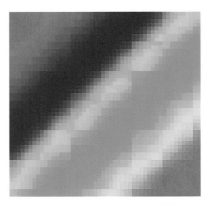

Result of saving noisy gradient as JPEG level 1

JPEG and ISO Speed

JPEG captures shot at low ISO ratings are relatively well behaved. But at higher speeds, they become progressively more difficult to handle. Figure 2-22 shows two JPEGs, one at ISO 100 and the other at ISO 800. There is also an image shot raw at ISO 100 and one at ISO 800. For the raw processed images, optimal sharpening was done in Camera Raw. The ISO 800 image had luminance noise reduction of 20, and the default color noise reduction for each was 25. The processed images were then output sharpened. For the JPEG versions, only output sharpening was done.

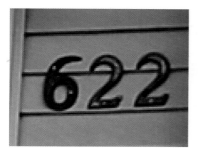

ISO 100 JPEG at 800% zoom

ISO 100 raw at 800% zoom

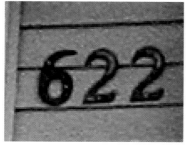

ISO 800 JPEG at 800% zoom

ISO 800 raw at 800% zoom

Figure 2-22 JPEG and raw ISO speed comparison

At ISO 100, the difference between the JPEG and the raw image is pretty minimal. One might argue that the sharpening included in the original JPEG file plus output sharpening was too strong, but since the capture sharpening was baked in the JPEG, we would have had to modify the output sharpening to get an optimal result—which, as we'll show throughout the rest of this book, should not be needed.

Where the raw and JPEG comparison really highlights the upside to raw and the downside of JPEG is at ISO 800. Sharpening the already brittle JPEG with its stronger noise became a real problem compared to the smoother raw image. This is what we laughingly call "pixel-peeping": zooming far into an image and becoming enraptured by pixels that are way outside of any reasonable visual reality. But it is useful to show what happens to your image even though it's on a micro scale.

LENSES AND IMAGE QUALITY

Regardless of the camera and sensor you use to make captures, the lens stands between your subject and your sensor. The quality of the lens, how well its autofocus is aligned, lens diffraction due to aperture settings, whether you used a tripod or a fast shutter speed… all of these factors affect image quality. Image sharpening may or may not be able to help eliminate or reduce many of these factors' effects on image quality. But if you are interested in achieving the maximum image quality your camera, lens, and sensor can deliver, you must address the following photographic factors before you make the capture.

Monochromatic Lens Aberrations

Slapping a cheap lens on a high-resolution digital camera is a shame— unless you want the creative effect of a digital Holga, a trendy camera with poor lenses. High-quality prime, fixed focal-length lenses will generally give better image quality than zoom lenses. But not all primes or zooms are equally good or bad. Individual copies of even expensive lenses can vary in their performance, so testing a new lens should be a mandatory exercise before buying one.

The quality of a lens is generally based on how well various lens defects or aberrations are handled. The aberrations discussed in this section are all monochromatic, meaning they impact lens performance even for a single color of light. Chromatic aberrations (CAs), discussed in the next section, lead to image-forming problems with different colors of light.

There are three lens aberrations that directly impact image sharpness: spherical aberration, astigmatism, and coma. Spherical aberration affects the whole image, while astigmatism, coma, and curvature of field mostly affect the edges and corners.

- *Spherical aberration* is the inability of all light rays to focus at the same point. Rays at the edge (marginal rays) of the lens come to focus closer to the lens than do rays parallel to the axis or center (paraxial rays). This causes the focus to drift as you stop down the lens. Some lenses use aspheric elements to better correct spherical aberration at wide apertures.

- *Astigmatism* is the inability of the lens to bring to focus both vertical and horizontal lines on the same plane. It will appear that lines of equal density (darkness) are less dense horizontally or vertically. Stopping down the lens (using a smaller f-stop) can improve astigmatism.

- *Coma* causes parallel oblique rays passing through a lens to be focused not as a point, but as a comet-shaped oval image. Stopping down the lens can improve coma.

- *Curvature of field* is another lens aberration that can impact critical focus. Field curvature results in the image from the lens being formed as a curved surface, not flat. As a result, when the center of the image is in focus, the edges are not, and vice-versa. Stopping down the lens may improve the overall sharpness, but it won't fix the field curvature. Figure 2-23 shows the impact of a curved field.

As you can see in Figure 2-23, a quality 50mm F1.4 prime lens is outperforming an inexpensive consumer-grade lens when it comes to field curvature. While stopping down (the same F/5.6 aperture was used on both lenses) would make some improvements, there is little one could do in post-processing to make the cheap lens corners as sharp as the prime lens corners.

Another aberration that has less impact on image sharpness but does impact image quality is *curvilinear distortion*. This results in lens barrel distortion (convex), where straight lines are bowed out, or pincushion distortion (concave), where straight lines are bowed inward. Photoshop's Lens Correction plug-in corrects for this defect. There are also third-party utilities, such as DXO (www.dxo.com) or PTLens, that can fix even more lens problems.

Figure 2-24 shows a curvilinear distortion comparison between a 50mm prime lens and a consumer grade 28-135mm zoom lens. Depending on focal length, the zoom lens suffers from variable amounts of barrel distortion. However, this zoom lens does show good corner sharpness, so correcting to the distortion would be possible in Photoshop. You would lose part of the image due to the corrections, as shown in the Lens Correction dialog in Figure 2-24.

Figure 2-23 Curvature of field of a 50mm prime lens compared to a cheap 18-55mm zoom lens

Full frame of the 50mm lens capture

Full frame of the 18-55mm zoom lens

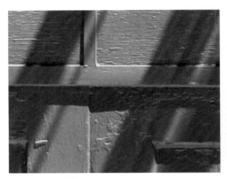

400% view of the 50mm lens, center crop

400% view of the 18-55mm zoom lens, center crop

400% view of the 50mm lens, upper-right corner

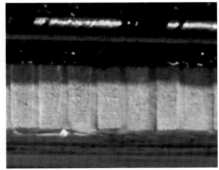

400% view of the 18-55mm zoom lens, upper-right corner

Figure 2-24 Curvilinear distortion of 50mm prime lens compared to a 28-135mm zoom lens

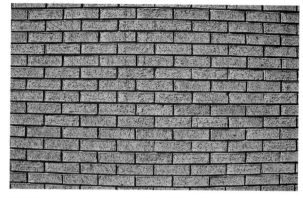

50mm lens capture showing no curvilinear distortion

28-135mm zoom lens showing barrel distortion (convex curvilinear distortion)

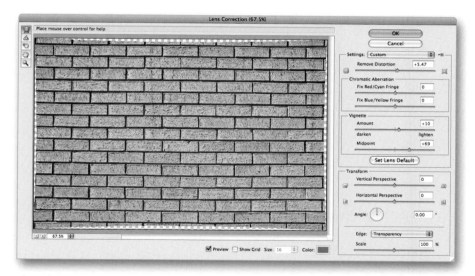

Photoshop's Lens Correction filter showing corrected barrel distortion

Chromatic Lens Aberrations

There are two types of chromatic aberration (CA), which differ from those before in that they impact lens performance with different colors of light:

- *Longitudinal chromatic aberration* is the inability of a lens to focus all wavelengths (colors) of light at the same plane on the lens axis. Shorter wavelengths come to focus in front of the focal plane, longer behind. This defect is not improved by stopping down the lens. This is normally noticeable only in cheaper, long telephoto lenses, and is reduced by the use of exotic glass elements, referred to as LD (low dispersion), ED (extra-low dispersion), AD (anomalous dispersion), and Fluorite. There is very little that can be done to correct this problem in post-processing.

- *Lateral chromatic aberration* is the lateral displacement of color images at the focal plane. This type of aberration is caused by different sizes of images produced by different colors, even though the image is all on the same plane. This CA produces color fringing of red or blue, and it is not improved by stopping down.

Lateral chromatic aberration is pretty easy to correct in post-processing, as shown in Figure 2-25. However, it's best to fix *any* CA before performing noise reduction or sharpening, both of which will make CA removal later more difficult. The Chromatic Aberration correction feature in Camera Raw fixes CAs in the proper place in the raw processing pipeline, at the same time as sharpening and noise reduction.

Stopping Down a Lens: An Aberration Cure-All?

Stopping down a lens greatly reduces spherical aberration and coma. It has a small positive effect on astigmatism and field curvature, but little or no effect on chromatic aberrations or distortion. So, it might be assumed that you should always just stop down to get better lens performance, right? Up to a point, this is true. Most lenses have a sweet spot where a given aperture provides an optimal image-forming capability. This optimal aperture is usually found when the lens is stopped down two to four stops from wide open. As a result, a fast lens with a very wide aperture such as F/1.4 will perform better at an aperture between F/2.8 and F/5.6. Stopping the lens down to F/8 or F/11 probably will not degrade performance, but stopping way down to F/22 or F/32 will, due to lens diffraction.

Figure 2-25
Lateral chromatic aberration before and after correction in Camera Raw

Full image shot with a Canon EF-S 10-22mm lens (known for CAs)

400% view of upper-left corner before CA correction

400% view with CA corrections

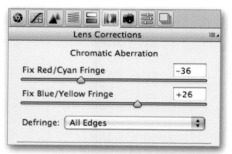

Lens Correction panel settings in Camera Raw

Lens Diffraction

Not really a lens defect per se, because diffraction is a property of light, lens diffraction is caused by the slight bending of light rays as they pass by (or through) a sharp edge such as a lens aperture. The smaller the aperture, the greater the effect of the diffraction will be on the overall image-sharpness reduction. Figure 2-26 shows the impact of depth of field and lens diffraction.

Figure 2-26 Impact of F-stop on depth of field and lens diffraction

Full image shot with a Canon 100mm F2.8 macro

100% view at F/4.0

100% view at F/11

100% view at F/32

In Figure 2-26, the 100% view shot at F/4.0 is sharp in the area of critical focus but suffers from limited depth of field. The F/11 shot shows good depth of field—the higher and lower coins are in sharp focus. But when the lens is stopped all the way down to F/32, the entire image gets softer because of lens diffraction. While sharpening may help reduce the softness of the lens at F/32, it would never match the real sharpness found in the image shot at F/11.

Lens Flare

Lens flare can also have a negative impact on image quality by reducing contrast and color saturation, but it's not really a typical lens defect in today's high-performance multicoated lenses. Flare can still happen when using too many lens filters, failing to use a lens shade, or, very commonly, simply having a dirty and grimy lens.

Some people seem to think it's a good idea to put a UV filter on the front of a lens to protect it. While this does offer lens protection, it also cuts down on image quality, especially if it's a cheap filter without perfectly flat optical properties.

PHOTOGRAPHIC ASPECTS OF IMAGE QUALITY

Remember the opening line of Chapter 1, about using a tripod if you want great prints? We said we were only half joking. Actually, we weren't joking at all. Shooting a camera from atop a tripod is an excellent way of getting a very sharp image if slower shutter speeds are required for a given shot. Sure, a lens that offers image stabilization (IS) can help overcome having to hand-hold a longer lens at slower shutter speeds. But there's no better way to reduce camera shake than setting your camera on a tripod, using a remote release, locking up the mirror, and setting a sandbag on top of everything to completely dampen vibration.

Figure 2-27 shows a comparison of images taken using a tripod and using a hand-held camera. It's pretty obvious that for optimal image quality, using a tripod and locking up the mirror (as well as using a shutter release and sandbag) can help substantially.

Figure 2-27
Impact of camera shake on image sharpness

Image shot with a Canon 300mm F2.8 lens at 1/320 of a second at F/7.1 and ISO 100

400% view of a capture with the camera on a tripod with mirror lockup, shutter release, and sandbag

400% view of a capture with the camera on a tripod using shutter release

400% view of a capture hand-held using IS

400% view of a capture hand-held without IS

400% view of a capture with ISO 400 and shutter speed increased to 1/1250 of a second

The best image sharpness in Figure 2-27 comes from the image shot on a tripod with the mirror locked up and a sandbag on the lens to further dampen any camera vibrations. Figure 2-28 shows a picture of Jeff shooting his 300mm F2.8 lens on a Canon EOS-1Ds Mark III on a tripod, mirror lockup and sandbag version.

Figure 2-28 Jeff shooting on a tripod with a sandbag resting on the lens

What, you don't want to have to carry a tripod and sandbag with you everywhere? We suppose that's reasonable, and one can get an image that rivals shooting on a tripod with a fast enough shutter speed, as in the last image in Figure 2-27. To increase the shutter speed, Jeff increased the ISO from 100 to 400. This allowed him to shorten the shutter speed from 1/320 of a second down to 1/1250 of a second. Combined with IS, this faster shutter speed rivals the capture shot on a tripod without the mirror lockup and sandbag. The only downside is the increased perception of noise due to the higher ISO. But, it is a reasonable trade-off to increase the ISO in order to capture a sharper image.

Even if you have a really good lens and are shooting with a fast shutter speed, if you rely upon autofocus, you are at the mercy of your equipment's autofocus accuracy. Front or back focusing of a lens can kill image sharpness just as surely as using cheap lenses or slow shutter speeds. If the autofocus misses the critical subject, you can't save the image by sharpening (although some improvement can sometimes be accomplished). Figure 2-29 shows an overall image and two cropped captures showing missed focus and critical focus.

Figure 2-29 Impact of focus alignment on image sharpness

Full image shot with a Canon 70-200mm F2.8 lens at 1/160 of a second at F/4.5 with IS and ISO 100

100% view of a capture with back focus problems

100% view of a capture with critical focus on the eyes

As good as Bruce and Jeff are at image sharpening, there's simply nothing we could do to make the back-focused image look like the image whose critical focus is accurate. If your camera and lens combination constantly front- or back-focuses, you should send them in for repair because the problem can be corrected. Some newer cameras actually enable the user to do a focus correction based on the actual lens and save it in the camera.

To make the process of adjusting lenses easier, Michael Tapes of RawWorkflow.com has created a product called LensAlign that provides a lens calibration system. The object is to set the LensAlign unit on a tripod in front of your lens and camera, and have the autofocus system focus on the main target. Care must be given to setting the unit up so that the target is square to and a specific distance from the camera. Then you shoot the target and inspect the lens ruler to discover at which point on the ruler the autofocus is focusing.

Figure 2-30 shows the result of an initial calibration shot and the result after adjusting the autofocus in the camera.

Front-focused on target (full capture)

Focus-corrected on target (full capture)

Canon EOS-1Ds Mark III with 50mm F1.4 lens AF Microadjustment + 14 to the back

Figure 2-30 Using LensAlign to adjust the front focusing of a 50MM F1.4 lens

Front-focused (detail)

Focus-corrected (detail)

SHARPENING AND THE IMAGE SOURCE

For the past 30 or so pages, we've shown examples of different image source types and their influence on sharpening and noise reduction. In some cases the differences are painfully obvious, while in others, they are rather subtle. Rest assured that this was a conscious decision on our part!

What lessons can we draw from the preceding examples?

- The need to address the image source specifically is not always clear-cut. In some cases, it may simply create extra work. In other cases, it's absolutely necessary if you want a usable image. Most real-world scenarios lie somewhere between these two extremes, but the better the fundamentals of the photography itself, the better the resulting image quality will be. There's a reason why some people buy expensive lenses, or large- or medium-format cameras, and plop their cameras on tripods in the search for ultimate image quality. And sharpening those images for optimal output can be a lot easier.

- The degree of enlargement is a key factor in determining the need for applying noise reduction and sharpening to the high-resolution data. We've shown you extremes—such as making a 20" x 30" print from a 35mm original, and making a 4.3" x 3" print from the same 35mm original. With greater enlargement, the need for sharpening tailored to the source becomes more likely. But the point at which it becomes necessary depends on both the source and the usage.

- With larger film formats or higher-resolution digital captures, the need to address grain and noise diminishes because the enlargement factor diminishes—unless, of course, you're pushing the limits to make the largest prints possible. In that case, you'll certainly get better results if you apply noise reduction and sharpening that is tailored specifically to the image source before applying final sharpening for output.

- ISO speed, whether with film or with digital captures, also plays a critical role. The higher the speed, the more noise, so for any given medium or any given use, specialized treatment will be required sooner at high ISO speeds than at lower ones.

- Underexposed digital images contain more apparant noise, and hence are more likely to need special handling than underexposed film images.

- The computer display can show you what is happening to the image pixels, but is a far-from-reliable guide to final printed appearance, because the size of the pixels on the display is typically much larger than the size of the pixels translated to print.

- Understanding all of these factors is key not only in learning how to apply sharpening tailored to the image source, but also in deciding whether and when to do so.

While it's undoubtedly the most complex part of the whole equation, the image source is only one of the factors we need to understand and, in some cases, address when we sharpen. The next factor, and one that we *always* have to address in sharpening, is the image content.

SHARPENING AND IMAGE CONTENT

While the range of influence of the image source can be quite subtle, the influence of the image content is quite obvious. In any given image, there exists a level of detail that we want to emphasize, but that level of detail varies from image to image. If we simply treat all images the same, we may end up either emphasizing unwanted detail or noise, or obscuring detail we really wanted to emphasize.

A "busy" image with lots of fine detail, like the upper image in Figure 2-31, needs a much different treatment than one with soft detail, like the lower image in Figure 2-31. Both images have been sharpened with the content taken into account, and both images have received two passes of sharpening. The first pass matched the sharpening haloes to the size of the details we want to emphasize. The second pass was tailored to the 150-line halftone process.

We'll look at the whole question of multipass sharpening in much more detail in Chapter 3, "Sharpening Strategies," but for the moment, let's focus on the issue of matching sharpening radius to image content. The images in Figure 2-31 and the subsequent examples have all had identical sharpening applied in the second phase. The only difference is in the first sharpening pass.

Special thanks to Martin Evening, who shot the image of Natasha that we're using for the example of the softer detail.

Figure 2-31 Sharpening optimized for image content

Both of these images have received multipass sharpening, with the first pass matched to the image content, and the second pass matched to the 150-lpi halftone process used to print this book.

Low-Frequency and High-Frequency Images

The top image in Figure 2-31 is known as a high-frequency image, because it has lots of sharp tonal transitions in a small area. The bottom image is of the type known as a low-frequency image, because the tone stays relatively constant over a given small area and the tonal transitions are gradual rather than sudden.

Many, if not most, images contain both high- and low-frequency components, but in the vast majority of cases, there's a single dominant tendency that we want to emphasize. If you're willing to do a good deal of manual work, you can even sharpen low-frequency and high-frequency elements separately in a single image, but you can obtain good results with relatively little work by sharpening in the first pass for the dominant characteristics of the image.

To make the low-frequency/high-frequency distinction a little clearer, Figure 2-32 shows a theoretical single row of pixels from each image in Figure 2-31, graphed according to their tonal values. The high-frequency image has sudden jumps in tonal value spread across a relatively small area, which is another way of saying that the image has lots of narrow edges. The low-frequency image features much more gradual transitions spread over a much wider area, indicating that the image contains big, wide edges.

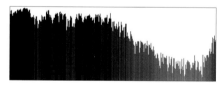

Figure 2-32
High-frequency and low-frequency images

A high-frequency image has many strong tonal transitions in a small area.

A low-frequency image has smooth tonal transitions spread across a large area.

Figure 2-33 shows an extreme example of what can happen if we apply the wrong sharpening in the first pass. For the high-frequency image of the trees, we used a radius of 1.5 pixels for the "incorrect" sharpening. For the low-frequency image, the radius amount was inverted, with the incorrect radius setting of .6 pixels. While coming from different image sources—the high-frequency image was from a Digital Rebel, and Martin's shot from a 1Ds Mark III—the optimal radius is dictated more by the edge width and frequency than by the image source.

A high-frequency image with a higher radius sharpening (incorrect)

A low-frequency image with a lower radius sharpening (incorrect)

Figure 2-33 High-frequency and low-frequency images with incorrect sharpening

In the left image in Figure 2-33, applying the wrong sharpening produces an image that actually has less textural detail. The wide sharpening haloes obscure some of the fine detail instead of making it more obvious, and the image seems blocky—the opposite of the result we wanted!

In the right image, applying the wrong sharpening produces a more obviously unacceptable result. Even with a model with good skin and makeup, the skin looks like sandpaper because the incorrect sharpening has introduced unwanted enhancement of the skin texture.

When we applied the wide-edge sharpening to the high-frequency image in Figure 2-33, we created sharpening haloes that were much wider than the details in the image, so it ended up looking soft and losing detail. When we applied the narrow-edge sharpening to the low-frequency image in Figure 2-33, we emphasized the small tonal transitions that represented texture rather than edges, producing the sandpaper effect.

A casual glance at Figure 2-33 might lead us to conclude that the incorrectly sharpened left image is undersharpened, while the incorrectly sharpened right image is oversharpened. In actuality, it's not the *quantity*, but the *quality*, of sharpening that's the problem. No matter how much we increased the intensity of the sharpening in the left image, we'd still wind up obscuring detail, because the haloes are too wide; if we backed off the amount of sharpening on the right image until the sandpaper disappeared, we'd have a soft, unsharpened image.

As we noted earlier, it's easy to mistake the wrong *kind* of sharpening for the wrong *amount* of sharpening. We'll discuss the tools and techniques that let us influence both the quality and the quantity of sharpening in much more detail in Chapters 4 and 5, but for now let's stay focused on the sharpening requirements themselves rather than how to obtain them.

At the beginning of this chapter, we emphasized the difficulty of using your computer display as a guide for print sharpening. Figure 2-34 shows sections of the images from Figure 2-31 printed at approximately the resolution of the display. They look quite ugly, but these are exactly the same pixels used to print Figure 2-31.

Figure 2-34
Sharpened pixels

This magnified view of the pixels used to print the images in Figure 2-31 corresponds approximately to what you'd see if you looked at the images on the computer display in Actual Pixels (100% zoom) view.

The magnified pixels look fairly hideous, especially in the upper, high-frequency image, but when they're rendered in print, the objectionable "jaggies" are simply too small for the eye to pick them out as distinct features. Instead, we see a sharp image.

What the computer display *does* show is the difference in the sharpening haloes between the high-frequency and low-frequency images. The high-frequency image has very small, high-contrast haloes, while the low-frequency image has larger, lower-contrast ones. Ultimately, you have to gain experience at judging sharpening with your own display, but the one factor you always need to bear in mind is the size of the pixels on final output. Faced with scary-looking images on screen, many of us end up undersharpening our images with the result being lower image quality in print.

Figure 2-35
How sharp is
sharp enough?

The image with no sharpening

The image with a single pass of sharpening tailored for the output process

How Sharp Is Sharp Enough?

Figure 2-35 shows different sharpening treatments of the same image, ranging from unsharpened to oversharpened. To some degree, sharpening is a matter of taste, but we suspect that most readers will agree that the image at the extreme left in Figure 2-35 is undersharpened (in fact, it isn't sharpened at all), and the one at the extreme right is oversharpened.

The difference between the two middle images is more subtle (but again, subtle differences are ultimately what this book is all about). Our opinion is that the image sharpened in two passes (the third from the left) has more of an illusion of "depth" than the one sharpened with a single pass (second from the left). The peeling bark has more texture, though not overly so, and the background foliage is more clearly defined. The highlights are a little less bright and contain more detail.

Now let's look at the actual pixels—you may find them surprising!

Figure 2-35
continued

The image with multipass sharpening for both content and output

The image with typical one-pass oversharpening

The image in Figure 2-36 with no sharpening, at the extreme left, looks soft in Actual Pixels view, and it's no surprise that it also prints that way, though it doesn't look as soft at the reduced print size in Figure 2-35 as it does in Actual Pixels view.

The image sharpened with a single pass for output, second from the left, looks reasonably sharp in Actual Pixels view, but still prints a little soft. It's acceptable, but it's less sharp than it could be.

The image sharpened with multiple passes looks downright crunchy in Actual Pixels view, yet it prints well. Note that while the edges appear jagged, the highlights and shadows still hold detail, and the sharpening contours, while strong, are relatively narrow, so they don't obscure any fine details. In short, the sharpening is matched to the image content.

The final image, at right, is indeed oversharpened—lots of pixels have been forced to pure white or solid black. But the underlying problem is that the sharpening haloes are too big, obscuring detail rather than emphasizing it.

Figure 2-36
Sharpening and pixels

The image with no sharpening

The image with a single pass of sharpening tailored for the output process

The combination of overlarge haloes and too much sharpening also causes some hue shifts, such as the bright lime greens in the upper-left corner that aren't present in any of the other versions.

In the real world, this is often what happens when a client looks at a proof and asks for "more sharpening." What they really need is a different *kind* of sharpening that is sensitive to the image content, but when they ask for more sharpening, that's exactly what they get, so highlights get blown to white and shadows get plugged to black, without actually fixing the problem.

The main argument that is raised against sharpening images more than once is that you'll end up with an oversharpened mess. It's certainly possible to destroy images with multiple rounds of sharpening, but as you just saw in Figures 2-35 and 2-36, it's equally possible to do so with just one ill-considered sharpening pass.

Figure 2-36
continued

The image with multipass sharpening for both content and output

The image with typical one-pass oversharpening

The relationship between pixels on the computer display and dots in the final print is sufficiently indirect that we can't really judge final output sharpness from the display without a good deal of experience. But as we've said before, looking at the pixels on the display is one of the essential paths to gaining that experience. The key point to remember is that optimally sharpened images often look ugly on screen, particularly at higher zoom levels.

We can't control the halftoning process, and unless you're unusually knowledgeable about screening algorithms, it's just about impossible to know which four pixels will go to make up a particular cyan, magenta, yellow, or black dot on the print. What you *can* do is to check that the sharpening haloes aren't too wide—they should be just wide enough to provide the appearance of sharpness in the print, but still too small for the eye to pick out the halo as a discrete feature. We use the benefit of the sharpening haloes without making them obvious in the print, which is the key to good sharpening.

This leads us to the last of the three factors we need to address when we sharpen: the softening introduced by the output process.

SHARPENING AND THE OUTPUT PROCESS

Just as the process of turning photons into pixels introduces softness, so does the process of turning pixels into marks on a substrate (typically, but not always, ink on paper). There are three basic types of printed output (these are discussed in more detail later in this chapter):

- *Halftone output* (see Figure 2-37), used on most printing presses and some color laser printers, turns the pixels into regularly spaced variable-sized dots. The spacing between the dots is called the screen frequency, and is usually expressed in lines per inch (lpi). Light tones are produced by small dots, dark tones by larger ones.

  This book is printed using a 150-lpi screen. Trade magazines typically use 133 lpi, newspapers use 85 or, on modern presses, up to 120 lpi. Glossy magazine covers and premium-quality print jobs use 175 lpi, and some fine art coffee-table books may use 200 or even 300 lpi, though the latter is still very rare.

Figure 2-37 Halftones and diffusion dithers

In a conventional CMYK halftone, dot placement is regular, and the illusion of different tonal values is produced by varying the size of the dots.

In a CMYK diffusion dither, the size of the dots is regular, and the illusion of different tonal values is produced by varying the dot placement.

- *Error diffusion dither output* (see Figure 2-37), used on almost all inkjet printers, many color laser printers, and on a few printing presses (where it's more commonly known as stochastic screening), turns the pixels into fixed-sized dots with variable placement. Light tones are produced by printing fewer dots in a given area, and dark tones are produced by printing more dots in that same area.

  Some inkjet printers offer variable-size dots. Don't confuse these with halftone dots, which are continuously variable in size—the inkjets that use this feature typically have only two dot sizes, the larger one being used only in dark areas.

- *Continuous-tone output* includes dye-sublimation printers, and printers such as the Fuji Pictrography and Frontier, the Océ LightJet, and the Durst Lambda, which use color lasers to expose traditional photographic paper. Unlike the first two printed-output types, this one prints dots that have the same properties as pixels—the dots are all the same size, and all three (cyan, magenta, and yellow) colors are laid down in the same dot, with varying density of each color to produce different tone and color values.

  With continuous-tone printers, the relationship between image pixels and print dots is direct—one pixel in the image produces one dot on the print—but the dots are round where the image pixels are square, and the edges are softer than pixels displayed on an LCD (though probably not on a CRT display). However, unless you're printing an unusually low-resolution image, the print dots are likely to be much smaller than the image pixels viewed on the display.

We can't control how pixels get turned into dots. What we *can* control is the resolution—the number of pixels per inch—we send to the print device and how we sharpen those pixels. Moreover, the resolutions we usually send to the various different print technologies aren't just picked out of thin air—they're based on the physiology of the eye itself, which imposes limits on the finest detail we can see.

Resolution and the Eye

It should be obvious, but we'll state it anyway: It takes two photoreceptors to detect a difference in luminance or color, because to detect a difference, you need two signals. It follows that the smallest difference we could possibly see is one that is projected onto two photoreceptors on the retina.

Human Visual Acuity

The generally accepted definition of normal (20/20) visual acuity is the ability to resolve a spatial pattern whose features are separated by one minute of arc, or 1/60 of a degree. This number comes directly from the retina. The lens in the eye projects one degree of the scene across 288 micrometers (or microns) of the retina.

In the fovea, the area of the retina where the photoreceptors are most tightly packed, a linear 288 micrometers contains about 120 photoreceptors. So, if more than 120 alternating black and white lines, or 60 cycles, are projected onto this area, someone with normal visual acuity will see a solid gray mass. Most printing processes exploit this fact to create the illusions of continuous tone from a bunch of discrete dots.

The actual size of the features that fall at the limit of visual acuity depend, of course, on viewing distance. With a little trigonometry, we can calculate the threshold of normal visual acuity for a given viewing distance. One minute of arc (1/60 of a degree) is 0.00029089 radians. We can calculate the limit L of visual acuity at distance D by this formula:

$L = D \star \mathrm{TAN}(0.00029089)$

Table 2-2 shows the limit of visual acuity at different viewing distances, and the minimum print resolution, in dots per inch (dpi), needed to provide the illusion of continuous tone to an observer with 20/20 vision.

Table 2-2 Viewing distance and resolution

Viewing distance (inches)	Limit (inches)	Resolution (dpi)
8	0.00232	428
12	0.00349	286
15	0.00436	229
18	0.00524	191
20	0.00582	172
24	0.00698	143

However, although useful, these numbers aren't set in stone for the following important reasons:

- Most of the work done to establish these limits uses black and white line pairs, but our ability to discern individual features diminishes as contrast is reduced. So in most real photographic imagery (which is *not* comprised of black and white line pairs), the practical limit may be larger, and, hence, the required ppi to provide the illusion of continuous tone may be lower.

- Conversely, some people have better than 20/20 vision. The maximum acuity of the unaided human eye is generally thought to be about 20/15 (meaning that the observer can distinguish details at 20 feet that someone with "normal" 20/20 vision could distinguish at only 15 feet), and with modern corrective lenses, 20/10 vision (where the observer can distinguish details at 20 feet that someone with 20/20 vision could distinguish only at 10 feet) may be achievable.

- A slew of other factors can come into play, including but not limited to defects in the eye's lens, the pupil size, the level of illumination, the duration of exposure to the target, the area of the retina that is stimulated, the state of adaptation of the eye, and eye movement.

So treat the numbers in Table 2-2 as useful guidelines rather than as absolutes. One reason for mentioning these numbers is to provide insight into the reasons that we print at the resolutions we typically use. Yet another equally important reason is to help us understand what we need to do to keep our sharpening haloes near the threshold of visual acuity. By doing so, we can produce prints that appear sharp, yet lack the obvious and disturbing sharpening haloes that mar so much of the work we see in print.

Viewing Distance

Bruce observed this phenomenon so many times that he couldn't resist commenting on it. He has often said that "when some otherwise-sane photographers learn that a print was produced digitally, the concept of 'normal viewing distance' suddenly changes from the distance at which they can see the image to one that is largely determined by the length of their noses." If you examine a 30" x 40" traditional darkroom print at such close proximity, you'll likely see unpleasant grain artifacts that become invisible when you move back far enough to see the image. It's the same with digital!

Figure 2-38 contains 75 line pairs per inch, with increasing contrast from solid midtone gray at the top to solid black and white at the bottom. As you move the image farther or closer to your eye, the point at which you can no longer discern the individual line pairs changes. As you move closer, you can discern the line pairs higher up the page, and if you move back far enough, the whole figure becomes one solid gray mass.

Notice that the right side of the figure is different from the left side. The difference is that the left side of the figure has had no sharpening applied, while the right side has been sharpened. As a result, you can discern the line pairs on the right side higher up than you can on the left side at any given viewing distance.

This is exactly what good sharpening does: increases localized contrast to reveal detail. But each printing process imposes its own requirements and limitations.

Figure 2-38 Line pairs with increasing contrast

PRINT RESOLUTION

When we print, we need to decide how many pixels per inch we send to the printing process. In part, the decision depends on how many pixels we captured in the first place. We can create more pixels by interpolation, but interpolation can't create detail—it simply takes the original pixels, spreads them apart, and creates new pixels with intermediate values in the spaces between the original ones.

When interpolation is combined with careful sharpening, it can improve the print results slightly on some images, but it tends to be a great deal of extra work for questionable return. Bruce recommended attempting it only when printing at the uninterpolated resolution has clearly failed. Jeff has seen where interpolation can help (covered in Chapter 5).

Interpolating downward to achieve the required output resolution is, however, necessary and normal. It's possible to drown printers in data: If you send far more data than the printer can resolve, it will either throw away the excess data (in which case you've just wasted some time) or, worse, it will attempt to use the extra data, with the result that detail gets blocked up instead of being resolved.

In either case, final sharpening for print *must* be done after any interpolation. If you downsample, the sharpening haloes can simply disappear as they're downsampled out of existence. If you upsample, the sharpening haloes become too large and hence visually obvious. The print sharpening must always be done at the final print resolution.

Halftone Output

The general rule of thumb for halftone output is to send a number of pixels per inch that corresponds to between 1.5 and 2 times the screen frequency in lines per inch. If the platesetter or the imagesetter is driven by PostScript (which they invariably are), anything over 2.5 times the screen frequency is automatically discarded, so it's an absolute certainty that there's no reason to send more than 2.5 times the screen frequency.

In the real world, we've yet to encounter an image that showed any visible difference when printed from 2.5 times the screen frequency instead of two times. But images with fine detail generally reproduce better when two times the screen frequency is used rather than 1.5, particularly at lower screen rulings. At higher screen frequencies of 175 lpi and greater, the difference becomes more subtle and is apparent on fewer images.

Figure 2-39 shows the same image printed from a 300-ppi file (native resolution, two times the screen frequency) and from a 225-ppi file (downsampled from 300 to 225 ppi, 1.5 times the screen frequency). Can you see the difference? There *are* differences—we had to sharpen the 225-ppi version more aggressively for output than we did the 300-ppi version—but they're quite subtle!

Figure 2-39 Resolution for halftone

This image had one pass of sharpening applied before downsampling to 300 ppi and one pass of sharpening for print.

This image had the same one pass of sharpening applied before downsampling to 225 ppi and one pass of sharpening for print.

Continuous-Tone Output

A great deal depends on the software used to drive the continuous-tone printer, but a useful rule of thumb is to send pixels at the printer's native resolution. Some older dye-sublimation printers may still insist that you do so, but most modern continuous-tone printers have sophisticated controllers that will perform the necessary interpolation to the printer's native resolution.

Some pundits advocate sticking to resolutions that are even multiples of the printer's native resolution. Doing so certainly simplifies the interpolation tasks that the software controller needs to conduct, but we've found the practice to be advantageous only with some older printers and with some entry-level dye-sub printers.

It's almost certainly a bad idea to send significantly *more* than the printer's native resolution, not because the interpolation algorithms will do a bad job, but simply because in doing so, you lose some control over the sharpening, since the sharpening haloes will be downsampled along with the rest of the image. But it's not worth downsampling an image that had been prepared at 305 ppi for a Fuji Frontier to 300 ppi before printing it on a 300-ppi Océ LightJet—the difference is just too small to worry about on normal images. (You may see a detectable difference on synthetic targets made up of black and white line pairs, but that difference disappears with even slightly lowered contrast.) Most minilabs and online services who offer continuous-tone output specify 300 ppi for high-quality printing. If you aren't sure about the optimal ppi for your preferred service, ask!

Error Diffusion Dither Output

Most inkjet and color laser printers use an error diffusion dither of some kind, though the details are usually proprietary. Most color laser printers quote a resolution of 600 or 1200 dpi, while most inkjet printers specify some multiple of these resolutions. Canon's photo inkjet printers range from 1200 x 1200 to 9600 x 2400 dpi; Hewlett-Packard's photo inkjets generally use 4800 x 1200 dpi; and Epson's inkjet printers typically specify 720 x 2880 or 1440 x 5760 dpi.

What these numbers represent is the *addressable* resolution of the printer—the accuracy with which it attempts to lay down droplets of ink. Their relationship to the pixel resolution of the image is fairly indirect, but the optimal ppi value is lower than these numbers may suggest. The conventional wisdom is that the "effective" resolution of Epson inkjets is 360 ppi, while that of the Canon and Hewlett-Packard inkjets is 300 ppi.

Notice that we didn't say dpi here. Inkjet printers eject tiny droplets of ink from nozzles rather than creating dots as in halftones. Most Epson printers can literally print 180, 3 picoliter droplets per inch, because that's how many nozzles the print heads contain. Newer printers have increased that count to 360 nozzles per inch. But take note that picoliter is a unit of measurement of volume, not dimension.

What Bruce's own testing indicated was that there's definitely no point in upsampling images to achieve a resolution higher than the native ones stated above, and little point in upsampling even to these resolutions. For large prints that are likely to be viewed from 20 inches or more, 180 ppi is probably plenty. However, if you are at the low end of acceptable resolution and you have an image with a lot of high-frequency texture and/or high-contrast diagonal lines (particularly problematic for inkjet printers), you may see a benefit by upsampling about 50% prior to applying the final sharpening for output.

However, if you're making small prints and you have real captured data (that is, with no interpolation) in excess of the native resolution, you may not want to downsample it to the native resolution. With Epson printers, there seems to be a small but useful advantage to sending 480 ppi of real data, *suitably sharpened*, to the printer. At higher resolutions, the advantage diminishes, and sending more than 720 ppi actually seems to degrade the image.

Some pundits claim that you'll always get better results if you print at even multiples of the native resolution. This holds true for line pair targets, but on real-world images the benefit is much less certain, and may often be outweighed by the damage done by resampling the image. We almost always print at the native capture resolution, and if that turns out to be 342 ppi rather than 360, or 191 ppi rather than 180, we simply don't worry about it.

Note that this is simply a statement of what we do, albeit based on considerable testing and experience. Each generation of new printers brings new capabilities and, probably, new challenges, so beware of any statements on optimal resolution for inkjet printers that claim to be definitive—and don't be afraid to put conventional wisdom to the test!

SHARPENING FOR OUTPUT

Whether you adopt the multipass workflow we'll advocate in Chapter 3 or the more traditional single-pass sharpening, output sharpening is where the strongest sharpening comes into play. The key point to bear in mind when sharpening for output is that it's resolution dependent—it's all about the size of the pixels.

Remember—you have no control over how the pixels get turned into dots, so all you can do is sharpen the pixels themselves. For any given size of output, you need to sharpen higher-resolution images more aggressively than lower-resolution ones to achieve the same perceived sharpness. More aggressive sharpening can mean wider haloes, higher contrast between dark and light contours, or a combination of both.

The goal with output sharpening is to produce a satisfactorily sharp image without introducing visually obvious sharpening haloes. To do so, the secret is to keep the size of the haloes below the threshold of visual acuity at the anticipated viewing distance—this is where the size of the pixels on output becomes a critical factor.

Bear in mind that the numbers given in Table 2-2 for the limits of visual acuity refer to very high-contrast edges, since they're based on black and white line pairs. In practice, you can take some liberties with these numbers. The following rules of thumb have served Bruce well:

- For smaller reproductions, such as small inkjet prints, magazine reproduction, or most of the images in this book, we try to keep the light and dark sharpening haloes to around 0.01 inches each. If we're printing to an inkjet printer at 360 ppi, that means that the sharpening haloes can be as wide as 3.6 pixels if the image content requires it, and if we're printing a 200-ppi image to a 133-line halftone, we need to keep the haloes to around one pixel for the light halo and one pixel for the dark one.

- For larger reproductions, we may relax these limits to make light and dark contours of around 0.02 inches. If we're making a large inkjet print at 180 ppi, which is the lowest resolution we would typically print, that still allows light and dark haloes of close to two pixels each. However, we still try to keep the haloes as small as possible, varying the contrast to make the contours stronger or weaker.

Paper stock also has an influence. Inks bleed more on uncoated papers than on coated ones, so sharpening for uncoated papers has to be stronger than that for coated papers to achieve the same degree of sharpness.

Figure 2-40 shows the same native-resolution pixels sharpened for different print sizes and processes, zoomed in approximately 400% to make the differences obvious. The sharpening for the 4" x 6" inkjet print appears the gentlest of the three, because the inkjet can actually resolve the fine detail that wider sharpening haloes would obscure.

Figure 2-40 Size-sensitive sharpening

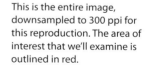

This is the entire image, downsampled to 300 ppi for this reproduction. The area of interest that we'll examine is outlined in red.

Detail of the image at capture resolution, sharpened for a 4" x 6" inkjet print at 480 ppi

Figure 2-40 *continued*

Detail of the image at capture resolution, sharpened for a 20" x 14" 85-line halftone print at 127 ppi (1.5 times the line screen frequency)

Detail of the image at capture resolution, sharpened for a 7.75" x 5" 175-line halftone print at 350 ppi

The haloes for the halftone sharpening are wider than for the inkjet, because it takes several pixels to make up one halftone dot. Therefore, rendering single-pixel details isn't possible (you could render single-pixel details by sending a lower-resolution image, but then you'd have obvious single pixels, which looks worse than bad sharpening). The haloes for the 85-line halftone need to be higher-contrast than those for the 175-line halftone to achieve the same apparent sharpness.

There's one last thing to note about output sharpening. Unlike the other sharpening factors we've discussed, the relationship between pixels and printer dots is fixed, for any given print process at any given resolution, and doesn't depend on image content or source. We'll discuss the implications of this in detail in Chapter 3.

INTRODUCTION TO CREATIVE SHARPENING

Creative sharpening, as we'll discover in subsequent chapters, is the middle part of a sharpening workflow; it starts with sharpening for source and content, and finishes with sharpening for output. In between is what Bruce and Jeff called "creative sharpening." Rather than spend a lot of time discussing creative sharpening and showing examples here, we'll do that in Chapter 6, "Putting the Tools to Work." But we wanted to briefly explain why there is this thing called creative sharpening, and that's because we often need to improve reality. The concept of improving reality is anathema to some photographers, and if you're one of them, feel free to skip this section— but do recognize that it's what some other photographers get paid to do!

We sometimes want to call extra attention to an element in an image by making it appear a little sharper than its surroundings. Headshots often benefit from a little extra sharpening around the eyes, for example. We call this kind of sharpening "creative sharpening" because, unlike the other kinds of sharpening we've discussed so far—source-sensitive, content-sensitive, and output-sensitive—creative sharpening can't be automated. It requires manual application and human decision-making.

There are a variety of reasons why one may need to apply a sharpening effect that does not relate to source, content, or output. That is considered "sharpening for effect." This also falls under the general umbrella of creative sharpening and shares the fact that, most often, these kinds of sharpening are optimal when done on a local basis, not global.

There are really no hard and fast rules, beyond those imposed by good taste, regarding creative sharpening. Obviously, if you overdo it, you'll wind up with a crunchy image; if you don't do enough, you'll waste time doing things that don't show up in the final image. But within those bounds, you have a lot of leeway.

A reasonable rule of thumb is to apply creative sharpening in such a way that it doesn't stick out from the rest of the image as an area that has obviously been more heavily sharpened—the transition between the areas that have received creative sharpening and those that have not should be imperceptible at Actual Pixels zoom or lower. The smoothness of the transition is more important than the actual appearance of the pixels on the screen, unless you're actually sharpening for on-screen viewing.

ONE SIZE DOES NOT FIT ALL

This chapter contains a lot of details, but the overall message is that, when it comes to sharpening, one size doesn't fit all. If you fail to take the image source into account, you end up sharpening noise as well as detail. If you ignore the image content, you may exaggerate unwanted detail or obscure wanted detail. And if you don't tailor the sharpening for the output process, your images will appear undersharpened or oversharpened.

The challenge, then, is to reconcile these disparate needs to produce optimally sharpened images. In the next chapter, we'll discuss a sharpening workflow that attempts to do just that.

CHAPTER
THREE

Sharpening Strategies
Why Use a Sharpening Workflow

In the last chapter, we saw that when sharpening, we must take into account a variety of different and often contradictory demands. In this chapter, we'll offer a means of reconciling these disparate demands, while pointing out the potential pitfalls in doing so.

Having tried for decades to meet all the requirements imposed by image source, image content, and image use in a single sharpening operation, we've reluctantly concluded that it is, in fact, impossible to do so. Of course, this conclusion flies in the face of conventional wisdom, which dictates that sharpening should be applied in a single pass as either the last or next-to-last step (before conversion to final CMYK in an RGB workflow) in the image reproduction chain. The conventional wisdom does have some foundation:

- Back when the drum scanner was king, images were usually scanned directly to RGB and automatically converted to CMYK, at reproduction size, with sharpening appropriate to the halftone screen applied by the scanner. The conventional wisdom workflow tries to replicate this.

- If downsampling is done after sharpening, the image has to be resharpened, because the haloes get downsampled out of existence.

- Multiple passes (of the wrong kind) of sharpening tend to ruin images.

These are all good points that deserve careful consideration, but let's look at the downsides to the conventional wisdom (aside from it coming from the last millennium and, therefore, being way out of date).

TRADITIONAL PREPRESS SHARPENING

First, let's be clear that traditional sharpening works reasonably well as long as it's done with the requisite skill and the built-in assumptions aren't violated. But there's a substantial difference between "reasonably well" and "optimally."

In the traditional sharpening workflow, sharpening is applied either as the final process (which allows tricks like sharpening only the black plate, so that eyelashes and hair get sharpened, but skin textures don't) or as the next-to-last process before conversion to final CMYK. It offers a simple workflow (which is no small advantage), but it also has its share of disadvantages.

One-Pass Sharpening Is Inflexible

A key assumption in the traditional sharpening workflow is that the final use is known *and* the image has been sized for that final use. Back in the Rubylith days, this assumption was generally valid because the size of an image reproduction was set by the supplied mechanical design. But as soon as page layout applications gave designers the ability to resize images in layout, that assumption went out the window because, of course, designers *will* resize the images in page layout.

Nowadays, it's common practice for prepress operations to act both as suppliers of original scans and as the final step in the output chain. As a result, it's not uncommon for scanned images to receive two rounds of sharpening behind the scenes: once at the time of the scan on the high-resolution image, and again on the resized image before output. The key point is that traditional sharpening was designed to be applied only to the final image at final output resolution. The further the image is from that state, the less successful the traditional sharpening approach is likely to be.

TIP: Buy unsharpened scans. If you're buying drum scans for images whose final use is unknown or to use as master images for multiple outputs, specify no sharpening during the scan process. Inappropriate sharpening is extremely hard to undo and, unless the images are scanned to their final output resolution, any sharpening applied during the scan is almost guaranteed to be inappropriate. Even if you opt to stay with a one-pass sharpening workflow, that workflow will work better when you reserve sharpening for the final output-sized image.

One-Pass Sharpening Is Often Overdone

Traditional sharpening, as it is commonly in use today, is sensitive neither to image content nor to final use. As a result, it's common to see grossly over-sharpened images, especially in the case where a sharpened scan receives a second round of sharpening at final output size.

Figure 3-1 shows an image scanned without sharpening, then sharpened carefully in two passes, and the same image sharpened during the scan and then again after resizing.

Figure 3-1 Oversharpening

This version of the image was scanned with no sharpening, then sharpened carefully in two passes: once on the high-resolution scan, then again at final output resolution after resampling to size.

This version of the image was sharpened during the scan, then sharpened again at final output size, using "standard" sharpening techniques.

While this kind of oversharpening is rare in high-end work (because someone has paid to make sure that it doesn't happen), it's depressingly commonplace in commercial publishing. However, this is not an argument against multi-pass sharpening; both versions of the image in Figure 3-1 received two sharpening passes. Rather, it's an argument against careless sharpening that fails to account for image source, content, and final use.

Figure 3-2 shows details of both images zoomed in 200%. You'll note that the oversharpened image has crunchy grain and overly bright-edged haloes. Both of these image attributes are undesirable and rather difficult to fix or eliminate. Once oversharpening has occurred, there is very little one can do to undo the damage done to the image.

Figure 3-2 Oversharpening viewed at 200% zoom

This is the optimally sharpened version, zoomed in.

This image received the "standard" sharpening technique. Note the excessive grain and edge haloes.

One-Pass Sharpening and Digital Capture

Traditional one-pass sharpening was very much tailored to scanned transparencies, since it essentially tries to simulate the sharpening that was built into drum scanners. It's possible to get good drum scans from color negative, but relatively few operators know how to do so.

Traditional Sharpening Is Global

A salient feature of traditional sharpening is that it's applied globally to the entire image. While this worked reasonably well with transparency scans, it generally fails to do justice to digital raw captures, where it sharpens the noise along with the edges.

The problem can become worse if unsophisticated global sharpening is applied by the conversion from raw camera capture into a rendered RGB image. Bear in mind that when you shoot JPEG, the camera itself performs a raw conversion, often with global sharpening applied as default.

Global sharpening in the raw converter followed by traditional sharpening produces images with sharp noise, but not necessarily with optimally sharp image detail.

Most raw converters offer the option to produce an unsharpened image, but many photographers decline to exercise this option because the results are obviously soft on the display. Yet many of the major stock agencies specify that submissions should be unsharpened. This is a recipe for soft images.

NOTE: When stock photo agencies ask for unsharpened images for digital submission, what they are really asking for are images that haven't been ruined by oversharpening. Since final output type, size, and resolution cannot be known in advance, photographers should not be tempted to apply any output sharpening to images supplied to stock agencies. Properly sharpening for output is the role of the final buyer, unless the agency offers that service. However, photographers should do careful preliminary "capture sharpening" and any "creative sharpening" as required by careful examination of the image.

Traditional Sharpening Fails to Exploit Digital Capture

By their nature, unsharpened digital captures produce images that both tolerate *and* require a good deal more sharpening than those from film. Most digital cameras actually include an optical low-pass filter to prevent color artifacting and Moiré patterns (discussed in Chapter 2, "Why Do We Sharpen?"), which has the effect of softening the image. As a result, traditional sharpening, which is optimized for transparency scans, often undersharpens digital captures.

Figure 3-3 shows the difference between a traditionally sharpened and an optimally sharpened digital raw capture.

Figure 3-3
Digital raw capture and undersharpening

This is the full-frame image from a Canon EOS-1Ds Mark III shot with a 300mm F2.8 lens at ISO 200. The full print size of this image was 18.75" x 12.5" at 300 ppi (pixels per inch).

This contact-print–sized version of the image was produced by applying zero global sharpening in the raw converter, followed by traditional one-pass sharpening at final print size. It's not really sharp at all.

This contact-print–sized version of the image was produced by applying optimal selective sharpening in Adobe Camera Raw, followed by output sharpening at print size. It's noticeably sharper than the version above.

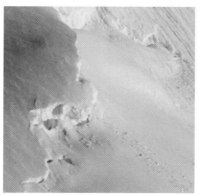

This is a 200% zoom view of the image without sharpening in the raw capture but with output sharpening.

This is a 200% zoom view of the image sharpened in Camera Raw with the following settings: Amount: 65; Radius: 0.7; Detail: 80; Masking: 10; Luminance: 8; and Color: 25. The output sharpening was suitable for 150-lpi (lines per inch) halftone with 300-ppi resolution.

This failure to understand the inherent properties of digital capture and the differences between digital capture and scanned transparencies has given rise to a considerable body of prepress myth regarding the perceived superiority of film over digital capture. But like it or not, digital capture has already largely replaced film for most commercial work, and the trend is clear and irreversible.

Traditional Sharpening Roots

Traditional sharpening is rooted in the drum scanner and, moreover, in the analog drum scanner. The earliest drum scanners, from the 1960s, were analog devices that produced actual CMYK film separations, and the sharpening was done optically. By the 1980s, drum scanners produced digital CMYK files from RGB scans, still with optical sharpening.

When the desktop revolution hit in the early 1990s, the old paradigm of scanning at final resolution for a specific use fell by the wayside. Adobe Photoshop 2.0 introduced CMYK support and changed print manufacturing forever—though not overnight. Proprietary systems from the likes of Scitex, Linotype-Hell, Crosfield, and Agfa continued to hold sway for much of the decade, but by 1999, Photoshop had become not only a ubiquitous noun, but also a verb.

Photoshop Sharpening Practice

As has often been the case when an analog process is replaced by a digital one, most practitioners of sharpening in Photoshop used Photoshop's sharpening tools to replicate the drum scanning workflow. There is still considerable debate as to whether to sharpen before or after conversion to CMYK (some even advocate converting to Lab and sharpening the Lightness channel), but it's generally agreed that sharpening must be done at the final output size and resolution, after all major tonal adjustments have been performed.

Traditional Sharpening Problems

The main problem with the traditional sharpening approach is that it tries to account for image source, image content, and output process in a single round of sharpening. After nearly 20 years of experience using Photoshop to produce images both on press and on desktop printers, Bruce and Jeff have concluded that it's simply impossible to address all three factors in one sharpening pass. The preceding pages of this book show the kinds of problems that arise when we attempt to do so. While the results aren't invariably bad, they're never as good as they could be.

Multipass Sharpening Problems

Many Photoshop users have, at some point, tried a multipass sharpening approach. A few have made it work, but the vast majority have wound up creating grossly oversharpened images, usually by falling into one or more of four potential pitfalls:

• Relying on the computer display to judge sharpness is a practice fraught with peril, yet until we make the print, it's all we have. The temptation is to make the image look sharp on screen, then to sharpen it again for output, often with unacceptable results.

• Failure to take image content into account in the first round of sharpening typically results in applying the wrong *kind* of sharpening for the image, so wanted detail may be obscured, and unwanted detail or noise may be exaggerated.

• Applying the first pass of sharpening globally, rather than through a mask that isolates edges, sharpens noise, flat-textured surface areas (such as skies), and the edges. When the second pass of sharpening is applied, the image becomes oversharpened.

• Applying the first pass of sharpening to the entire tonal range, rather than protecting the extreme highlights and shadows, almost guarantees that the second pass of sharpening will create blown highlights and plugged shadows.

The good news is that all of these problems are avoidable given sufficient attention, care, and skill. Building a multipass sharpening workflow is not a trivial undertaking, but neither is it impossible—otherwise we wouldn't have bothered writing this book!

A MULTIPASS SHARPENING WORKFLOW

It's impossible to address the varying needs of the image source, the image content, and the output process in a single pass, because each imposes requirements that can contradict the others. The solution, then, is to build a multipass sharpening workflow that addresses the individual needs separately.

Each component has its own requirements, and by ignoring everything else, we can tailor each sharpening pass to address a specific issue.

Phase One: Capture Sharpening

When the first edition of the book was released, some people were somewhat confused about the definition and role of capture sharpening. Bruce had written about sharpening for the image source as well as the image content as though they were two different sharpening passes. They weren't. The intent was to describe two different aspects that needed to be considered when doing sharpening at the early input stage, which Bruce called "capture sharpening."

Whether the capture is on film and scanned or made with a digital camera, the concept remains the same. You must apply initial sharpening to the image, and this initial sharpening must consider two components very carefully: the image source and the image content. Done properly, both components can be addressed in a single round of capture sharpening.

The goal of this first pass of the sharpening workflow is to create an image that responds well to subsequent rounds of sharpening aimed at the image content and at the output process. We recommend performing any major tonal correction before doing any sharpening or noise reduction, because sharpening and noise reduction can't easily be undone if it's done before the tone and color correction.

Figure 3-4 shows an image in Camera Raw at the default sharpening settings. (We'll follow this image through the entire sharpening workflow.) Optimizing Camera Raw's sharpening settings is one example of capture sharpening. Note that the tone and color correction settings have already been determined; only the sharpening and noise-reduction settings are being addressed at this stage.

Optimizing for the Image Source

Optimization for the image source is dictated by two factors: the noise signature and the amount of detail the system can record. The inherent softness of most digital captures (due to the anti-aliasing filter) requires actual sharpening, where with film the emphasis may be on grain reduction instead.

Optimizing digital captures. With digital capture, the lens is more often than not the practical limiting factor on the amount of detail the system can record, but the optical low-pass (anti-aliasing) filter found in the majority of digital SLRs sets an absolute limit.

Figure 3-4 Capture sharpening's default settings in Camera Raw

For those few cameras that lack an anti-aliasing filter, it may be worthwhile making lens-specific settings, but in general we can come up with a single sharpening routine that is optimal for a given camera. High-ISO shots and significantly underexposed images may need special handling of noise, in either the raw converter or in Photoshop. Severe noise may call for a dedicated third-party noise-reduction plug-in.

With normal exposures at low ISO settings, it's often enough to simply avoid sharpening the noise by protecting the extreme shadows.

Figure 3-5 shows the beginning of the process of optimizing the settings. In general, the controls of Camera Raw are set out in the logical order of use. It should be expected, however, that adjusting subsequent settings may require modifications of previously made adjustments. In this figure, the Option key (Mac) or Alt key (Windows) is being held down while adjusting the Amount slider. This instructs Camera Raw to display the luminance image data that will be sharpened in the processing pipeline. In addition to sharpening only the luminance data, Camera Raw also rolls off the extreme highlight and shadow detail so that image sharpening won't cause clipping.

Figure 3-5 Adjusting the Amount parameter

The preliminary Amount adjustments using the luminance preview as a guide to adjustment. This is the first stage of adjusting for both image source and content.

Optimizing film captures. It's a little more difficult to make generalizations about film capture, since the scanner represents a huge variable in both tonal rendering and resolution. With film, the amount of resolvable detail may be limited by the film grain or by the lens. On most film captures, the first pass is less about sharpening the image and more about mitigating the film grain. At one extreme, 35mm color negative requires strong grain reduction, while at the other extreme, large-format (4" x 5" or 8" x 10") transparencies can usually skip the first pass altogether.

We'll discuss specific techniques you can use to achieve these ends in Chapter 5, "Industrial-Strength Sharpening Techniques." Photoshop invariably offers several different ways to accomplish any given task, and for the moment, it's more important to understand the goals of the different stages in the workflow than it is to focus on the details of the techniques needed to attain those goals.

Optimizing for Image Content

As you saw in Chapter 2, a busy, high-frequency image with lots of fine detail demands a different kind of sharpening than does a low-frequency image with soft, wide edges. This phase of the sharpening workflow is where that difference is taken into account.

Figure 3-6 shows the live edge mask being generated on the fly by Camera Raw. The mask plays a dual role: It prevents sharpening areas of flat texture, leaving headroom for the final output sharpening, and it provides some control over the width of the sharpened edges. Again, the preview is being generated by holding down the Option (Alt) key while adjusting the slider.

Figure 3-6 Adjusting the Masking setting to concentrate the sharpening on the edges, not the surfaces.

The layer mask offers some limited control over the width of the sharpening halo, but it's vital to match the actual sharpening settings to the image content rather than relying on the mask. We'll discuss techniques for building and applying layer masks, and applying sharpening through them, in Chapter 4. For now, it's enough to remember the simple rule that white reveals and black conceals. (Logically enough, intermediate shades of gray apply varying opacities to the masked layer proportional to the shade of gray.)

The layer mask's real job is to protect the areas we don't want to sharpen at this stage, which is everything except the obvious edges. Note the qualifier, "obvious"—almost all images contain a mixture of low-frequency, mid-frequency, and high-frequency edges. In this phase of workflow, you need to decide the dominant tendency and sharpen accordingly.

Content optimization shares some of the properties of source optimization —the sharpening is applied in luminosity blend mode to eliminate the possibility of color shifts, and the sharpening is focused mostly on the midtones while highlights and shadows are protected. The sharpening radius is tuned to the image content we want to emphasize rather than being dictated by the properties of the sensor.

Figure 3-7 shows the final, optimized capture sharpening settings for this image. The radius setting of 0.8 is intended to concentrate the sharpening on the high-frequency edges of the image. The Detail setting was also increased to reduce halo dampening, and a slight amount of Luminance noise reduction was added. The Color noise reduction was also reduced because this capture had less need. The aim of these settings is to optimize the capture sharpening of the image prior to opening in Photoshop, which will bring us to the next phase: creative sharpening.

Figure 3-7 The final capture-sharpening settings used for this image

Phase Two: Creative Sharpening

Creative sharpening isn't required for every image (if you're shooting 500 plumbing widgets on white seamless backgrounds, creative sharpening probably isn't in the budget), but on some images, subtle sharpening (or blurring) moves can make a big difference.

For example, on headshots we often add a little extra sharpness to the eyes and hair. Sometimes skin texture needs a little softening. And of course, while one way to make a subject stand out from its surroundings is to sharpen it, it's sometimes more effective to blur the surroundings (which makes the subject appear sharper without actually sharpening it).

Figure 3-8 shows some examples of creative sharpening and blurring. They represent subjective decisions made on our part with which you may well disagree, but they serve to illustrate the point that localized control of detail can be a creative tool. The Progressive Sharpening layer is a result of running multiple passes of an increasing radius in the Unsharp Mask filter while fading each step. The Box Blur layer is being used to soften the corners of the image, while the Midtone Contrast is increasing the contrast of only the image's midtones. All three of these creative sharpening steps (and more) will be shown in detail in Chapter 5, "Industrial-Strength Sharpening Techniques."

Figure 3-8 This figure shows the result of three different creative sharpening steps: Progressive Sharpening, Box Blur, and Midtone Contrast.

There are few rules for creative sharpening beyond those dictated by taste: You have to learn the behavior of your display so that you can make reasonable judgments as to how far to push the sharpening, and there's no shortcut for doing that.

As with all the previous steps in the sharpening workflow, it's a good idea to leave headroom for the final output sharpening by protecting the extreme highlights and shadows, and to do your creative sharpening on the native-resolution image. We'll discuss specific techniques for creative sharpening in Chapter 5.

Phase Three: Output Sharpening

The final step in the sharpening workflow compensates both for the softness introduced by the output process and for the softening induced by resizing to final output resolution. At this stage in the workflow, all the other factors that affect sharpening have already been addressed, so this step can focus (no pun intended) entirely on the output process.

Since the relationship between input pixels and output dots is always the same for a given output process, it's possible to create a single optimal sharpening routine for each different output process and resolution. It's true that different platesetters or different inkjet printers use subtly different screening algorithms, but all we can do is sharpen the pixels—we can't control how they get turned into dots—and, in practice, these small differences are below the threshold that we can address by sharpening pixels.

Figure 3-9 shows the final image resizing and output sharpening.

You'll note in Figure 3-9 that the image has been resized and resampled to 4.25" x 2.8" at 300 ppi. The output sharpening was applied after the resize/resample and broken down into two layers: the Light Contour and Dark Contour. Again, we'll describe the process of creating output sharpening in detail in later chapters.

By far the most important factor when output sharpening is the pixel resolution you send to print, because that resolution dictates the size of the pixels and, hence, the size of the sharpening haloes. Up to this point in the workflow, we've tried to avoid obvious sharpening haloes. For output sharpening, however, we want haloes that may be obvious on the computer display when viewed at actual pixels (or higher) zoom, but that will still fall below the threshold of visual acuity at reasonable viewing distance for the print.

Matte papers need slightly more sharpening than glossy or luster papers to achieve the same apparent sharpness, since the ink bleeds a little more on matte papers, but the difference is quite small. It's up to you to decide whether it's worthwhile making separate sharpening routines for the same device on matte and glossy papers. It's almost certainly overkill to make more than two paper-specific routines.

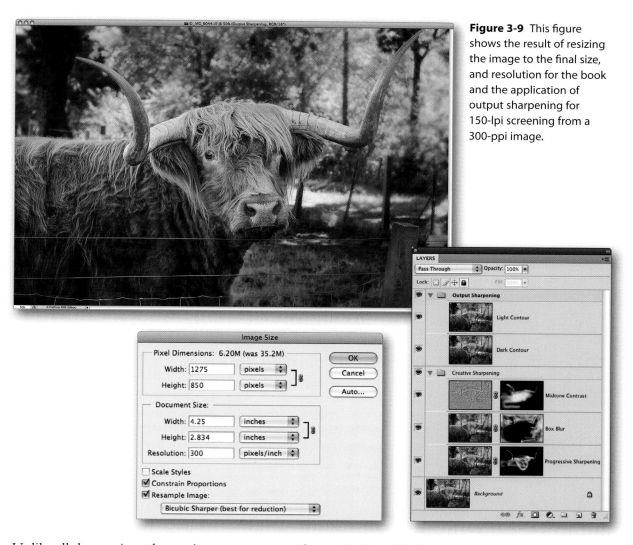

Figure 3-9 This figure shows the result of resizing the image to the final size, and resolution for the book and the application of output sharpening for 150-lpi screening from a 300-ppi image.

Unlike all the previous sharpening passes, output sharpening is applied globally to the entire image, with no masking, and often to the entire tonal range without protecting the highlights and shadows. It's by far the simplest of the sharpening passes, but it's a vital one.

Figure 3-10 shows the final result of capture sharpening, creative sharpening, and output sharpening.

Figure 3-10 This figure shows the result of a multi-pass sharpening workflow.

Identifying Hamish: A Case for CSI

When Jeff was preparing screenshots for this edition of the book, he thought he recognized this Highland steer as being Hamish from *Real World Camera Raw with Adobe Photoshop CS4*—or at least he thought he did. How many Highland steers could Bruce have photographed while visiting Scotland?

Figure 3-11 shows both images.

The metadata indicates that image _MG_5589 was shot on August 4, 2005, and image _MG_6044 was shot four days later, on the 8th. Jeff thought the odds were pretty good that this might be a case of Bruce revisiting a likely subject and that both shots were of Hamish—whose horns, apparently, the Scots have a hard time keeping American tourists from grabbing.

There are enough points of similarity in the steer's nose that Jeff feels confident that even the TV show *CSI* would conclude that both images are of the same Highland steer (even though in the two shots, Hamish tried to disguise himself by parting his hair differently).

Figure 3-11 The identification of Hamish

The original image _MG_5589 from *Real World Camera Raw with Adobe Photoshop CS4*

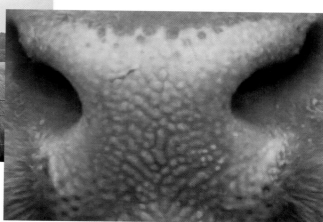

The 200% zoom of the steer's nose

The original image _MG_6044 from the last edition of this book, *Real World Image Sharpening with Adobe Photoshop CS*

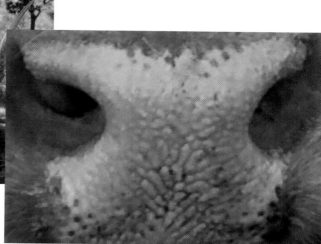

The 200% zoom of this steer's nose

BENEFITS OF A MULTIPASS SHARPENING WORKFLOW

If care and craft are applied to the development of a sharpening workflow, the benefits of such workflow far outweigh what may be seen as more steps and more work. Even in a high-production environment, a properly designed workflow can lead to improved results with more efficient processes.

Use-Neutral Capture-Sharpened Master Images

The combination of source and content optimization produces a "use-neutral" master image that can be repurposed for different outputs. The optimized image can be downsampled or, to a lesser extent, upsampled, then sharpened for the specific use at hand. This is a very different model from the traditional sharpening workflow, where sharpening starts from scratch at every different use. The presharpened image becomes a digital asset, ready for a wide range of output uses.

Of course, there are limits. Film grain makes scanned images less amenable to resizing than digital captures, but experience suggests that we can upsample presharpened digital captures to 200% or downsample to 10% without additional handling beyond output sharpening.

Fixed Output Sharpening

A second benefit of this workflow is that, since all the image-specific and source-specific issues have already been addressed, output sharpening becomes a fixed, determinate process that requires no decision-making. Since the relationship between input pixels and output dots (or output pixels, if the output is to the display) is fixed—that is, it doesn't vary from image to image—it becomes possible to create optimal routines for output sharpening that do not and need not vary with image source or content.

In the future, such sharpening routines may be embedded in printer drivers or RIPs (raster image processors), where they can be applied automatically. (Many workflows already rely on in-RIP separations and in-RIP trapping, so in-RIP sharpening doesn't seem like much of a stretch.) At this stage in the workflow, only these factors influence sharpening:

- The type of output (halftone, continuous-tone, inkjet, etc.)

- The image size and resolution

- The paper type (glossy/coated papers need slightly less—and different—sharpening than matte/uncoated ones to achieve the same apparent sharpness)

All these factors are known at print time, so output sharpening becomes a simple matter of selecting and running the appropriate routine. This is one of the benefits with Adobe Lightroom's Print module. Output sharpening can be applied on the fly during the printing process, which greatly aids output efficiency and consistency.

CREATING A MULTIAPPLICATION SHARPENING WORKFLOW

So far we've not really broken down the various sharpening tools available in Photoshop, Camera Raw, and Lightroom. In Chapter 5, we'll concentrate on explaining the relative benefits and various sharpening techniques available in these applications. But we wanted to give an outline and a flowchart in this chapter.

Which application you use for which function will play a role in defining your own personal sharpening workflow. Figure 3-12 shows a potential sharpening workflow deploying Photoshop, Camera Raw, and Lightroom for various tasks. As you can see, there are various options depending on whether the source image is a scan or a capture. Lightroom can be used for database organizational tasks while also developing capture sharpening settings in the Develop module.

Figure 3-12

A multiapplication
sharpening workflow chart

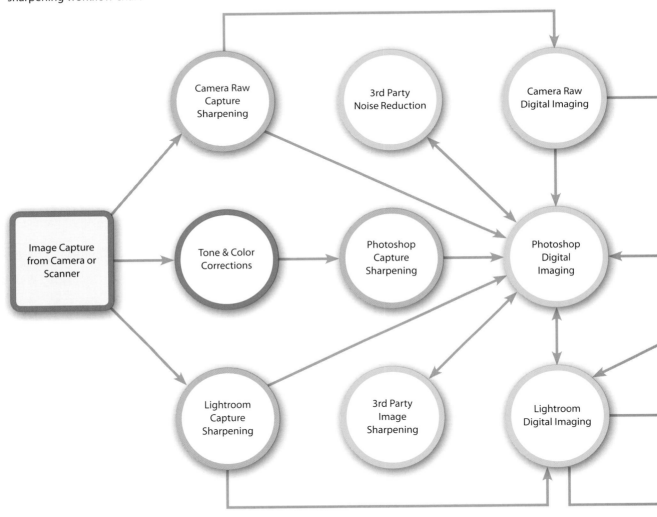

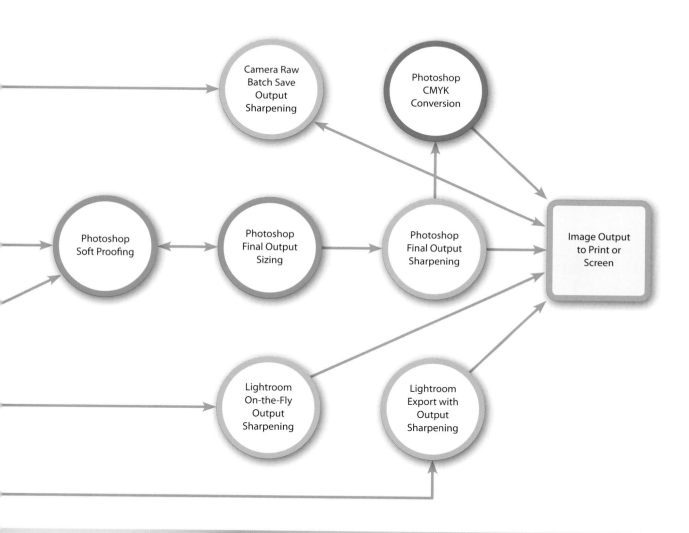

Output Prep   **Output Sharpening**   **Final Output**

Sharpening in Photoshop

As the granddaddy of digital-imaging applications, there's no doubt one can "do it all" with Photoshop (or one of its third-party plug-ins). Photoshop's main sharpening tools are the Unsharp Mask and Smart Sharpen filters. There are a wide variety (some might say dizzying variety) of other methods of sharpening using a variety of other tools, filters, and layers. Noise reduction can also be handled using the Reduce Noise filter or other filters and tools. Figure 3-13 shows the main tools in Photoshop's arsenal.

Figure 3-13 Photoshop's main sharpening and noise-reduction toolset

Smart Sharpen filter

Unsharp Mask filter

Reduce Noise filter

The massive power and complicated flexibility of Photoshop must also be considered a usability weakness. While all the tools provide virtually unlimited functionality, it's left to the user to figure out what tool to use, and in what order, to accomplish a sharpening workflow. Then, as if Photoshop weren't enough functionality, you have a healthy third-party developer community offering specialized tools that further extend Photoshop.

Sharpening in Camera Raw

Camera Raw 5.2+, which works with Photoshop CS4, offers the potential for a complete sharpening workflow. In practice however, Camera Raw really excels in capture sharpening.

Figure 3-14 shows Camera Raw's main sharpening toolset for capture and creative sharpening. The Detail panel allows four parameters under Sharpening and two under Noise Reduction. We would argue that the Luminance noise-reduction slider is really the fifth sharpening slider, because unless you fine-tune the Luminance noise reduction, you won't be able to fine-tune the Detail slider of Sharpening.

The Detail panel for capture sharpening

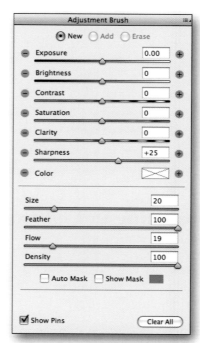

The Adjustment Brush for creative sharpening

Figure 3-14 Camera Raw's main sharpening and noise-reduction toolset

Camera Raw does have a localized sharpening channel available as an Adjustment Brush. However, Jeff believes that the Sharpness slider of the Adjustment Brush is a good placeholder for a tool yet to be developed, as the current implementation leaves a lot to be desired. As it stands in Camera Raw 5.x, it's not really ready for prime time as a creative sharpening tool. Ironically, Clarity (with either negative or positive numbers) is a very useful creative sharpening tool.

NOTE: Camera Raw 5.0, which shipped in October 2008, was updated with new functionality in version 5.2 at the end of November 2008. One of the big changes to 5.2 was output sharpening being added to the Camera Raw 5.2 Workflow Options dialog. This was consistent with Lightroom 2.2 and was part of the agreement between Adobe and PixelGenius to incorporate Bruce Fraser's PhotoKit Sharpener's output sharpening philosophies into Lightroom and Camera Raw.

As far as the output sharpening available in Camera Raw, it works in version 5.2 and above, but only in very limited uses where the exact final size and resolution can be determined and set inside of Camera Raw. Figure 3-15 shows the Camera Raw Workflow Options dialog. Since Output Sharpening must be applied only after the final size and resolution can be determined, that limits the type of output for which Camera Raw can be used.

Figure 3-15 Camera Raw's output sharpening in the Workflow Options dialog

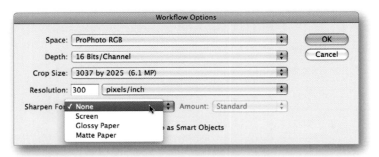

Sharpening in Lightroom

Lightroom shares the same processing pipeline found in Camera Raw. So, while usability may vary, the same parameters set in Lightroom and Camera Raw will produce the same rendered result. The primary differences are usability and user interface.

Lightroom also shares the relatively limited creative sharpening tools found in Camera Raw's Adjustment Brush. We suggest very limited use of the Sharpness slider in the Adjustment Brush, as over-application cannot be undone once an image has been processed as a rendered image file.

Figure 3-16 shows Lightroom's capture and creative sharpening options.

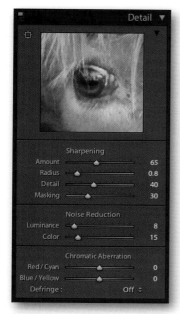

Figure 3-16 Lightroom's main sharpening and noise-reduction toolset

The Detail panel for capture sharpening

The Adjustment Brush for creative sharpening

Lightroom's output sharpening is arguably much more refined and useful than what is currently found in Camera Raw. Since Lightroom can sharpen on the fly when sending an image to a printer, there's no need for resizing and resharpening different versions of the same image. Lightroom takes the current capture sharpening, applies it to the image in memory, resizes (and/or resamples) the image for the image cell size, and sharpens the image data on the way to the printer. This on-the-fly print sharpening is one of the reasons that printing out of Lightroom is one of the program's most popular features.

Figure 3-17 shows print sharpening in Lightroom's Print module and Export dialog box.

Figure 3-17 Lightroom's output sharpening

Output sharpening for prints in the Lightroom Print Job panel

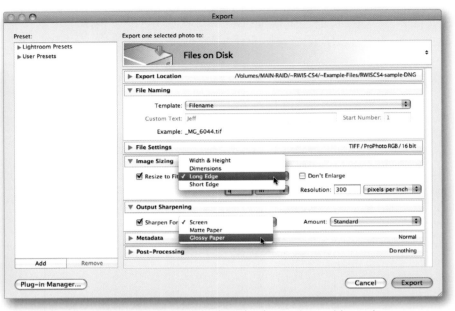

Output sharpening in Lightroom's Export dialog box, also showing image sizing options

Lightroom can also deploy output sharpening when exporting images, as shown in Figure 3-17. Lightroom offers more control over final image size and resolution than Camera Raw does, so the option to use output sharpening upon export is enhanced.

Output Sharpening in Practice

In this book, we're limited to showing the output sharpening for the 150-line screen used to print it. But within these constraints, we *can* show how output sharpening interacts with the previous stages of the sharpening workflow on the same images downsampled to different resolutions.

Figure 3-18 shows several versions of an image. All versions were produced from the same native-resolution master file. The only differences are in the output resolution and the output sharpening that accommodates it, and whether or not it had been optimized for source and content.

Figure 3-18 Output sharpening and resolution

Contact-print size at 300 ppi, unsharpened

Contact-print size at 300 ppi, sharpened for 150-lpi screen

Contact-print size at 225 ppi, sharpened for 150-lpi screen

There may be very little visible difference between the two sharpened images, since the difference between 300 ppi and 225 ppi will show subtle differences in print. In practice, you need to send somewhere between 1.5 and two times the halftone line screen for adequate halftone dot creation. We tend to stick with the 2x figure because our experience shows it's optimal for photography.

Output sharpening is very much like traditional prepress sharpening. You'll see that the versions without optimization for source and content aren't unacceptably soft, but you'll also see that the optimized versions are sharper, without appearing oversharpened. The optimizations for source and content allow us to take the same master file and produce optimally sharp versions of the image at different sizes and resolutions simply by downsampling and applying the appropriate output sharpeners.

Output Sharpening and the Display

Just to round out the picture, Figure 3-19 shows a zoomed detail of the optimized and output-sharpened image that corresponds roughly to viewing the image pixels on screen at 200% and 400% zoom. We included these views not because attempting to judge sharpness by looking at pixels at 200% or 400% zoom is a useful or even rational activity—it isn't—but simply to dramatize the fact that images that are well sharpened for output will almost certainly look scary on the computer display.

We fully admit that Figure 3-19 forces you to engage in an unseemly activity commonly called "pixel-peeping." Photoshop CS4 even allows you to extend the degree of peeping to an eerie 3200% zoom. While we'll admit to sometimes gleaning useful image info from 400% zooms, we've never gotten anything useful out of looking at an image at 3200%.

As we explained back in Chapter 2, it's nearly impossible to judge final print sharpness from the display. At the risk of some redundancy, we reiterate the point here because it bears repeating. One of the biggest leaps of faith in the entire Photoshop universe is sending pixels that look hideous on screen to a printing device. But if the pixels don't look seriously crunchy on the display, you're almost certainly undersharpening your images. The only reliable way to evaluate print sharpening is to sharpen the image, print it, and look at the print!

Figure 3-19 Comparing unsharpened and output-sharpened images zoomed in

Image at 200%, unsharpened

Image at 200%, creative and output sharpened

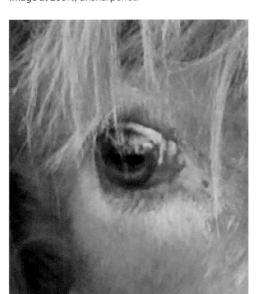

Image at 400%, unsharpened

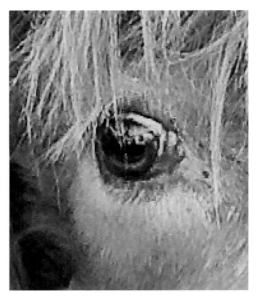

Image at 400%, creative and output sharpened

FROM THEORY TO PRACTICE

Thus far, the focus of this book has been to expound the theory of a workflow-based approach to sharpening images. In the ensuing chapters, we'll shift that focus to concentrate on the practical application of the theory. Good sharpening requires mastery of a significant body of technique and knowledge of some of the murkier depths of Photoshop. So in Chapter 4 we cover all the tools we use, and in Chapter 5 we cover all the techniques and tricks that we use in our own sharpening workflow, including nondestructive layer-based sharpening and the all-important use of layer masks.

CHAPTER FOUR

Sharpening Tools

Learning to Sharpen

Thus far, this book has been fairly long on theory and short on practice. In this chapter, we'll switch focus to looking in depth at what the tools Adobe Photoshop, Adobe Camera Raw, and Adobe Lightroom offer for sharpening images, and how to use them effectively in a capture-to-output sharpening workflow. The tools themselves are important, but there's a world of difference between simply running the Unsharp Mask filter on a flattened image and running it on a layer with an edge mask: The former uses a tool, while the latter employs a technique.

So in this chapter, we'll explain the basic tools, but we'll also discuss using those tools in ways that may not be obvious. Of course, Photoshop always offers multiple ways to carry out any given task. It's not our intention to cover every possible way to sharpen pixels. To do so would greatly lengthen this book, and take us into territories that our friend and colleague Fred Bunting eloquently describes as "more interesting than relevant."

Instead, we'll cover the tools that we've tested exhaustively, that we use on a daily basis, and in which we have total confidence. If a treasured trick of yours isn't covered here, don't worry—it's entirely possible that you know something that we don't. By the same token, if we debunk a cherished myth, rest assured that we do so without malice—at some point in time, they were very likely myths that we, too, cherished.

Sharpening Tools in Photoshop

Photoshop offers a variety of sharpening tools, ranging from the indispensable Unsharp Mask filter to the extremely hard to control Sharpen tool. But Photoshop also offers ways to sharpen images using features that don't provide any hint by their names that sharpening is one of their capabilities. Everyone has their preferred sets of tools, but few of us actually spend time analyzing what they do, so before examining the tools themselves, let us show you an easy way to see the effects of different sharpening routines.

Analyzing Sharpeners

One very easy way to compare the effect of different sharpening routines is to look at what they do to a variety of edges with different contrast. Figure 4-1 shows a simple test file that you can make yourself, which contains a single edge with varying contrast from solid black on white to midtone gray on midtone gray.

Figure 4-1
Sharpener analysis target

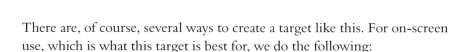

There are, of course, several ways to create a target like this. For on-screen use, which is what this target is best for, we do the following:

1. Create a new document, either RGB or Grayscale, 512 pixels wide by 50 pixels tall.

2. Fill it with a black-to-white gradient using the Gradient tool.

3. Select either the top or the bottom half of the image (the selection should be 512 pixels by 25 pixels—you can use the Info palette and/or the rulers to get the selection the right size).

4. Invert the selected area (choose Image > Adjustments > Invert, or press Command-I).

5. Crop the image in half horizontally from the right edge to obtain an image that looks like Figure 4-1, 256 pixels wide by 50 pixels tall.

If you zoom to around 400% or 500%, the target will still fit most screens, and you can easily see what happens at the pixel level. This target helps you understand what different sharpening tools do to edges, with the important caveat that their behavior on real images may be more complex than on this simple target.

The Sharpen Filter

Located on the Filter > Sharpen submenu, the Sharpen filter applies a simple, nonadjustable sharpening routine that creates a single-pixel halo for the light contour and a single-pixel halo for the dark contour. The haloes reach maximum intensity (solid black and pure white) when the difference between the light and dark sides of the edge is 169 levels.

Sharpen is virtually identical to running the Unsharp Mask filter (discussed later in this chapter) with Amount at 130, Radius at 0.4, and Threshold at 0. Figure 4-2 shows the target from Figure 4-1 after applying the Sharpen filter.

Figure 4-2
Sharpen filter

The Sharpen More Filter

As its name suggests, the Sharpen More filter, also on the Filter > Sharpen submenu, is a stronger version of Sharpen. It also creates a single-pixel halo, but reaches maximum intensity sooner, when the difference between the light and dark sides of the edges is 85 levels.

Sharpen More is virtually identical to running the Unsharp Mask filter with Amount at 390, Radius at 0.4, and Threshold at 0. Figure 4-3 shows the target from Figure 4-1 after applying the Sharpen More filter.

NOTE: Frankly, we don't use this or the Sharpen filter, because we can obtain the same results using the Unsharp Mask filter.

Figure 4-3
Sharpen More filter

The Sharpen Edges Filter

Sharpen Edges, which appears on the Sharpen submenu of the Filter menu between Sharpen and Sharpen More, is a little different than those filters: Its effect can't be replicated exactly using Unsharp Mask. However, Unsharp Mask with Amount at 140, Radius at 0.4, and Threshold at 3 comes very close—the Unsharp Mask produces very slightly stronger contrast in the midtones. Like Sharpen, Sharpen Edges reaches maximum intensity at a difference of 169 levels. The main difference between the two is that Sharpen Edges has a gentler start on values that differ only slightly.

Sharpen Edges isn't really any more useful than Sharpen or Sharpen More—the difference between what it does and what we can accomplish with Unsharp Mask is so small as to be merely academically interesting, and the lack of control makes it inflexible.

Figure 4-4 shows the target from Figure 4-1 after applying the Sharpen Edges filter.

Figure 4-4
Sharpen Edges filter

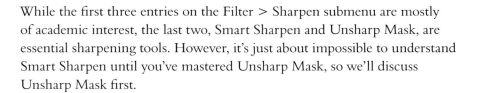

While the first three entries on the Filter > Sharpen submenu are mostly of academic interest, the last two, Smart Sharpen and Unsharp Mask, are essential sharpening tools. However, it's just about impossible to understand Smart Sharpen until you've mastered Unsharp Mask, so we'll discuss Unsharp Mask first.

The Unsharp Mask Filter

The Unsharp Mask filter is by far the most important item in the sharpening toolbox—if we were forced to rely on a single sharpening tool, we'd choose Unsharp Mask for its speed, power, and flexibility. In short, Unsharp Mask is indispensable! Unlike Sharpen, Sharpen Edges, and Sharpen More, all of which simply apply preset routines, the Unsharp Mask filter offers a great deal of control over sharpening.

Figure 4-5 shows the Unsharp Mask filter dialog box at its default settings: Amount at 100, Radius at 1, and Threshold at 0. Note, however, that the settings are sticky (remembered) between filter applications, so you'll see the default settings only once.

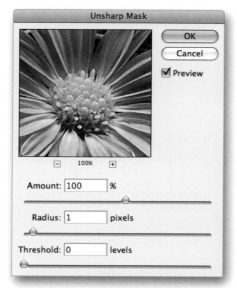

Figure 4-5 Unsharp Mask dialog box

Mastery of these three Unsharp Mask controls is the key to good sharpening:

- Amount
- Radius
- Threshold

Amount

The Amount control sets the intensity of the sharpening halo—the increase in contrast along edges. At low settings, it takes more difference between levels for the sharpening haloes to reach pure white and solid black; at higher settings, it takes less difference.

Figure 4-6 shows the effect of the Amount slider at constant Radius and Threshold settings.

Figure 4-6 Amount control

The Amount slider at 100, 200, 300, 400, and 500, with Radius 0.4 and Threshold 0. The red lines indicate the point at which the sharpening haloes reach maximum intensity at the selected Radius.

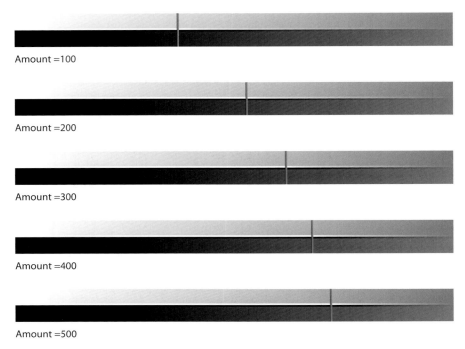

Amount =100

Amount =200

Amount =300

Amount =400

Amount =500

Radius

The Radius control sets the width of the sharpening haloes, though it also has some effect on their intensity. However, because it was designed by engineers rather than photographers, the number you enter into the Radius field doesn't actually produce haloes of that size (not that it's possible to produce a sharpening halo 0.4 pixels wide).

What the Radius setting actually does is a little more complicated than adding a determined pixel halo. The Unsharp Mask filter changes pixels one at a time, examining the surrounding pixels to determine the difference in contrast between the subject pixel and its neighbors. The Radius setting tells the filter how many surrounding pixels to take into account when calculating the new value for the subject pixel.

The net effect is that low Radius settings produce narrow sharpening haloes and higher settings produce wider ones. (At very high settings, the sharpening haloes collide and merge into one another, so the effect changes from a pure sharpening to an overall contrast adjustment—see "Local Area Contrast," later in this chapter.)

Figure 4-7 shows the effect of the Radius setting at constant Amount and Threshold settings. (We've zoomed and cropped the target to exclude the higher-contrast edges so that the difference between settings is more obvious.) Lower settings produce narrower haloes and higher settings produce wider ones, but the width of the haloes also depends on the contrast of the edge that's being sharpened.

Figure 4-7 Radius control

With Amount at 200 and Threshold at 0, the effect of the Radius setting at 0.4, 0.8, 1, 1.2, 1.5, 2, 3, and 5, from top to bottom

The red line shows the point at which the sharpening haloes reach maximum intensity.

The width of the haloes increases with contrast at any single Radius setting.

Notice that the intensity of the haloes increases with Radius—at higher settings, the sharpening haloes reach solid black and pure white earlier than they do at lower settings. However, Radius has a much smaller effect on intensity than Amount does.

The Radius control determines the "flavor" of the sharpening. Low-frequency images with wide edges and soft detail require higher Radius settings than high-frequency images with narrow edges and sharp tonal transitions. One of the most important aspects of sharpening images for content is matching the Radius setting to the edges in the image.

One aspect of Unsharp Mask that's less than optimal is the fact that it increases the width of the sharpening haloes as the contrast of the edge being sharpened increases. This is rarely the behavior we want.

Threshold

Threshold delays the onset of the sharpening haloes by telling the Unsharp Mask filter to ignore a certain amount of difference between pixels before applying any sharpening. Figure 4-8 shows the effect of the Threshold setting at constant settings for Radius and Amount—we've cropped the target to show the areas of interest.

The Threshold control is designed to allow you to protect textured areas, such as skin tones or slightly noisy skies, from being sharpened. At low settings (1 to 4), it works reasonably well on lightly textured areas, but may not provide enough protection. At higher settings, Threshold has a tendency to create unnatural-looking transitions between the sharpened and unsharpened areas. Because of this tendency, generally we rely on edge masks to protect textured areas rather than using Threshold. We'll cover techniques for doing so later in this chapter.

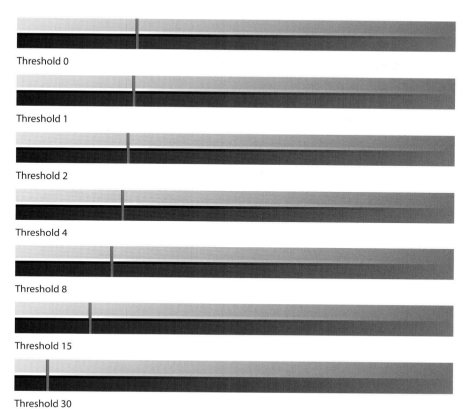

Threshold 0

Threshold 1

Threshold 2

Threshold 4

Threshold 8

Threshold 15

Threshold 30

Figure 4-8
Threshold control

Effect of the Threshold control with Amount at 200 and Radius at 0.4

The red line shows the point at which the sharpening haloes reach maximum intensity.

Working the Controls

Whether we apply Unsharp Mask globally or through a layer mask, we always set the Radius first, because more than any of the controls, it dictates the character of the sharpening. Many different combinations of Amount and Radius produce the same apparent amount of sharpening, but with subtly different characteristics.

As you increase the Radius, you need to reduce the Amount, and vice versa, to maintain the same degree of apparent sharpness. Figure 4-9 shows the same image detail with two very different Unsharp Mask settings that nevertheless produce approximately the same degree of sharpness.

The difference between the two versions below is extremely subtle—we'd be surprised if you can see it—but that subtle difference becomes more obvious when a second round of sharpening is applied for the output. Figure 4-10 shows the same image detail-sharpened for output, along with a 400% zoomed-in view of the output-sharpened pixels.

Before output sharpening, the two versions seemed identical, but after output sharpening we begin to see subtle differences. The high-frequency detail on the flower center is revealed more clearly in the lower, small-radius version than in the upper, larger-radius version. Examination of the zoomed-in pixels confirms this—the detail on the yellow center has higher contrast, and hence is more visible, in the small-radius version.

Figure 4-9
Amount and Radius

Unsharp Mask with Amount
150, Radius 1.5, Threshold 0

Unsharp Mask with Amount
500, Radius 0.4, Threshold 0

Figure 4-10 shows something else important: While targets like the one first shown in Figure 4-1 can help us understand a good deal about the basic behavior of sharpening tools, the application of those tools to real photographic images is a good deal more complicated, because edges in real images are often more complex than a single row of dark pixels against a single row of white pixels.

The behavior of the target might lead you to expect that the versions of the image in Figure 4-10 that were sharpened with a Radius setting of 1.5 might feature wider sharpening haloes than the one sharpened with a Radius setting of 0.4. Yet in practice the haloes have essentially the same width in both versions, because the image edges themselves constrain the width of the haloes. The higher-Radius version simply ends up with weaker contrast on the haloes.

Figure 4-10 Amount and Radius with output sharpening

Unsharp Mask with Amount 150, Radius 1.5, Threshold 0

Unsharp Mask with Amount 500, Radius 0.4, Threshold 0

Unsharp Mask Limitations

Unsharp Mask is an immensely useful and powerful tool, but it suffers from two significant limitations:

- The Threshold control isn't terribly good at protecting noisy or lightly textured areas from sharpening. At low settings, it may not provide enough protection, while at higher settings it can produce unnatural-looking transitions. More significantly, the Threshold control wipes out midtone sharpening, which is often where we need it most.

- Unsharp Mask always sharpens high-contrast edges more than low-contrast ones, which is usually the exact opposite of the behavior we need. On edges that are already at maximum contrast (solid black and pure white), Unsharp Mask simply widens the sharpening halo—a behavior that's almost always undesirable.

Local Area Contrast

Earlier in this section we mentioned using Unsharp Mask with a smaller Amount setting and larger Radius to adjust what some people call the "local area contrast." Substantially increasing the Radius to 50 or more actually inverts the edges and introduces a contrast adjustment that is image dependent. Thus, the image edges are used to adjust the tonal curve. This image-adaptive adjustment isn't really a sharpening effect from the Unsharp Mask filter, but it can produce useful results. Figure 4-11 shows the Unsharp Mask dialog box with lowered Amount and higher Radius.

Local area contrast image adjustments are similar to the Clarity slider of Camera Raw and Lightroom. Yet there is a different method of producing what we refer to as "midtone contrast" adjustments using the High Pass filter on an image layer set to Overlay blend mode.

Figure 4-11 Local area contrast

Unsharp Mask with Amount 25,
Radius 50, Threshold 0

Image before local area
contrast adjustment

Image after local area
contrast adjustment

The Smart Sharpen Filter

The Smart Sharpen filter is a good deal more complex than the Unsharp Mask filter because it offers more options. Figure 4-12 shows the Smart Sharpen dialog box in Basic mode.

Figure 4-12
Smart Sharpen dialog box

Smart Sharpen has no Threshold control, only Radius and Amount, but the additional controls it offers add up to many different permutations:

- The Basic and Advanced radio buttons control whether the Shadow and Highlight tabs become available. In Advanced mode, these two additional tabs let you shape the tonality of the light and dark contours, allowing you to reduce the sharpening on high-contrast edges (see Figure 4-13).

- The Remove menu lets you choose one of three flavors of sharpening. Remove Gaussian Blur works essentially the same as Unsharp Mask, Remove Lens Blur uses a different sharpening algorithm that attempts to differentiate actual edges from image noise, and Remove Motion Blur lets you (within limits) undo motion blur caused by subject or camera movement.

- Selecting the More Accurate checkbox makes the filter run more iterations, producing a significantly different result than when it's unselected. It also makes the filter run more slowly.

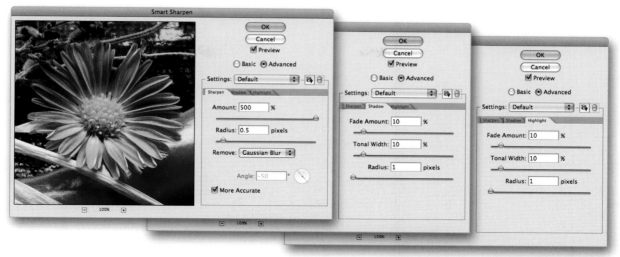

Figure 4-13 Smart Sharpen dialog box's Advanced tabs

Smart Sharpen also allows you to save commonly used parameters and call them back up as needed. Figure 4-14 shows the Save and Trash buttons, the New Filter Settings dialog box, and the saved setting in Smart Sharpen's drop-down menu.

Save and Trash buttons   New Filter Settings dialog box

Figure 4-14
Saving Smart Sharpen settings

Saved settings in the drop-down menu

Gaussian Blur

When Gaussian Blur is selected from the Remove menu, the More Accurate checkbox is unselected and the filter is in Basic mode. It behaves identically to Unsharp Mask with the same Amount and Radius settings and Threshold at 0.

When the More Accurate checkbox is selected, the filter behavior changes, producing a wider halo with gentler contrast. Figure 4-15 shows the difference between Gaussian Blur, Basic mode, with More Accurate unselected (which is the same as Unsharp Mask), and Gaussian Blur, Basic mode, with More Accurate selected.

Figure 4-15 Smart Sharpen, Remove Gaussian Blur, Basic mode, with and without More Accurate

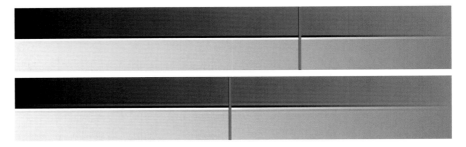

When More Accurate is unselected (upper image), Smart Sharpen with Gaussian Blur behaves exactly like Unsharp Mask. When More Accurate is selected (lower image), Smart Sharpen produces a wider, lower-contrast halo. The red line indicates where the sharpening haloes reach maximum intensity.

On real images, Gaussian Blur with More Accurate selected produces much weaker sharpening than when it's unselected, so much so that small-radius sharpening is very weak indeed. Figure 4-16 shows an image detail that had Smart Sharpening applied for content before being sharpened for output, using Amount 500 and Radius 0.5, with More Accurate unselected, and with More Accurate selected.

Both versions are acceptable, but the one that had the More Accurate button unselected has a little more snap. Numerous similar examples have led us to conclude that in the majority of cases, Smart Sharpen with Gaussian Blur in Basic mode offers little or no advantage over Unsharp Mask.

Figure 4-16 Smart Sharpen, Remove Gaussian Blur, Basic mode, with and without More Accurate

Smart Sharpen, Amount 500, Radius 0.5, More Accurate unselected, followed by output sharpening

Smart Sharpen, Amount 500, Radius 0.5, More Accurate selected, followed by output sharpening

Gaussian Blur Advanced Mode

When the Advanced radio button is selected, the Shadow and Highlight tabs (see Figure 4-13) become active. These tabs let you fade the contrast of the dark and light sharpening contours, respectively.

Both tabs offer the same three controls: Fade Amount, Tonal Width, and Radius, which together determine the way the Shadow (dark) and Highlight (light) contours along edges have their intensity reduced.

- *Fade Amount* controls the degree of fading of the Shadow or Highlight contour.

- *Tonal Width* controls the tonal range across which the fade applies, starting from solid black (level 0) for the Shadow contour and pure white (level 255) for the Highlight contour.

- *Radius* works akin to the Radius control in Photoshop's Shadow/ Highlight image adjustment command, specifying the neighborhood the filter evaluates in determining whether a pixel is a Shadow or Highlight pixel and hence is affected by the Shadow and Highlight tab settings.

When used in conjunction with Gaussian Blur, the effect of the Radius setting is barely detectable (and is detectable only by doing actual pixel-value comparisons—you can't see it). However, it has an obvious effect, not on the image, but on the speed of the filter—it's much, much slower at high Radius settings than at lower ones!

Figure 4-17 shows the effect of the Advanced mode options at several different settings. The difference between (Advanced) Radius set at 1 and the much slower (Advanced) Radius set at 100 is detectable, though not terribly visually significant, when the Tonal Width is set to a low amount, but it's basically insignificant at higher Tonal Width settings.

The ability to fade the highlight and shadow contours, and thus force more of the sharpening into the midtones, is useful for early-stage sharpening for image content, but you can lose a lot of time fiddling with settings that make almost no difference to the result!

Figure 4-17 Smart Sharpen, Gaussian Blur, Basic and Advanced modes

These figures differ only in the Advanced options. All were made with Amount at 500 and Radius at 0.4. The Fade Amount, Tonal Width, and Advanced Radius settings were applied equally in the Shadow and Highlight tabs.

The red lines indicate the maximum intensity of the sharpening haloes—in some cases, it's a range.

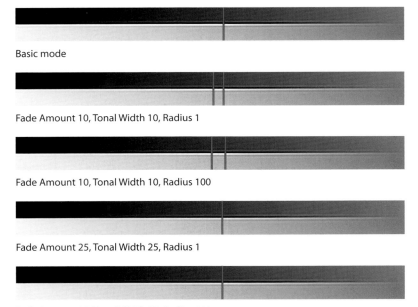

Basic mode

Fade Amount 10, Tonal Width 10, Radius 1

Fade Amount 10, Tonal Width 10, Radius 100

Fade Amount 25, Tonal Width 25, Radius 1

Fade Amount 25, Tonal Width 25, Radius 100

Lens Blur

Choosing Lens Blur from the Remove menu makes Smart Sharpen use a different algorithm that sharpens the midtones rather more aggressively than either Unsharp Mask or Smart Sharpen with Gaussian Blur. The More Accurate and Advanced options modulate the effect of the sharpening much like they do when Gaussian Blur is selected.

Figure 4-18 compares the Lens Blur and Gaussian Blur "flavors" of sharpening at two different strengths, with More Accurate on and off.

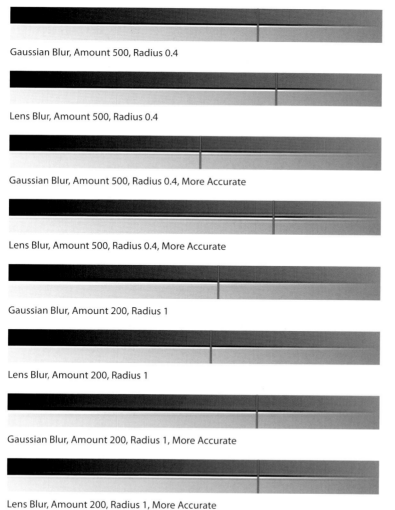

Gaussian Blur, Amount 500, Radius 0.4

Lens Blur, Amount 500, Radius 0.4

Gaussian Blur, Amount 500, Radius 0.4, More Accurate

Lens Blur, Amount 500, Radius 0.4, More Accurate

Gaussian Blur, Amount 200, Radius 1

Lens Blur, Amount 200, Radius 1

Gaussian Blur, Amount 200, Radius 1, More Accurate

Lens Blur, Amount 200, Radius 1, More Accurate

Figure 4-18 Smart Sharpen, Gaussian Blur, and Lens Blur compared

Lens Blur tends to sharpen the midtones more aggressively than Gaussian Blur, and maintains tighter haloes as edge contrast increases.

The red lines indicate the maximum intensity of the sharpening haloes.

The More Accurate option works approximately the same with Lens Blur as it does with Gaussian Blur, making a slightly wider but gentler sharpening halo. The most obvious difference between Gaussian Blur and Lens Blur is that the latter does a much better job of controlling the width of the halo along high-contrast edges than does Gaussian Blur, which creates ever-widening haloes as contrast increases.

Lens Blur Advanced Mode

The Advanced option enables Smart Sharpen's Shadow and Highlight tabs, allowing you to fade the light and dark contours of the sharpening haloes. The controls operate similarly to the way they do with Gaussian Blur (including the dramatic slowdown produced by high Radius settings in the Shadow and Highlight tabs), but the effect of the Shadow and Highlight Radius settings is a little more discernible than with Gaussian Blur, as shown in Figure 4-19.

Figure 4-19 Smart Sharpen, Lens Blur, Basic and Advanced modes

These figures differ only in the Advanced options. All were made with Amount at 500 and Radius at 0.4. The Advanced options were applied equally in the Shadow and Highlight tabs.

The red lines indicate the maximum intensity of the sharpening haloes—in some cases, it's a range.

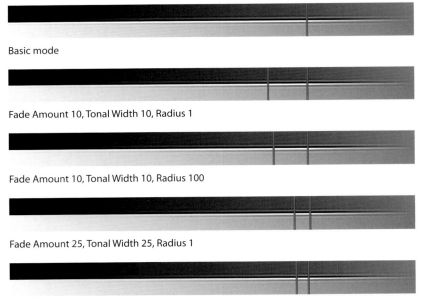

Basic mode

Fade Amount 10, Tonal Width 10, Radius 1

Fade Amount 10, Tonal Width 10, Radius 100

Fade Amount 25, Tonal Width 25, Radius 1

Fade Amount 25, Tonal Width 25, Radius 100

With Lens Blur, the Advanced options do a better job of sharpening midtones while protecting extreme highlights and shadows than they do with Gaussian Blur. But the effects of the Radius setting are still quite subtle, and the extreme slowdowns caused by high Radius settings in the Shadow and Highlight tabs provide an exercise in frustration.

WARNING: Advanced options persist even when they're hidden. One of the more infuriating aspects of Smart Sharpen is that switching from Advanced to Basic mode doesn't actually turn off the settings in the Shadow and Highlight tabs—it just hides them. So it's all too easy to fade the highlights and shadows without meaning to. The only safe solution is to always use Advanced mode, and always check the settings in the Shadow and Highlight tabs before doing anything else. Otherwise you may find yourself getting entirely unexpected results.

Figure 4-20 shows the same image detail unsharpened and then sharpened with Unsharp Mask, and finally Smart Sharpen using the Gaussian and the Lens options. All of the images were then sharpened for output.

Figure 4-20 Unsharp Mask and Smart Sharpen comparison

Original unsharpened image

Unsharp Mask, Amount 500, Radius 0.5

Smart Sharpen with Gaussian Blur, Amount 500, Radius 0.5, Fade Amount 25, Tonal Width 25, Radius 1

Smart Sharpen with Lens Blur, Amount 500, Radius 0.5, Fade Amount 25, Tonal Width 25, Radius 1

Smart Sharpen does a good job on the high-frequency detail (though the difference between the Gaussian and the Lens options is very subtle indeed), but copes less well with the soft edges where the Lens option can introduce undesirable edge artifacts. It should be noted that all of the sharpening in Figure 4-20 was done without the benefit of using an edge mask, which we consider a requirement when using these tools for capture sharpening.

Motion Blur

The third and final Smart Sharpen flavor, Motion Blur, is (as its name suggests) designed to undo motion blur caused by subject or camera movement. Don't expect miracles—those happen only on TV crime shows—but with care, Smart Sharpen with Motion Blur can do a reasonable job of extracting detail from a moving subject. Figure 4-21 shows one such example of a more theoretical nature.

When Motion Blur is selected from the Remove menu, one additional control, Angle, becomes enabled. The Angle setting is the key parameter in using Smart Sharpen's Motion Blur mode to undo motion blur. Just click to drag the angle or enter in a rotation by degree. Once the Angle is correct, the next step is to set the Radius and Amount, followed by the options in the Shadow and Highlight tabs.

Figure 4-21 shows the Motion Blur tool's theoretical capabilities. It's actually doing a reasonable job of unblurring the artificially blurred image with only a few defects. The Motion Blur option is using a deconvolution algorithm to reverse the effects of the convolution—in this case, the motion blur that was intentionally applied to the circles. To determine the optimal deconvolution that would remove the blur, the exact nature of the cause of the blur or its point spread function (PSF) needs to be determined. The Smart Sharpen Motion Blur removal uses the Amount and Radius as well as angular direction settings to attempt to unblur the motion.

> **NOTE:** When the Hubble Space Telescope was first launched into space, scientists were dismayed to discover that the telescope's mirrors were flawed, which caused distorted and blurry images. Yet because the exact nature of the mirror flaws were known, deconvolution image processing could substantially sharpen the images. However, as with Smart Sharpen, it was only an improvement, not a fix. Since the Hubble mirror was so precise but too big to replace in space, the solution was to design new optical components with exactly the same error, but in the opposite direction, to be added to the telescope at the servicing mission. This was effectively like applying glasses to correct the spherical aberration.

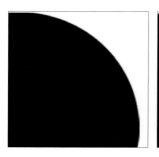

Figure 4-21 Smart Sharpen with Motion Blur

The original image

Original image blurred 20 pixels with Motion Blur

The blurred image unblurred using Smart Sharpen's Motion Blur option

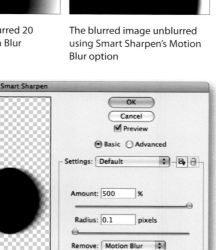

Dialog box showing 0.1 Radius (image still blurred)

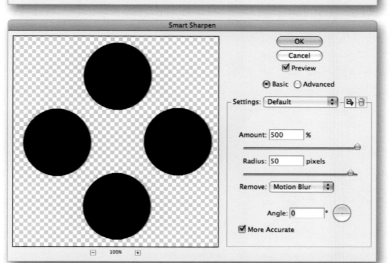

Dialog box showing 50-pixel radius (image is unblurred)

The unblurring of the image can certainly be useful, but in the real world, it can do only so much. Since there is no way to create a mathematically precise PSF, Smart Sharpen can go only so far with the deconvolution. Currently the maximum radius is only 64 pixels, which often falls short of fixing many images. Additionally, if either the subject or camera blur is not in an exact straight line, the unblurring can't really fix the blur. We find that the Motion Blur removal can only help, not remove, the blur.

Figure 4-22 shows the use of Smart Sharpen to reduce (not totally eliminate) motion blur.

Figure 4-22 Smart Sharpen with Motion Blur

The full image

Detail image showing Smart Sharpen Amount of 54% and a Radius of 39.7

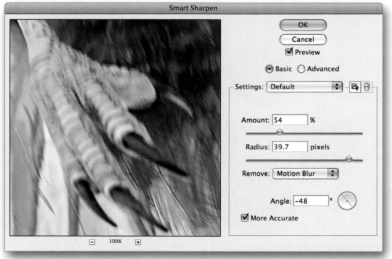

Unlike the other Smart Sharpen flavors, Motion Blur rarely works when it's applied to an entire image. It's best used for unblurring specific subjects in the image, and the work goes much faster if you make a rough selection of the subject, then copy it to a new layer. Once the sharpening is applied, you can either erase the unwanted areas from the rough selection or mask them using a layer mask, as we did in the example shown in Figure 4-23.

Detail before Smart Sharpen

Detail after Smart Sharpen

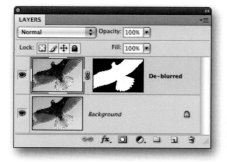

Layer panel showing the layer mask allowing the sharpening only in the center of the bird.

Figure 4-23 Smart Sharpen with Motion Blur detail before and after

Smart Sharpen Issues

Smart Sharpen is an intriguing tool that has won its share of devotees. We confess that we can't number ourselves among them. We do use Smart Sharpen for some tasks—the Motion Blur option is the only game in town for undoing motion blur, and Smart Sharpen works very well indeed for on-screen output, which typically involves fairly small files. On print-resolution images, however, Smart Sharpen is often infuriatingly slow.

The persistence of the Shadow and Highlight settings when the filter has been switched back to Basic mode has undoubtedly caused a great deal of head-scratching, and is at best a questionable design decision. And while the Shadow and Highlight tabs attempt to address a real issue—reducing the intensity of the highlight and shadow contours—they simply don't offer the degree of control we need. As a result, we still rely on the Unsharp Mask filter for the majority of our sharpening tasks.

The Sharpen Tool

Before continuing with Photoshop's array of sharpening tools, we would be remiss if we didn't mention the one tool in Photoshop that's actually named the Sharpen tool. It's a brush-based tool that shares a slot in Photoshop's toolbox with the Blur tool and the Smudge tool. At its default setting of 50% opacity, it applies sharpening that is similar (but not identical) to the Sharpen filter—it's a little more aggressive in the midtones than Sharpen.

Figure 4-24 shows the results of the Sharpen tool applied up to five times. A single-pixel halo quickly turns into a grid of parallel lines.

Used sparingly, at low opacities, the Sharpen Tool is moderately useful for adding a slight increase in sharpness to a specific area in the image. But caution is most definitely required, because repeated applications of the Sharpen tool can quickly destroy images! That's why we suggest building your own sharpening brush, which will be covered in the next chapter.

Figure 4-24 Sharpen tool

 Sharpen tool icon

Sharpen tool, one application

Sharpen tool, two applications

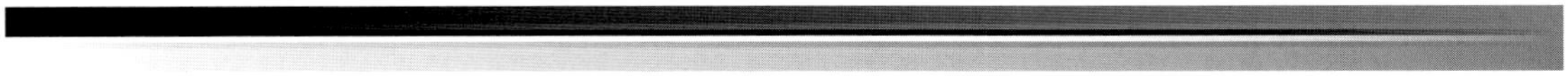

Sharpen tool, three applications

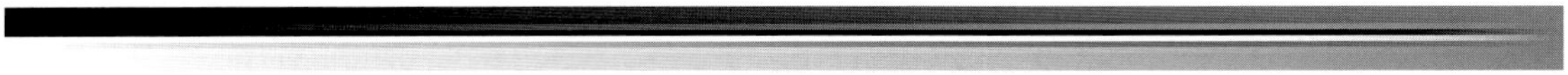

Sharpen tool, four applications

Sharpen tool, five applications

However, it's relatively rare for us to simply apply Unsharp Mask globally to an image. Instead, we use an edge mask, described later in this chapter. At first glance, making edge masks may seem to require more work than Smart Sharpen, but much of that work can be automated, and the actual routines run quite quickly.

But before we get to making masks, we have an additional "tool" to discuss, even though there's no name for it in Photoshop: We call it the Overlay/High Pass method.

The Overlay/High Pass Method

There is no actual tool in Photoshop named "Overlay/High Pass": You need to make this custom tool—or method, if you will—in Photoshop yourself. Overlay/High Pass refers to using an Overlay blend mode on an image layer and then applying the High Pass filter to that layer, resulting in an important custom tool for image sharpening. We wish the Photoshop engineers would turn this into an actual tool, but until they do you must use this method to make your own. It's worth the effort.

Figure 4-25 High Pass filter

The original sharpener analysis target before application of the High Pass filter

The High Pass filter of 4-pixel radius applied to the original sharpener analysis target

The High Pass Filter

The High Pass filter actually does what its name suggests—it passes high-frequency image data, such as edges of an image, but blocks lower frequencies. The end result is that anything in the image that is not an edge gets turned into middle gray while the high-frequency edge is preserved based on the pixel radius.

Figure 4-25 shows what happens with the High Pass filter being applied to the original sharpener analysis target in Figure 4-1, at the beginning of this chapter. Admittedly, our sharpener analysis target is a theoretical image, but it does endeavor to show what the filter is doing.

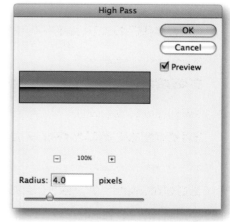

The High Pass filter dialog box

The Overlay Blend

Showing the sharpening effects on an image requires a series of steps that you must follow to prepare your image for applying this method. Figure 4-26 shows the image we'll be using as an example as well as the steps required for Overlay/High Pass sharpening.

1. Start with an image and drag the layer's icon to the New Layer icon on the Layers panel.

    This will duplicate the Background image layer.

2. Change the layer's blending mode from Normal to Overlay. This can be done in either the Layers panel or the Layer Style dialog box.

Figure 4-26 Overlay/High Pass steps

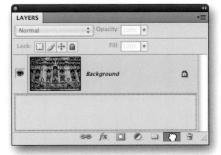

Original image (full frame)

Duplicating the Background layer

Setting the Background copy to Overlay in the Layers panel

Layer Style is a big and somewhat intimidating dialog box that may be overkill for simply changing the blend mode. But this dialog box will become a cornerstone of sharpening techniques outlined in the next chapter, so get used to it. (It won't bite, and Photoshop always has Undo in case you make an error.)

Once the Background copy layer is set to the Overlay blend mode, you'll note that the image gains contrast. This is to be expected and is the basis of how we'll use this blending mode. The Overlay blend mode is a procedural blend that lightens the image's lighter areas while darkening the darks. The cutoff is middle gray (level 128 in an RGB file). Above 128, Overlay uses a Screen mode to lighten the image. Below 128, it uses Multiply to darken the image. If the tone is exactly level 128 (as measured by the Eyedropper Tool), then nothing occurs.

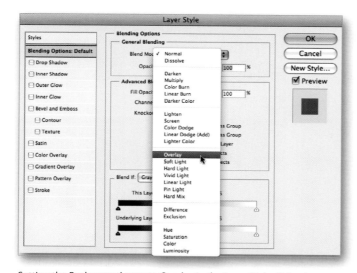

Setting the Background copy to Overlay in the Layer Style dialog box

Background copy layer set to Overlay

Effect of the Overlay blend on the image (detail)

Image preview in the High Pass filter dialog box

3. Finally, use the High Pass filter to turn everything that isn't an edge into level 128 gray, which will do nothing to the underlying image.

We're using the combination of the Overlay blend mode's inherent contrast boost with the High Pass filter's ability to find the edges while turning the non-edge image areas to a null gray. Adjusting the radius of the High Pass filter controls the width of the area where the image contrast is boosted. A Radius of .5 or 1 will increase the contrast in only a very small area. Figure 4-27 shows the result of applying various Radius settings to the image.

Figure 4-27 Overlay/High Pass sharpening results

The original image unsharpened

High Pass filter Radius set to .5

High Pass filter Radius set to 1

High Pass filter Radius set to 2

High Pass filter Radius set to 4

As you can see in Figure 4-27, the higher the Radius setting, the wider the sharpening haloes that are created. At this zoom (200%), the haloes are very obvious. That's because the haloes are actually about six times wider than they would be for the actual print resolution of about 12" x 18" at 300 ppi.

One limitation of the Overlay/High Pass sharpening method is there is no simple way of controlling the relative amount of the effect, other than using the layer's opacity to reduce the strength or duplicating the layer to increase the strength, as shown in Figure 4-28.

TIP: The Overlay blend mode isn't the only procedural blend mode that can be useful with the High Pass filter. Soft Light and Hard Light are modified versions of Overlay; their names describe their effects. Vivid Light, Linear Light, and Pin Light modes can also be used, though the odds are you'll need to substantially reduce the opacity or face over-blown effects. Of the procedural blend modes, only Overlay has a symmetrical effect on both shadows and highlights, and, as such, is the most useful blend mode for image sharpening.

Figure 4-28 Overlay/High Pass tool layer opacities

The Layers panel showing the opacity being reduced to 50%

High Pass filter Radius set to 4 with the opacity reduced to 50%

High Pass filter Radius set to 50 with the opacity reduced to 50%

High Pass filter Radius set to 2 with the sharpening layer duplicated to double the effect

The power of the layer blending and the flexibility of combining layer masks to localize the effect of the Overlay/High Pass method makes this sharpening tool worth the extra effort to create it. Plus, it can be easily automated by creating an action, which will be discussed in depth in Chapter 6, "Putting the Tools to Work."

We've covered the obvious and not so obvious sharpening tools found in Photoshop. That's not to say there aren't third-party tools that can be interesting and useful––there are. But this book is about sharpening in Photoshop, and inside of Photoshop you'll find plenty of tools that can sharpen your images. There is one additional and very important tool that anybody practiced in the art of image sharpening must know: creating an edge mask (and the edge mask's alter ego, the surface mask) to control how areas of an image do or don't get sharpened.

Edge and Surface Masks

The High Pass filter is an example of how an algorithm that can find image edges use the edges to modify the image. Unfortunately there is no simple tool inside of Photoshop to generate an edge or surface mask. Creating these masks is essential for producing images with optimized sharpening and noise reduction. So, like the Overlay/High Pass sharpening method, you will need to create your own tools. Figure 4-29 shows the image we'll be using to create an edge mask as well as the Channels panel.

> **NOTE:** This section is about creating edge masks, which are very similar to surface masks. Since the method outlined here is designed to find, create, and enhance the edges, the inversions of the edges are considered the surfaces, or non-edge portions, of the image. Sometimes by simply inverting the edge mask (Image > Adjustments > Invert), a suitable surface mask will be the result. However, the surface mask will often need special modifications to spread or contract the mask. We'll cover that in the next chapter.

Figure 4-29 Loading and saving the luminosity of an image as a channel

The original image in color

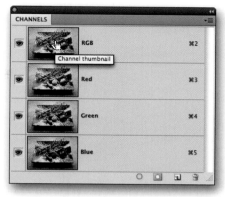

Command-clicking (Mac) the RGB composite channel to load the luminosity as a selection

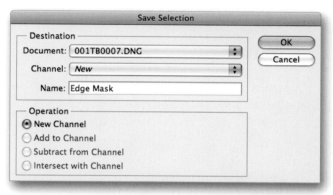

Saving the selection as a channel

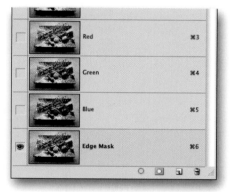

The selection saved as a channel named Edge Mask

Edge Mask Beginnings

To create an edge mask, it is ideal to start with the luminosity of the image. There are a variety of methods, including using a copy of the Green channel of an RGB image or using a Calculations command to generate a specialized channel from other channels. In this basic look at creating an edge mask, we'll use the simplest method: Command-clicking (Mac) or Control-clicking (Windows) the composite RGB channel in the Channels panel. You can also use the Command-Option-2 (Mac) or Control-Alt-2 (Windows) keyboard shortcuts. This loads the image's luminosity as an active selection. From there, save the selection as a channel for further work.

Once you have the basic channel created, target the channel and select Filter > Stylize > Find Edges. Not unlike the High Pass filter, Find Edges looks for edges and separates them from the rest of the image. Since the filter results in an inverted image, the result will need to be inverted again so the actual edges will end up becoming the selection (the white portions of the mask). If you were creating a surface mask, you would leave the image the way the Find Edges filter left it. Figure 4-30 shows these three steps.

Figure 4-30
Edge mask beginnings

The saved luminosity selection as a channel

Result of running the Find Edges filter

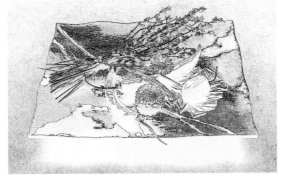

Inverting the channel to make the edges the active selection

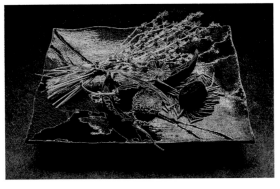

Tuning the Mask

If you were to use the edge mask in this current condition, the results of the sharpening would be too abrupt because the resulting selection would be too hard. So the next step we take is to soften the edges by using the Filter > Blur > Gaussian Blur filter to essentially feather what will end up being the edges of the selection. (The Gaussian Blur filter is the same algorithm as the Select > Modify > Feather command.) After blurring, we need to apply a tonal adjustment to the image. By clipping the highlights and shadows, we'll add contrast to the mask in order to adjust where the sharpening will and won't get applied. Figure 4-31 shows the result of blurring and adjusting the levels in the channel.

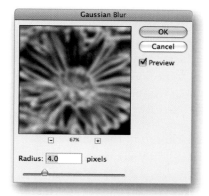

Applying a 4-pixel Gaussian Blur

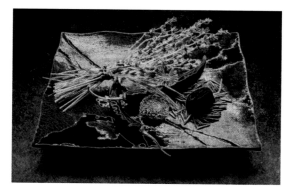

Result of the blur

Figure 4-31
Tuning the mask

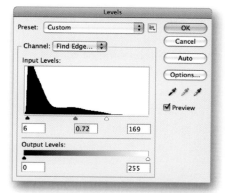

Adjusting the tone of the mask using levels

Result of the tone adjustment

The steps shown in 4-31 are not written in stone. There are a variety of methods of modifying the edge mask to fine-tune the results to apply sharpening to specific parts of the image. By using Find Edges and making further modifications, we're actually using the image itself to adapt the edge mask to the image. We could, of course, manually paint away any areas in the mask where we don't want sharpening by painting black in the mask or add sharpening by painting white. Anything that alters the tonality of the mask will end up impacting how and where the final sharpening will or won't be applied.

Preparing the Image for Sharpening

To prepare the image for sharpening, you could simply load the edge mask as a selection and apply any of the sharpening tools we've already outlined. However, that wouldn't be optimal, as the resulting sharpening would be applied to the RGB color image. Sharpening the color data can result in sharpening artifacts being introduced into the color portions of the image. What we need to do is sharpen a *copy* of the image with the layer's blending mode set to Luminosity.

Figure 4-32 shows the steps to duplicate the Background layer and adjust the blending mode as well as renaming the layer—in this case, to the amount we'll end up sharpening the image. How do we know the amount? Well, we've done this a time or two.

Using the Edge Mask Channel

Once the new layer is set to Luminosity, the next step is to load the Edge Mask channel as an active selection. You can do so by choosing Select > Load Selection and picking the Edge Mask channel. (You can also Command-click (Mac) or Control-click (Windows) the channel.) After the selection is active, the Edge Mask selection is turned into a layer mask. The final step is to run the Unsharp Mask filter to apply the edge sharpening. Figure 4-33 shows this process.

Figure 4-32 Duplicating the layer and setting to Luminosity blend

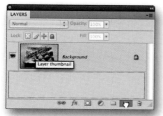

Dragging the Background layer to the New Layer icon

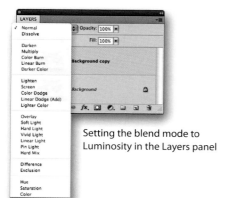

Setting the blend mode to Luminosity in the Layers panel

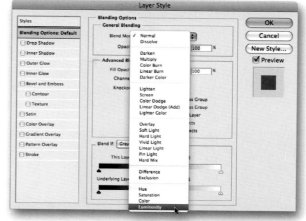

Setting the blend mode to Luminosity in the Layer Style dialog box

Renaming the new layer

Figure 4-33 Sharpening using the Edge Mask channel as a layer mask

Edge Mask channel as active selection

Selection turned into a layer mask

Applying the Unsharp Mask filter

Creating an edge mask can take at least ten separate steps with a lot of potential for additional fine-tuning steps. Performing these steps manually for each and every image you want to sharpen would be needlessly complicated and inefficient. The ideal is to automate them. We'll cover how to record these steps as actions in the last chapter, but let's jump ahead slightly and show the result of Camera Raw's ability to create an edge mask on the fly. Figure 4-34 shows the Photoshop ten-step edge mask and compares it to Camera Raw's parametric edge mask.

Edge mask created in ten steps in Photoshop   Edge mask created in Camera Raw with one slider

Figure 4-34 Comparing Photoshop and Camera Raw edge masks

You'll note minor variations between the Photoshop and Camera Raw edge masks. In actuality, the Camera Raw edge mask is merely a preview and not the actual mask. The preview also sometimes appears a bit higher-contrast than how the edge mask is actually being applied in Camera Raw. Nevertheless, it's pretty remarkable that a single slider in Camera Raw can take the place of so many steps in Photoshop. Makes one wonder why Photoshop doesn't have its own edge mask tool!

The edge mask is a fundamental tool for image sharpening but its alter ego, the surface mask, is critical for the next series of tools in Photoshop: the noise-reduction tools.

NOISE REDUCTION IN PHOTOSHOP

As we learned in Chapter 2, "Why Do We Sharpen?", noise or film grain is a fact of life for photographers. If you use a higher ISO or underexpose your image, the reduction of photons collected by the sensor or film results in more obvious perceptible noise. Shooting with a higher ISO often requires noise-reduction strategies in order to optimize an image for reproduction. Sometimes simply downsampling the image will be a sufficient noise-reduction tool. Other times you'll need to deploy more aggressive reduction tools.

One thing to keep in mind, however, is that these are noise-*reduction* tools, not noise *elimination* tools. A certain degree of noise is expected or even desirable. If you totally eliminate noise or film grain, not only will the image look synthetic, but it will also have lost a large amount of actual image detail. That is the ultimate challenge of noise reduction: reducing the noise while preserving real image detail.

Just as it's easy to overdo sharpening, it's also easy to overdo noise and grain removal, leading to two undesirable conditions:

- Overly aggressive noise removal produces soft, unnatural-looking images that scream "digital" and, in extreme cases, appear to have been run through the Median filter.

- Many noise-reduction tools, including Photoshop's Reduce Noise filter, have a tendency to produce images that aren't as easily sharpened, because as soon as you apply sharpening, artifacts from the noise removal pop into view.

In many cases, the best way to handle noise is to simply protect it from being sharpened. But in extreme cases—for example, high-ISO or heavily underexposed digital captures, or scans from high-speed film, especially color negative—you may have to reduce the noise before you start sharpening.

TIP: It's worth noting that the market for third-party noise-reduction plug-ins is one of the most competitive segments of the greater Photoshop plug-in market. If you routinely have to work with very noisy images, we suggest you consider one of the many third-party solutions available, because almost all of them do a better job than can be achieved with Photoshop's tools.

The Reduce Noise Filter

Photoshop's Reduce Noise filter can do a creditable job, though as noted previously, frankly it's not as good as most third-party plug-ins. The danger with Reduce Noise is that you wind up creating an image that can't be sharpened. Figure 4-35 shows an example.

Figure 4-35 Reduce Noise dangers

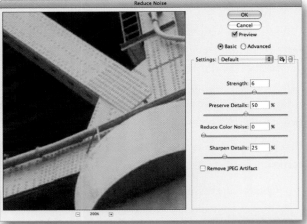

The original full-frame image, shot at ISO 1600 with a Canon Digital Rebel XT

Reduce Noise with the Basic button selected with noise-reduction settings

Original image without noise reduction at 800% zoom

The Reduce Noise version appears to eliminate most of the noise, but...

...sharpening starts to bring the noise back but also introduces ugly artifacts, which is as bad as (if not worse than) the original noise!

Reduce Noise Advanced Options

As with Smart Sharpen, clicking the Advanced button changes the interface and brings up a Per Channel option to apply differing amounts of noise reduction based on the channel. This is useful for film scans, as the Blue channel is often noisier than the other channels. As with Smart Sharpen, however, the settings you apply when in the Advanced mode continue to be in play when you select the Basic button. For this reason, we suggest always using the Advanced mode. Figure 4-36 shows the Advanced options.

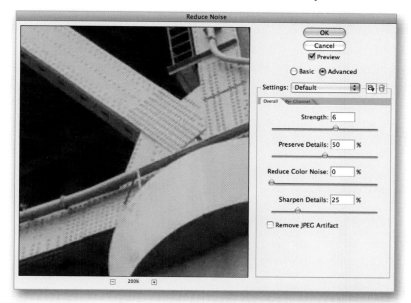

Figure 4-36
Reduce Noise Advanced

Reduce Noise with the Advanced button selected showing the Overall tab

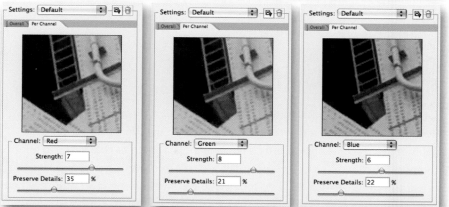

Reduce Noise with the Per Channel tab showing the Red, Green, and Blue Channel settings

When selecting the Advanced options, the Per Channel settings override the Overall settings for Strength and Preserve Details. The only Overall settings that will be applied will be the Reduce Color Noise, Sharpen Details, and the option to Remove JPEG Artifact. If you process raw files from Camera Raw or Lightroom, the optimal place for doing color noise reduction would be in that processing pipeline. Reapplying color noise reduction in Reduce Noise is not suggested, as it will potentially blur the color data and leads to color bleeding across color boundaries.

Saving Reduce Noise Presets

Like Smart Sharpen, Reduce Noise allows you to save commonly used settings as a preset to be applied more efficiently. Figure 4-37 shows the Save and Trash icons in the Reduce Noise dialog box, as well as the New Filter Settings dialog box and the Settings drop-down menu. To save settings, click the Save New Filter button and name the saved setting, which will then appear in the drop-down menu.

Figure 4-37 Reduce Noise saved settings

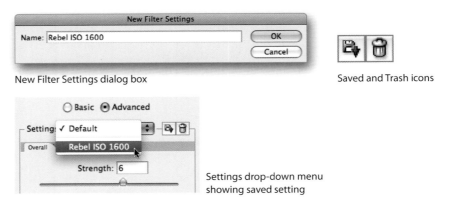

New Filter Settings dialog box

Saved and Trash icons

Settings drop-down menu showing saved setting

Strength vs. Preserve Details

As with all noise-reduction tools, the primary challenge is to reduce the noise while preserving the edge detail in the image. We strongly suggest applying Reduce Noise on only a copy of a pixel layer so that you can adjust the opacity and create your own surface mask to more accurately attack the noise and preserve details. The technique for creating the layer and mask is essentially the same as that for a sharpening layer with an edge mask, only the edge mask for noise reduction isn't inverted, so the edges show as black and hence are protected from the noise reduction.

The Surface Blur Filter

Tucked into the Blur filter group is a little known and rather underused blur filter that's useful for reducing noise. The filter has a Radius setting and a levels threshold. Combined, the settings allow the blur to be applied on the non-edge areas of an image—hence the name Surface Blur. It should be noted that this is a rather un-subtle tool. It's very strong; used too strongly, it can quickly turn your photographic image into an impressionistic mess. However, used with a degree of finesse and with the addition of a surface mask, Surface Blur can reduce some of the most stubborn noise, particularly noise that is amplified by strong boosts in post-processing exposure adjustments.

Figure 4-38 shows the Surface Blur dialog box as well as the surface mask we've created for use with Surface Blur and Despeckle.

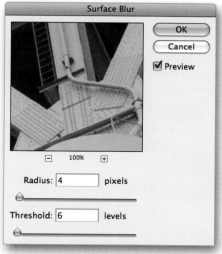

Surface Blur dialog box

Detail of the surface mask that was created by making an edge mask slightly more blurred than normal and inverted to select the surfaces instead of the edges

Figure 4-38 Surface Blur and surface mask

The key to using Surface Blur successfully is to localize the application both by using a surface mask as well as using reduced opacity. We've often found that applying Surface Blur and applying the result at 50% opacity allows a reduction in the perception of strong noise. The noise is still there because the opacity is reduced. But the gentle use lessens the strength of the naturally present noise.

Noise Reduction with Despeckle

The Despeckle filter is useful for dealing with mild-to-moderate luminance noise (as opposed to color noise). The secret is to apply Despeckle differentially to the three color channels—the red channel usually has the least noise, and the blue channel usually has the most.

Figure 4-39, below, shows the result of this technique, which is a simple filter menu command (Filter > Noise > Despeckle), in action along with additional noise-reduction tools. When overdone, this technique can produce color shifts, but it provides an easy way of knocking back some of the worst of the noise. As with all sharpening and noise-reduction tools, it's best applied to a copy of the image.

Comparing Noise Reduction Tools

In Photoshop, there's often not a single "perfect tool" you can call on to solve your imaging needs, and this is certainly true with noise reduction. Many times you'll need to combine multiple tools to achieve optimal results. In this section we'll compare the preceding noise-reduction tools as well as a couple extras: a third-party tool (Noiseware™ from www.imagenomic.com) and Photoshop's own Camera Raw. There will be two sets of comparison images, one set for pixel-peeping at a screen zoom of 400% and a contact-sized print set to 300 ppi and sharpened for output. The original, an ISO 1600 digital capture from a Digital Rebel XT, is a 6 MP capture and would reproduce at 11" x 7" at 300 ppi.

Comparing at 400% Zoom

Figure 4-39 shows an array of six images of a small portion of the original capture. At 400%, the image on screen would be effectively 12 times the actual size (at 100% of a 100-ppi display, the image would be three times the original, so at 400% it would be an additional four times bigger). So while what we are seeing is accurate, it is not at all representational of final output reality. In fact, viewing these images in the book is even further removed from reality, because the results have been put though the halftone screening process to produce 150-lpi halftone dot.

Figure 4-39 Comparing noise reduction at 400% zoom

Image processed with zero noise reduction and Camera Raw default sharpening

Prcocessed in Photoshop's Reduce Noise filter with Strength 6, Preserve Details 50%, and Sharpen Details of 24% with no surface mask

Processed using a Surface Blur Radius of 4 pixels, Threshold of 6 levels, and the same surface mask used in Figure 4-38

Processed using Photoshop's Despeckle command with two applications on the Green channel and one each on the Red and Blue channels, and the same surface mask used in Figure 4-38

Processed in a third-party noise-reduction tool at the tool's default setting and no additional edge mask

An optimized image processed through Camera Raw with the following Detail panel settings: Sharpening Amount 50, Radius 0.7, Detail 65, and Masking 10. The Luminance noise reduction was 60 and Color was 20.

There are some interesting conclusions to be drawn from this comparison. First, looking at the noise results of image processing at a 400% zoom isn't particularly enlightening. Yes, you can see what the pixels look like, but you can't really see what they mean in terms of signal-to-noise. Camera Raw, which is often criticized for inferior noise reduction, fares pretty well compared to Reduce Noise. Surface Blur with a surface mask does a good job (better than Despeckle) of substantially minimizing noise without too much obliteration of image detail. The third-party plug-in at default appears best, which isn't surprising—as with all things in life, you tend to get what you pay for.

Comparing at Contact-Print Size

In the grand scheme of things, what really matters about noise reduction is what do the results look like in *the real world*? Going back to the concept of a contact print, introduced in Chapter 2, the following images are crops of the full frame at 300 ppi, then output sharpened for this book's 150-lpi halftone screen. Let's see if these contact prints confirm or conflict with your impression of the noise-reduction tools' results when viewed at the previous 400% zoom.

Figure 4-40 shows the contact-print size of each of the noise-reduction examples.

If you're not quite sure what to think about this comparison, let us take this opportunity to tell you what we think. We think that by the time the image has been processed, cropped, and output sharpened for reproduction, the differences between these results are very subtle indeed. We would argue that, in many respects, the image processed in Camera Raw has perhaps the best combination of noise reduction without artificial, detail-losing smoothing. It looks more *photographic*.

We also think that Reduce Noise is a fine and dandy tool if used well, but if you have a few extra shekels, investing in a third-party noise-reduction tool is well worth the money. While we use Noiseware, that's not to say that any of the others are not equally useful when compared to Photoshop's toolset.

Figure 4-40 Comparing noise reduction at contact-print size

Image processed with zero noise reduction and Camera Raw default sharpening

Processed in Photoshop's Reduce Noise filter with Strength 6, Preserve Details 50%, and Sharpen Details of 24% with no surface mask

Processed using a Surface Blur Radius of 4 pixels, Threshold of 6 levels, and the same surface mask used in Figure 4-38

Processed using Photoshop's Despeckle command with two applications on the Green channel and one each on the Red and Blue channels, and the same surface mask used in Figure 4-38

Processed in a third-party noise-reduction tool at the tool's default setting and no additional edge mask

An optimized image processed through Camera Raw with the following Detail panel settings: Sharpening Amount 50, Radius 0.7, Detail 65, and Masking 10. The Luminance noise reduction was 60 and Color was 20.

Third-Party Solutions

In extreme noise situations, many third-party plug-ins do a better job than can be achieved using Photoshop's tools. ABSoft's Neat Image, Visual Infinity's Grain Surgery, PictureCode's Noise Ninja, and Imagenomic's Noiseware Professional all provide industrial-strength noise reduction with a great deal of control over the process. (If we've failed to mention your personal favorite, it's simply because the aforementioned plug-ins are the ones with which we're most familiar.)

Here are a few general guidelines for using third-party noise-reduction solutions:

- Always do noise reduction before sharpening unless the sharpening and noise reduction are integrated in the same processing pipeline. If you sharpen first separately, you'll almost certainly make the noise worse. The noise-reduction tool will have to work harder, and will probably wipe out the sharpening you did anyway.

- If you perform noise reduction on a layer, you can reduce the noise slightly more than you actually want, then fine-tune the noise reduction by tweaking the layer opacity.

- Don't overdo the noise reduction. A certain amount of noise is usually preferable to an image that looks like it's been blurred.

In practice, we find we need to resort to third-party tools only with high-ISO (1600 or greater) or severely underexposed (more than 1 f-stop) digital captures, or with scans from color negative. In virtually all other situations, the techniques presented here work well.

Ironically, it was during the preparation of these images for the book that a key aspect of noise reduction and image sharpening sort of fell into place—the ideal place to accomplish the noise reduction is in conjunction with and in the same process as the capture sharpening. This isn't such an earth-shattering revelation, since Bruce had advocated something similar in the first edition of this book. But the principal has been driven even further home now: If at all possible, do your capture sharpening and at least the primary noise reduction in your raw processor, particularly if that raw processor happens to be Camera Raw or Lightroom.

SHARPENING AND NOISE REDUCTION IN CAMERA RAW AND LIGHTROOM

In the preceding pages, we've covered the numerous Photoshop tools for the sharpening and noise reduction of digital images. However, for digital capture (and even TIFFs from film scanners), processing images in the Camera Raw/Lightroom processing pipeline offers many advantages, including the following:

- The image adjustment settings in Camera Raw and Lightroom are parametric adjustments that can be revisited and changed right up to the point when the final output file is rendered. Much has been made of "nondestructive" workflows (which we think is marketing hype), but it is relevant to the extent that your original will always stay original with parametric editing until you decide to process—if you even need to process. In the case of Lightroom, some images may never need to be rendered because the imaging controls and output are sufficient to handle a photographer's needs.

- Whether you are sharpening a single image or hundreds or thousands of images, applying the settings can be as simple as applying a preset or copying and pasting the settings in Camera Raw (via Bridge) or syncing Lightroom. If you want to apply sharpening and noise reduction in Photoshop, those files must be opened in Photoshop for processing and then saved. While batch operations can certainly automate the process, the Photoshop-based process is still far more time consuming.

- A strong argument can be made that the optimal time to do image sharpening and noise reduction would be combined with the rest of the raw image processing and demosaicing. As we've shown, it's important to do the noise reduction either before sharpening or at least during the raw processing. Doing the sharpening and noise reduction directly inside of Camera Raw or Lightroom offers the ability to leverage both the sharpening and noise-reduction tools for optimal image quality.

We would not be honest and forthright if we didn't state right here that both Bruce and Jeff have a vested interest in advocating and evangelizing image sharpening in Camera Raw and Lightroom, since both of us were directly involved in certain aspects of the products' sharpening development. We also coauthored another book dedicated to Camera Raw, *Real World Camera*

Raw in Adobe Photoshop CS4. So, it's only natural to have a certain degree of paternalistic pride in the results of our efforts. However, don't confuse that pride with blind faith and love. We are perfectly capable of getting into the correct peoples' faces in an effort to make sure Camera Raw and Lightroom do the best image processing possible. We are also completely gratified that those same faces on the Camera Raw and Lightroom teams are strongly self-motivated towards those same goals. So, with this caveat stated, let's get down to the business of learning how to use Camera Raw and Lightroom for sharpening and noise reduction.

Comparing Camera Raw and Lightroom's Environments

Both Camera Raw and Lightroom employ the same processing pipeline, assuming an equivalent version of each application. At the time of this writing, the current shipping versions were Camera Raw 5.4 and Lightroom 2.4. The matching *.x* number guarantees that the underlying processing engines are capable of exactly the same image processing and rendering. So whether Camera Raw 5.4 or Lightroom 2.4 processes an image, with all other factors such as color space and image size being equal, both applications produce the same results.

However, usability and the user interfaces vary, sometimes considerably. Figure 4-41 shows both Camera Raw 5.4 and the Develop module of Lightroom 2.4.

The sliders are named the same, although Lightroom combines the Chromatic Aberration and Defringe controls in the Detail panel; in Camera Raw, those controls are in the Lens Corrections panel. In Lightroom, you have a 1:1 (or 2:1 if you change it) live preview and the ability to use the Targeted Adjustment tool to change where the preview is from; in Camera Raw, you just see a message that says "Zoom preview to 100% or larger to see the effects of the controls in this panel."

Why? For several reasons. First and foremost, as we've already said repeatedly, the only zoom where one image pixel equals one display pixel is 100% (or 1:1 in Lightroom). The moment a screen zoom is anything lower than 100%, substantial inaccuracies occur because of screen dithering. Second, it's a lot faster to not have to even try to render the sharpening and noise reduction at smaller screen zooms, thus Camera Raw and Lightroom will render the rest of the image adjustment settings more quickly.

Figure 4-41 Comparing Camera Raw and Lightroom

Camera Raw 5.4 Detail panel

Lightroom 2.4 Detail panel of the Develop module

The real reason, though, is that Thomas Knoll doesn't think it's a good idea to render previews of sharpening and noise reduction at anything other than 100% zoom or above. We are being a bit facetious when we say that—but only a bit. If Mr. Knoll doesn't think something is the right thing to do, he simply doesn't do it. It takes a pretty compelling argument to change his mind.

The Camera Raw and Lightroom Sharpening Philosophy

Some people complain that the sharpening tools in Camera Raw and Lightroom aren't good enough or strong enough, and that other tools are needed. We agree with using additional tools, but we disagree that the Camera Raw/Lightroom tools aren't good enough. Many people fail to fully understand the applications' sharpening philosophy.

The image sharpening tools in Camera Raw and Lightroom are designed for capture sharpening only, not sharpening for effect. The intent is to use the tool to adjust an image to be "good at 100%." This means no undersharpening in expectation of additional sharpening down the road. It also means no oversharpening to try to compensate for final output. In order to fully understand the philosophy, you must fully understand the sharpening workflow that Camera Raw and Lightroom were designed around: capture, creative, and output sharpening.

At this point, Lightroom 2.x has fully formed capture and output sharpening components. Camera Raw has the same fully formed capture sharpening component but only a simple and limited output sharpening implementation (which we are sure will be improved). Neither application has a fully formed creative sharpening component as of yet, which is why we still need Photoshop for creative sharpening and sharpening for effect.

Analyzing Camera Raw and Lightroom's Sharpening Tool

We're going to return to the original sharpener analysis target that was explained back in Figure 4-1. Instead of opening the target in Photoshop, we'll be opening the TIFF file inside Camera Raw and Lightroom to show you what the controls do relative to Photoshop's sharpening tools.

Evaluating Radius

Figure 4-42 shows the original target and four additional targets whose Radius settings have been adjusted. The sharpening Amounts for each of these four adjusted examples are pegged at the maximum of 150 to better show off the somewhat subtle nature of Camera Raw and Lightroom's sharpening. We say subtle because they're designed for capture sharpening, not sharpening for effect.

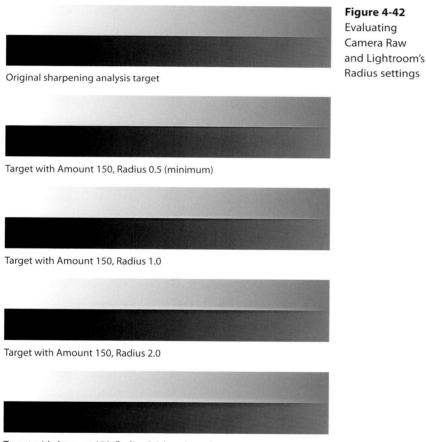

Figure 4-42
Evaluating Camera Raw and Lightroom's Radius settings

Original sharpening analysis target

Target with Amount 150, Radius 0.5 (minimum)

Target with Amount 150, Radius 1.0

Target with Amount 150, Radius 2.0

Target with Amount 150, Radius 3.0 (maximum)

As mentioned earlier, like the radius control of the Unsharp Mask filter in Photoshop, Radius is the control that sets the width of the sharpening haloes. The Radius setting tells the filter how many surrounding pixels to take into account when calculating the new value for the subject pixel.

However, the Radius settings in Camera Raw and Lightroom do not operate exactly the same as the Radius settings in either the Unsharp Mask or Smart Sharpen filters. Since the processing space for all sharpening in Camera Raw is linear luminance data, the Radius setting in Camera Raw is slightly different than Photoshop's filters. A Radius of 0.5 in Camera Raw 5.4 is about the same as 0.3 in Unsharp Mask.

That said, the net effect of Camera Raw/Lightroom's Radius settings is the same as Unsharp Mask or Smart Sharpen; low Radius settings produce narrow sharpening haloes and higher settings produce wider ones. For high-frequency images, you'll want to use a Radius setting below 1.0, and for low-frequency images, a setting above 1.0. How much below or above the default setting of 1.0 you go depends on the image (which means it's your responsibility to determine the optimal setting).

Evaluating Detail

Perhaps the most confusing of all of the image sharpening settings, regardless of the tool, is the Detail slider in Camera Raw and Lightroom. It's difficult to understand because Detail actually controls multiple parameters with a single slider. While the default setting is 25, the actual middle of the slider effect is 50. When moved lower than 50, Detail kicks in a halo suppression component that will help reduce the strength of the haloes the sharpening produces. Moving the slider to the right turns off halo suppression and concentrates the sharpening amount towards the higher frequencies of the image.

The Detail setting is highly dependent on the Radius settings. The lower the Radius, the more the increase of Detail's concentration on the high-frequency texture.

Setting Detail to the maximum of 100 will make the Amount and Radius settings behave in a similar manner to Unsharp Mask in Photoshop. However, there is nothing in Unsharp Mask that can replicate the effect of reducing the Detail setting when halo suppression kicks in. Figure 4-43 shows the impact of going from a Detail setting of 0 to 100.

One of the things that should jump out at you is what the higher Detail settings are doing to the actual texture of the gradations in the target. At a setting of 50 or above, the sharpening algorithm is actually accentuating the noise Photoshop puts into its Gradient tool. Yes, it's sharpening the noise! At the lower Detail settings, the noise is not being over accentuated—in fact, with a Detail setting of 0, there's very little effect of sharpening taking place.

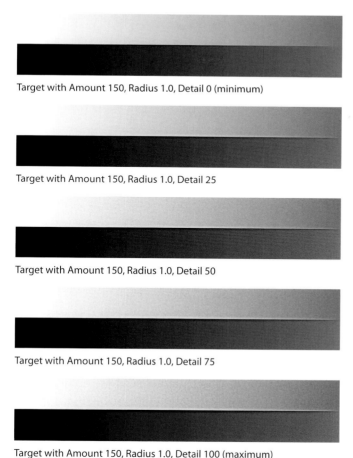

Figure 4-43
Evaluating
Camera Raw
and Lightroom's
Detail settings

Target with Amount 150, Radius 1.0, Detail 0 (minimum)

Target with Amount 150, Radius 1.0, Detail 25

Target with Amount 150, Radius 1.0, Detail 50

Target with Amount 150, Radius 1.0, Detail 75

Target with Amount 150, Radius 1.0, Detail 100 (maximum)

Detail Settings and Noise

As you can see in Figure 4-43, if you have noise in your images, increasing the Detail slider can substantially increase the perception of the noise. Some might say the higher Detail settings could be called noise enhancers, and they would be correct. However, what is not quite so obvious, largely because the Camera Raw engineers wanted separate categories for sharpening and noise reduction, is that adjusting the Luminance noise-reduction slider has an impact on the strength of the Detail slider's impact. By adding noise reduction, you can mitigate the increase in the Detail slider's negative impact. Figure 4-44 shows what happens when you add noise reduction to higher Detail settings.

Figure 4-44 Evaluating noise reduction's impact on Detail settings

Target with Amount 150, Radius 1.0, Detail 100, Luminance 50

Target with Amount 150, Radius 1.0, Detail 100, Luminance 100

As you can see, adding noise reduction has the impact of somewhat undoing the increase of the Detail settings' impact on high-frequency enhancement. However, while the noise reduction can help cancel out the increase in Detail's high-frequency enhancement, don't forget that the Detail slider doesn't just do one thing—the other impact the slider has is to suppress haloes. So, you can increase Detail's numbers to reduce the halo suppression and increase the Luminance noise reduction to cut down on the high Detail setting's negative impact on noise.

In effect, the Luminance slider is the fifth sharpening slider. To optimally tune sharpening requires that you also adjust Luminance noise reduction. If you fail to adjust both interactively, you are leaving image quality, in the form of optimal sharpening, on the table.

Masking

As we saw in the "Edge and Surface Masks" section, creating a mask based upon the edges within an image can be a laborious series of steps in Photoshop. In Camera Raw and Lightroom, the process has been distilled down to moving a single slider. Figure 4-45 shows previews of the edge mask being created on the fly. To see the preview, the Option (on a Mac; Alt in Windows) key was held while adjusting the Masking slider.

We didn't bother showing a target with Masking set to 0, as of course it would be a white frame. In Figure 4-44, where the target is showing white, the sharpening effect will be applied at the full strength of the settings contained in Amount, Radius, and Detail. Note that Masking has no impact on Luminance noise reduction. As you increase the Masking setting, more of the image will be protected from the sharpening effect, up to the maximum of 100, where the edges are about the only things still showing. However, it should be noted that even if the mask preview is 100 black, Camera Raw and Lightroom will still apply a slight degree of sharpening. We have been told this is a bug, not a feature, and will probably be modified in the future.

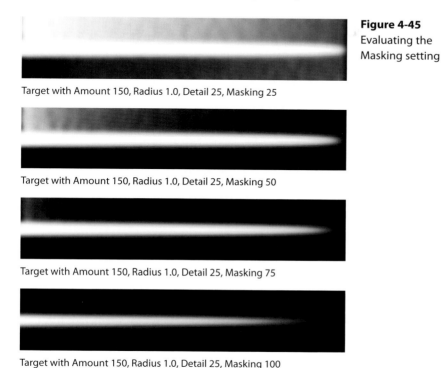

Figure 4-45
Evaluating the Masking setting

Target with Amount 150, Radius 1.0, Detail 25, Masking 25

Target with Amount 150, Radius 1.0, Detail 25, Masking 50

Target with Amount 150, Radius 1.0, Detail 25, Masking 75

Target with Amount 150, Radius 1.0, Detail 25, Masking 100

Using Camera Raw or Lightroom for Image Sharpening

It's all well and good to look at a bunch of targets, but to fully understand how to use the tools, you have to use the tools on real images. We're going to show the process of sharpening an image by using the Option/Alt special sharpening preview. You should note that the preview will show only when the zoom is 100% (1:1) or larger. You also need to hold down the Option (Mac) or Alt (Windows) key while adjusting a parameter for the preview to appear.

While the parameters are arranged top to bottom, we generally don't adjust Amount first; we usually adjust Radius based on the overall needs of the image's edges. Once the Radius is set, we then start adjusting the Amount. Since we're going to follow the individual controls, we are going to go in order, top to bottom, in this example.

It should also be noted that once set, *any* of the parameters are likely to be adjusted or tweaked, perhaps even multiple times. It is not at all unusual to work back and forth between Radius and Detail and to readjust the Amount, or to adjust Luminance noise reduction and then readjust Detail. Often we'll test the validity of some of our settings by adjusting the Amount ridiculously high (over 100) for the purpose of seeing what's happening to the pixels. Be sure to reduce it back to reasonable levels before finishing.

Let's quickly walk through each of the sharpening controls.

Adjusting Amount

Amount is the strength setting that takes all the other settings and applies a volume control. The default is 25, and that was selected as somewhat representative of the old Camera Raw 3.x single slider sharpening control.

Figure 4-46 shows the luminance sharpening preview and the Amount setting adjusted to 65. The additional settings are still at default.

Virtually every image will need to be adjusted upwards in the Amount setting. The default of 25 is a legacy holdover. Depending on your image source, the setting may need to go up only a bit. But if you are shooting with a camera that has a strong antialiasing filter (such as Canon digital cameras), the Amount may need to go way up. Figure 4-47 shows the lower and upper ranges of the Amount setting.

> **TIP:** If you find yourself constantly adjusting any Camera Raw or Lightroom parameter each and every time you use it, you really should consider changing the Camera Raw/Lightroom default for your camera. This applies not only to sharpening but any of the parameters. You should also note that Camera Raw and Lightroom both share the same defaults. So if you change the default in Camera Raw, Lightroom will pick up that new default and use it for the camera. You can also make the default specific to camera serial numbers as well as ISO settings, so you can have a camera-specific default that will be dependent upon the shot ISO.

Figure 4-46
Adjusting Amount

Camera Raw Detail panel

Adjusted image preview

Lightroom Detail panel

Figure 4-47
Amount setting's lower
and upper limits

Amount at 0 (no sharpening)

Amount at 150 (maximum)

Some people may wonder why the Amount goes up to 150 instead of top-
ping off at 100. During the development of the new sharpening routines, we
found images whose settings for Radius, Detail, and Masking were simply
too weak at 100. So the decision was made to allow the parameter to be set
to 150. There was a precedent with Camera Raw's Brightness setting, which

used to be limited to 100 but was later increased to 150. We will say, however, that unless you really fine-tune the Detail slider very low and have a very high Masking setting, the odds of needing to go above 100 isn't very high.

Adjusting Radius

Probably the single most important parameter to adjust in the Camera Raw/ Lightroom sharpening scheme is the Radius setting. Not only does the Radius sharpening amount depend on it, but both Detail and Masking depend on it as well. How the Detail slider "tweens" between halo suppression and high-frequency enhancement depends on the Radius setting. Mask creation also depends on the Radius setting, because increasing the Radius parameter makes the mask edges wider. Figure 4-48 shows our image being previewed, and the Camera Raw and Lightroom Detail panels.

Figure 4-48
Adjusting Radius

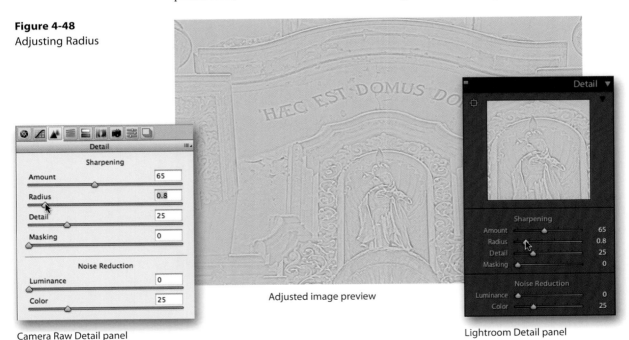

Adjusted image preview

Camera Raw Detail panel

Lightroom Detail panel

When your image has a preponderance of high-frequency textual detail, you really must lower the Radius setting down from the default of 1. All of the other adjustments you make to the image are so dependent on the proper Radius setting that failing to nail this setting is the root cause of most people's problems with Camera Raw/Lightroom sharpening. Figure 4-49 shows the lower and upper limits of the Radius setting on this image.

If one were to err, it could be argued it's better to err on the side of a smaller Radius setting as opposed to a larger setting. We've rarely ever found a use for a setting above 2, and the more useful low-frequency setting tends to be 1.5. Putting the Radius setting too high can have a negative impact on Detail and Masking, which also interact with whatever the currently set Radius parameter is set to.

Radius at 0.5 (minimum)

Radius at 3.0 (maximum)

Figure 4-49
Radius setting's lower and upper limits

Adjusting Detail

If you want a short and concise definition of Detail, try this: Detail is a multifrequency halo suppression adjustment for the Amount and Radius parameters. Does that help? We thought not…but don't feel bad. Even the engineer who wrote the code for Detail can't really explain precisely what it does. The bottom line is, season to taste and be sure you factor in the Luminance noise reduction as an additional modifier to the Detail setting. Figure 4-50 shows the adjusted Detail setting and the preview.

For this image, adjusting the Detail setting upwards to 60 helps bring out the super high-frequency detail in the stone and the carvings. The halo suppression at 60 is almost off. We don't know the exact point where the suppression quits entirely, but we can't see much if any evidence of suppression above 75. At one point in the development of these new sharpening parameters, the default Detail setting was 50. However, it was thought to be too aggressive when comparing the legacy sharpening settings, so the default was reduced to 25. We don't disagree with that decision, however we point this out to suggest that for many users, changing their defaults might be a fruitful endeavor (read: Change your default to 50). Figure 4-51 shows the lower and upper range of the Detail setting.

Figure 4-50
Adjusting Detail

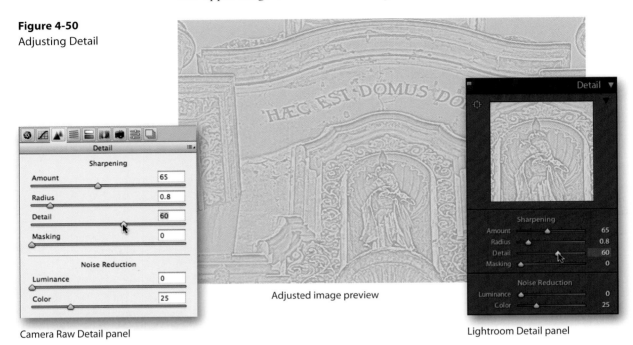

Camera Raw Detail panel

Adjusted image preview

Lightroom Detail panel

Figure 4-51 Detail setting's lower and upper limits

Detail at 0 (minimum)

Detail at 100 (maximum)

Adjusting Masking

At this point, the main sharpening settings have been applied. We still need to adjust the Masking setting and do a tiny tweak to the Luminance noise reduction. By default there is no Masking setting being applied. It is set to 0 for several reasons. First, since creating the edge mask is processor intensive, the thought was that to force a user to take the processing hit on a mask generation wasn't efficient. But the primary reason is that since the mask is so image dependent, it's pretty difficult if not impossible to have a one-size-fits-all mask. You need to see the impact that the mask has on the image to determine what setting to use.

Make no mistake about using the Masking in Camera Raw and Lightroom. For optimal image sharpening, you must use some masking for virtually every image you process. The only question is how much?

Figure 4-52 shows adjusting the Masking parameter as well as a slight tweak to the Luminance noise reduction.

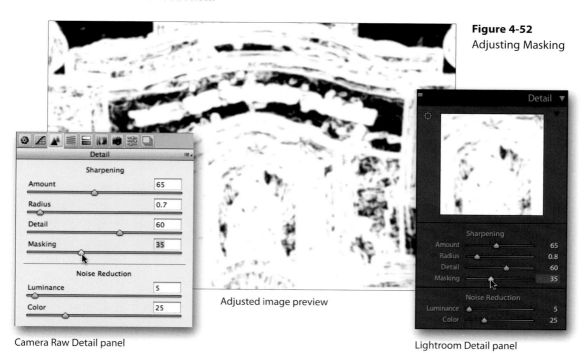

Figure 4-52
Adjusting Masking

Adjusted image preview

Camera Raw Detail panel

Lightroom Detail panel

The Masking for this image didn't need to be too high. The primary goal was to keep the sharpening from hitting the sky and any other large surface areas. Generally a minimum setting of between 10 and 25 is enough to keep too much of the sharpening effect from falling onto the surfaces and concentrating the sharpening to the edges. Remember, as of Camera Raw 5.4 and Lightroom 2.4, some sharpening will always be applied to the entire image. It's important to make the determination where to back it off and where to concentrate the effect. Also remember that the proper Radius setting is important too. Figure 4-53 shows lower and higher Masking previews for this image.

Figure 4-53 Lower and higher Masking settings

Masking at 10 (minimum of 0 would show a white screen)

Masking at 90 (maximum 100 would be almost completely black)

Normally, the process of arriving at the optimal settings for a given image would involve adjustment and then readjustment of all of the sharpening parameters and the Luminance noise reduction. To achieve the optimal results, there really is no alternative to using your eyes (and mind) to judge the impact of the sharpening parameters on your image. Granted, that's a pretty user-intensive process. However, once you master the Camera Raw/Lightroom sharpening toolset, it's not hard to put most images into one of a relatively few categories and, as a result, be able to apply relatively accurate presets to large numbers of images very quickly in Bridge or Lightroom. We'll cover the use of presets in the next chapter.

Comparing Default and Optimized Sharpening Parameters

While looking at the images zoomed in is useful for arriving at the optimal sharpening settings, the true test of optimization accuracy is to process the image out and combine it with output sharpening and then output the image. While we're limited to showing only 150-lpi halftone output in this book, this output is still a useful relative target for evaluation.

Figure 4-54 shows the full image optimally capture sharpened in Camera Raw, downsampled using Bicubic Sharper to the output size, then output sharpened for print in the book. The same figure also shows the results of outputting the image at contact-print size with the sharpening "defaults" and then optimally set.

Figure 4-54 Comparing default to optimized sharpening

Image optimized and downsampled, then output sharpened (full frame)

Image set to default sharpening, then output sharpened (contact size)

Image set to optimal sharpening, then output sharpened (contact size)

For those people who have not yet mastered the intricacies of using Camera Raw or Lightroom's sharpening tool, we hope this has been helpful. For those who had previously thought that the sharpening was inferior, we hope that learning how to use the tool will change your opinion. Now, the next step is to try to convince you that noise reduction in Camera Raw/Lightroom isn't half bad either.

Using Camera Raw or Lightroom for Noise Reduction

Some people have given Camera Raw and Lightroom a bad rap for producing mushy, soft, and impressionistic rendering of camera noise. For some cameras whose noise signature is particularly poor, or for those people who are driving the real ISO into unrealistically high numbers, or for people who seem predisposed to ETTL (considerable underexposure), we suppose the Noise Reduction portion of the Detail panel leaves something to be desired. Rest assured, everyone: The elves that work on the Camera Raw processing pipeline are actively engaged in substantially increasing the image quality that comes out of the pipeline. But even as it stands, for most cameras at most ISO settings, properly used in conjunction with appropriate image sharpening settings, Camera Raw and Lightroom are capable of producing very good image quality. Of course, to achieve this, one must be fluent with the use of the controls, so let's look at them now.

The Noise Reduction Controls

Really, the important control one needs to learn how to finesse is the Luminance slider in the Noise Reduction portion of the Detail panel. As with the Sharpening controls, the only way to see what's going on is to zoom in to 100% (1:1) or closer to see the actual impact on the pixels. We often find it useful to zoom in to 200% (2:1) to get a better feel of what the image noise signature looks like and to gauge how much noise reduction to apply.

Figure 4-55 shows a digital capture done with a Canon EOS 10D (the same poor camera we beat up in Chapter 2, we're afraid), downsampled and reproduced full frame here in the book. The image was optimized for sharpening and noise reduction in Camera Raw, downsampled, and output sharpened for the book. The native size of the capture would have been 10.25" x 6.875" at 300 ppi.

The capture was shot at 1600 ISO and a -1.35 Exposure setting was needed to reduce the bright windows, but a Brightness setting of +130 was needed to lighten up the resulting tone curve. As a result, the shadows did get an increase in processing with an attendant increase in perceived noise.

Figure 4-55 Full-frame digital capture at ISO 1600

At this reproduction size, the image in Figure 4-55 looks relatively noiseless. Part of that was due to downsampling, which has the effect of substantially reducing noise all by itself. The other part was the noise reduction applied in Camera Raw.

Figure 4-56 shows the same image with a screen zoom of 300% (3:1). At this zoom, the noise is large and ugly. Something needs to be done about it, right? Let's see what can be done.

Figure 4-56 300% zoom view of the digital capture at ISO 1600

- Adjusting the Luminance noise reduction: To successfully make accurate adjustments to the Luminance noise reduction, one must make all of the other sharpening adjustments as well. Remember that there is an interrelationship between the Detail slider and the Luminance noise-reduction slider. Figure 4-57 shows the final Detail panel settings for both Sharpening and Noise Reduction.

  When you compare the images from Figures 4-56 and 4-57, the reduction in the apparent noise is considerable. But because the image sharpening is optimized, the overall image appearance is not particularly soft. Has the noise been completely eliminated? No. To completely obliterate it would also mean a loss of image detail as well as the noise elimination. But Camera Raw has done a useful amount of noise reduction to the point that, for many purposes, no further noise reduction would need to be done.

- Adjusting the Color noise reduction: This discussion is really short because in general, Camera Raw and Lightroom do a wonderful job of color noise reduction, so for the most part you can ignore this setting. We've tried to find a visually good sample of an image that needed *less* than the default. Alas, we've failed. On occasion we have found images that needed more. The only caution we make when increasing the Color noise reduction is to be sure you are actually seeing color noise (learn how to recognize it) and that you use only the amount needed to eliminate it. Unlike Luminance noise reduction, there is no reason not to eliminate noise as long as the settings you use don't also blur the color boundaries of objects.

Figure 4-57 Optimized Sharpening and Noise Reduction settings

Adjusted image at 300% zoom

Camera Raw Detail panel

Lightroom Detail panel

COMBINING CAMERA RAW, LIGHTROOM, AND PHOTOSHOP'S TOOLS

We're going to keep this section short because this is the very tip of a very big and important subject we'll be covering in depth in Chapter 5, "Industrial-Strength Sharpening Techniques." But we thought it would be useful to show, on the same example image we've been working, how to combine the best of all the applications' toolsets.

Figure 4-58 shows three contact-print-sized images. Each image was processed, then output sharpened for book reproduction. The first one was output at the camera default sharpening of Amount 25 and zero noise reduction. The next is the image where we optimized both the Sharpening and Noise Reduction parameters. The last image was then opened in Photoshop for a gentle dose of the Reduce Noise filter and added using a surface mask to preserve the edges.

Figure 4-58
Comparing the results

Processed with Camera Raw defaults

Processed with optimized Camera Raw settings

Processed in Photoshop using Reduce Noise and a surface mask

We think you'll agree that each step we took was an upgrade to the overall image quality. Leaving the image at default gives a grainy, noisy result whose details aren't as sharp as the noise. Optimizing the sharpening and the noise reduction is a clear improvement in image quality—the image details are sharper than the noise. Yes, it looks like a higher ISO shot, but the noise is not as objectionable as the first example. The last image is the overall best image quality. There are still some telltale signs of the image having come from a higher-ISO capture, but those signs are very subtle.

Figure 4-59 shows the layer stack as well as the surface mask that was generated for the final image.

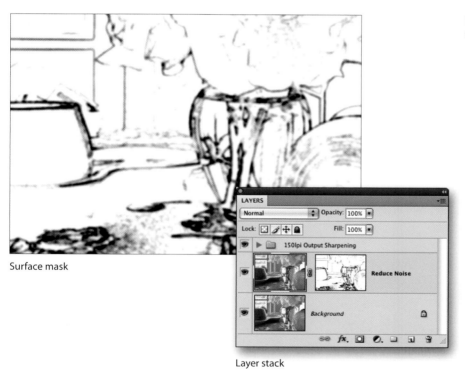

Surface mask

Layer stack

Figure 4-59 The image tuned in Photoshop

It should be clear after reading this chapter that knowing how a particular sharpening or smoothing tool works is only part of the answer. Learning to work with various tools and creating layers and masks provides you with much more control and flexibility than when you simply use the tools to burn changes into the pixels of a flattened image.

But as we all know, there's no such thing as a free lunch, and the downsides of doing everything on layers are that the files become very large, and also very complex. If you plan to leave the layers intact for maximum flexibility, *name them* in a way that you know will make sense to you several years hence. Otherwise you'll find yourself spending considerable amounts of time just figuring out what each layer does when you come to revisit the image.

In the next chapter, we'll show you how to assemble the various tools covered in this chapter into a complete arsenal of advanced techniques dedicated to getting the best image quality available while automating the work wherever possible.

CHAPTER FIVE

Industrial-Strength Sharpening Techniques

Using the Tools

Knowing your way around Adobe Photoshop CS4, Adobe Photoshop Camera Raw, and Adobe Photoshop Lightroom's sharpening tools is a good start, but learning how to actually deploy them is the key to mastering sharpening, especially if you plan to use the workflow-based approach to sharpening that we outlined in Chapter 3, "Sharpening Strategies." Multipass sharpening must be approached with care and diligence, lest you end up with an oversharpened mess.

This chapter will break down the techniques based on the sharpening phases of capture sharpening, creative sharpening, and output sharpening. We'll describe techniques for controlling sharpening not only while it's being applied, but also after it's been applied. We'll show you how to sharpen nondestructively, so that if things go horribly wrong you still have an escape route. We'll also explain how to confine sharpening to specific tonal ranges and image areas, so that you can sharpen edges without affecting textured areas or sharpening noise.

LAYERS, BLENDING, AND MASK-MAKING TECHNIQUES IN PHOTOSHOP

When you run the Unsharp Mask filter on a flat image, you have very limited control after you've applied the sharpening. You can immediately use the Fade command to reduce the strength of the sharpening or to apply it with a blend mode, but a single mouse-click can render Fade unavailable, as shown in Figure 5-1.

Figure 5-1 Using the Fade command

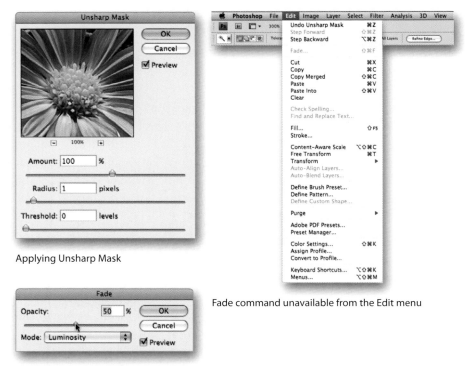

Applying Unsharp Mask

Fade command unavailable from the Edit menu

Adjusting the Fade command for Luminosity blend and 50% opacity

If you apply sharpening or noise reduction on a layer instead of on a flat image, a whole range of post-application tweaks become available. Much of this section is devoted to these tweaks, such as using blending modes, luminosity targeting, and the creation of edge and surface masks to localize the effects of sharpening or noise reduction. We'll start off by talking about the effects we'll be applying to layers and how to create those layers.

Sharpening on a Layer

In Chapter 4, "Sharpening Tools," we showed you how to duplicate the Background layer to apply sharpening or noise reduction on a separate layer above. This provides the benefits of offering various layer-blending modes and the ability to alter the opacity (or strength) of the sharpening or noise-reduction effect. This is fine with basic image editing, but if you have a complicated image with a bunch of stacked layers, simply duplicating the Background layer will be insufficient. You need a method of creating a layer intended for sharpening based on the visible layers you have checked.

Before you can run, you must learn to walk, so first let's look at the basics of creating sharpening layers. There are really only two ways:

- If the image is a flat file, duplicate the Background layer.

- If the image is a layered file, press Option (Mac) or Alt (Windows) while selecting Merge Visible from the Layer menu, or press Command-Option (or Alt)-Shift-E.

Figures 5-2a and 5-2b show both methods.

You can then apply sharpening to the new layer, leaving the Background or underlying layers untouched.

Drag the Background layer…

…to the New Layer icon in the Layers palette…

…to create a sharpening layer

Figure 5-2a
Creating a sharpening layer on a flat file

Figure 5-2b
Creating a sharpening layer
on a layered file

Hold down Option (Mac) or
Alt (Windows) while selecting
Merge Visible from the Layer
menu…

…to create a sharpening layer

Advanced Option/Merged Procedures

To take advantage of automating the Option/Merged process (which we really encourage you to do), you may need to alter the steps you take when recording an action to automate this process. Figure 5-3 shows the process of recording an error-proof action.

Figure 5-2 showed a simple method of making an Option/Merged layer, but doing so does not control exactly where and how the layer is created. We'll cover writing actions in further depth in the last chapter, but it's important to start to develop logical thinking regarding the steps that many of the techniques in this chapter will require. Figure 5-3 shows a more complicated layer stack where not all layers are visible—an important consideration when doing the Option/Merged command, since many times there may be layers you don't want captured in the resulting merged layer.

Figure 5-3 Recording specific steps in an action

1. Select the Background layer.

2. Hold down Option (Mac) or Alt (Windows) while selecting Merge Visible from the Layers panel menu.

3. The new layer is created above the Background layer.

4. Select the Bring to Front command from the Layer > Arrange flyout (or use the keyboard shortcut).

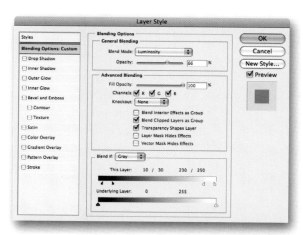

6. Adjust the Layer Style options.

5. Rename the layer.

The final recorded action

The Action panel shows that selecting the Background layer was a recorded step. This is important because the Background layer is about the only layer you can be relatively assured of having in an image. Recording this as a step will mean that no matter what layer or mask may be active in the layers stack, the Background layer will always start as the active target, and the merged layer will always show up immediately above. From there it's a matter of moving the layer to the top of the layer stack, renaming the layer, and adjusting the blending and opacity.

> **TIP:** Reduce opacity before sharpening. If you reduce the sharpening layer's opacity to, for example, 66% before sharpening, you can use the Layer Opacity slider in the Layers palette to increase or decrease the strength of the sharpening after it's been applied.

Luminosity Blending

One of the key benefits of sharpening on a layer is that you can set the layer's blending mode to Luminosity, thereby avoiding the possibility of sharpening-induced hue shifts.

Some Photoshop gurus recommend converting images to Lab mode, sharpening the Lightness channel, then converting back to RGB. However, unless the image actually requires some other operation that demands Lab mode, roundtripping from RGB to Lab to RGB is a somewhat destructive process on 8-bit/channel images (you lose anywhere from 20 to 35 of the 256 levels available due to quantization error) that can lead to unwanted hue shifts and possible posterization. On 16-bit/channel images, the quantization error is not an issue, but the conversion to Lab and back is time consuming and may force you to flatten the image.

Applying sharpening with the Luminosity blend mode produces results that, while not identical to converting to Lab then sharpening the Lightness channel, still provide the same main benefit of doing so—the sharpening changes only luminosity, not hue or saturation.

Sharpening Tonal Ranges

Yet another benefit to sharpening on a layer is that you can constrain the sharpening to a specific tonal range. This is particularly useful in the early stages of the sharpening workflow, when it's essential to protect the extreme highlights and shadows so that there's enough headroom for final sharpening for output.

The key set of controls for this are the Blend If sliders in the Layer Style dialog box, which you can open by selecting one of the commands from the Layer Style submenu on the Layer menu, or, more conveniently, by double-clicking the layer's icon in the Layers palette. Note that you have to double-click either the layer thumbnail or the blank area to the right of the layer name—double-clicking the layer name simply makes the name editable!

Figure 5-4 shows the Layer Style dialog box.

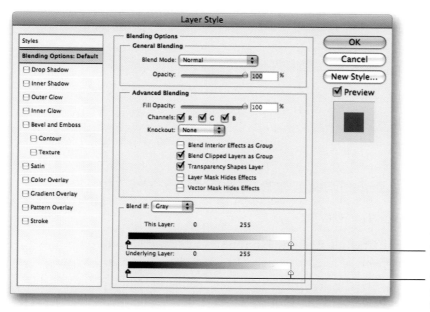

Figure 5-4 The Layer Style dialog box and the Blend If sliders

These sliders control which values will be applied from the overlying layer.

These sliders control which values in the underlying layer will accept values from the overlying layer.

The Blend If sliders are located at the bottom of the dialog box. The top slider controls which values in the overlying layer are applied to the image, while the bottom slider controls which values in the underlying layer(s) receive values from the overlying layer. Figure 5-5 shows the sliders in action.

Figure 5-5 The Blend If sliders in action

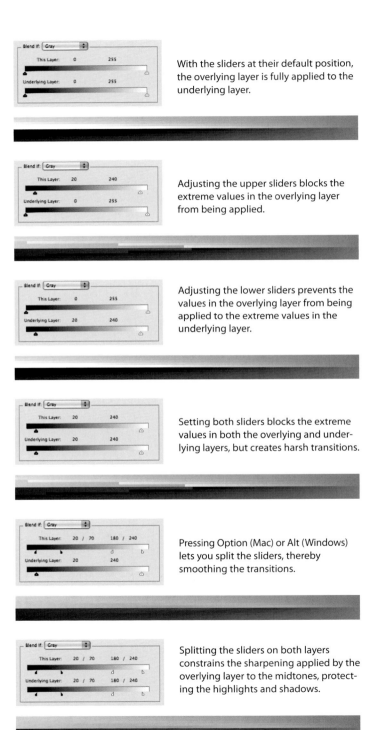

With the sliders at their default position, the overlying layer is fully applied to the underlying layer.

Adjusting the upper sliders blocks the extreme values in the overlying layer from being applied.

Adjusting the lower sliders prevents the values in the overlying layer from being applied to the extreme values in the underlying layer.

Setting both sliders blocks the extreme values in both the overlying and underlying layers, but creates harsh transitions.

Pressing Option (Mac) or Alt (Windows) lets you split the sliders, thereby smoothing the transitions.

Splitting the sliders on both layers constrains the sharpening applied by the overlying layer to the midtones, protecting the highlights and shadows.

Midtone Sharpening

The Blend If sliders are the key to applying strong sharpening to the midtones while protecting the highlights and shadows. Using the sliders, it's possible to apply strong sharpening, yet confine it to the midtones, as shown in Figure 5-6.

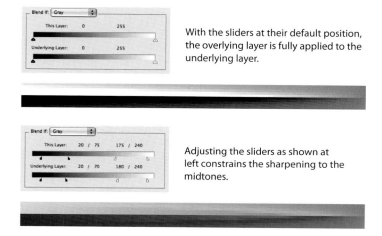

With the sliders at their default position, the overlying layer is fully applied to the underlying layer.

Adjusting the sliders as shown at left constrains the sharpening to the midtones.

Figure 5-6
Midtone sharpening

We also use the Blend If sliders to apply midtone contrast, the lack of which is often confused with a lack of sharpness.

Sharpening Layer Controls

In practice, we often combine all the techniques discussed thus far on a single sharpening layer, starting with either a layer created by duplicating the Background layer on a flat file or a new layer created by using Option-Merge Visible on a layered file.

We set the layer to Luminosity blending and 66% opacity. We set the Blend If sliders to apply sharpening only to the midtones, we create an edge mask and apply it to the layer, and then we sharpen the layer. But we still have a significant amount of control after applying the sharpening:

- We can increase or decrease the global strength of the sharpening by adjusting the layer opacity up or down.

- We can adjust the strength of the sharpening along edges by editing the layer mask to lighten or darken the edges in the mask—this is made easy by using the endpoint controls in Levels.

- We can adjust the transition between sharpened and unsharpened areas by adjusting the contrast of the mask, using either Curves or the gray slider in Levels.

- We can adjust the width of the sharpening haloes by blurring the mask with Gaussian Blur, then editing with Levels or Curves to maintain the original tonality.

- We can fine-tune the tonal range to which the sharpening is applied by adjusting the Blend If sliders.

This type of layer-based sharpening lends itself well to automation using actions. Most of the difficulties in doing so are a matter of taking into account the various assumptions and dependencies actions always entail.

One of the appealing aspects of automated sharpening layers that use these techniques is that they can be run as batch processes to make a large number of images good automatically, yet still provide enough control after sharpening to make the handful of hero images that justify handwork great, rather than just good.

Splitting the Sharpening Haloes

When adjusting a single sharpening layer, sometimes it becomes difficult to target the specific luminance ranges. Depending on the tonal range of the image, you may need to target the darks more or sometimes the lights. By splitting up the light and dark haloes, you can control the relative amounts of sharpening far more accurately.

Figure 5-7 shows the image we'll use to adjust the luminance targets for sharpening. The image has an Unsharp Mask filter applied with the Amount setting at 200 and Radius at .6. The sharpening was done on a separate layer set to Luminosity blend and an opacity of 66% (Figure 5-8).

- Adjusting the light haloes: In Figure 5-9, which shows the light contours being adjusted, we've set the white clip to be 250. We don't want to drive any textural tones to pure white. We've set the blend to taper in until level 220, where the full effect of the sharpened layer will be applied down to 140, when we once again taper off until level 110. This set of blending options concentrates the sharpening for this layer to target the quarter tones of the image. The overlay in the middle becomes the split point between the lights and the darks.

Figure 5-7

Bruce's tiger photo with a sharpening layer

The Layers panel

Full image

Targeting the layer

Adjusting the Blend If settings

Figure 5-8

Adjusting dark haloes

Targeting the layer

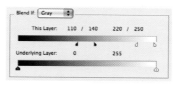

Adjusting the Blend If settings

Figure 5-9

Adjusting light haloes

It's tough to visualize how the blend split impacts an image, so Figure 5-10 shows the original unsharpened and sharpened images, and the two separate blend layers.

Figure 5-10 Comparing blend targeting

Unsharpened image

Sharpened image with both targeted layers visible

Blend If settings targeting the dark haloes (light halo layer is invisible)

Blend If settings targeting the light haloes (dark halo layer is invisible)

Be aware that the Photoshop working space you choose to use has an impact on the Blend If split points. Bruce and Jeff use Pro Photo RGB almost exclusively. Pro Photo RGB has a gamma of 1.8. If you use Adobe RGB (or, heaven forbid, sRGB), the gamma of those spaces is 2.2. (Actually, sRGB has a slightly modified 2.2 tone curve, but that's not relevant for this discussion.) As a result, you may need to slightly alter the split point up or down, and you may also need to vary the shadow halo blends. Gamma 2.2 is a steeper tone curve, and therefore shadow three-quarter tones tend to be emphasized. Narrowing the shadow feather of 15 to 40 down to 10 to 30 may help with the gamma adjustment tweaks. In terms of the light halo clip point, there shouldn't be much need to alter those other than fine-tuning them for your own taste.

Jeff is often asked whether or not it matters which of the Blend If sliders are adjusted. (The top set of sliders, labeled "This Layer," refers to the layer that is being blended down. The bottom set of sliders, "Underlying Layer," dictates the area of the bottom layer that gets blended into.) Yes, it does matter, but in the case of image sharpening or noise reduction, it matters very little. Since the intention is to roll off or otherwise reduce the impact of the effects on extreme highlights and shadows, the net impact is so similar as to not matter.

There are times, particularly if you use any of the Advanced Blending options in the middle of the Layer Style dialog box, where it does indeed matter whether you are adjusting the top or bottom sliders. The most critical adjustment point, in the case of splitting the haloes, is where you set the top of the dark and bottom of the light haloes. Our setting of 110 to 140 is a very gentle split point. If you narrow the numbers, you get a more specific cutoff between the light and dark haloes. If you do narrow the blend, be sure to check the results so that they are as expected.

Between adjusting the overall opacity and the blending options, you can acquire a lot of control over how and where sharpening and noise reduction will get applied. However, to fine-tune *exactly* where the effects occur, you need to deploy layer masks.

Layer Masks

A significant benefit to applying sharpening on a layer is that you can use a layer mask to localize the sharpening to specific areas of the image. You can adjust the transition between sharpened and nonsharpened areas by adjusting the blur and contrast of the layer mask. You can, within limits, adjust the width of the sharpening haloes by blurring, then adjusting the contrast, of the mask.

We use layer masks with sharpening or noise-reduction layers in two distinct ways:

- Edge or surface masks localize effects along the edges or surfaces in the image.

- Brush masks let you paint the effect in (and out) by painting on the layer mask with white or black.

Edge Masks

Creating an edge mask is a multistep process. The first step is to create a new channel that has good contrast along the edges you want to sharpen. In many cases, you can simply duplicate the red or green channel (the blue channel usually has more noise, and hence isn't a good candidate). In Chapter 4, we showed the ability to load the Luminance image info by Command-clicking (Mac) the RGB composite channel. You can also use the keyboard shortcuts of Command-Option-2 (Mac) or Control-Alt-2 (Windows). This loads the image's luminosity as an active selection. From there you save the selection as a channel for further work.

Figure 5-11 shows the image we'll be using for this edge mask example. This is the full-frame image downsampled and output sharpened for print.

We used Command-click on the RGB composite channel to load the luminosity of the image as a selection and saved the selection as a channel. Figure 5-12 shows the luminosity of the center portion of the image.

Figure 5-11 Full-frame image of the western slope of the Sierra Nevada Mountains

Figure 5-12 Center crop of the luminance channel

NOTE: In the previous edition of this book, Bruce outlined a procedure for using the Calculations command in Photoshop to combine the Red and Green channels using a Pin Light blending and saving this as a channel. Bruce used this approach while Jeff appreciated the more immediate method of Command-clicking the RGB composite channel. A careful examination will indeed reveal very slight differences between the two techniques. We'll leave it to the reader to test the very "Brucian" alternative of using Calculations and determine if it matters.

Figure 5-13 shows the result of applying the Find Edges filter under the Stylize submenu in the Filters main menu. This is a one-trick pony. The results depend entirely on the edges in your images, and it's up to you to modify the edges as you see fit. Figure 5-13 will need to be inverted to act as an edge mask. Further modification will require blurring and toning to achieve the optimal edge or surface mask result.

Figure 5-13 Result of running the Find Edges filter

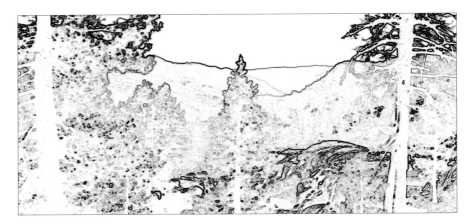

Figure 5-14 shows the original edge mask (Figure 5-13 inverted) as well as four different blurred results. Adding blur will soften the transitions between edge and surface areas. For high-frequency images, blur at a lower amount to preserve the edges for sharpening. For wider edges you'll often need to soften them with a higher Radius. With surface masks for noise reduction, it's typical to blur the mask a lot.

As you can see, very small amounts of blurring can have a big impact in the edge-width transitions. Figure 5-15 shows before and after applying the 3-pixel blurred edge mask.

The aim of the edge mask is to cut back on the harshness of the effect that sharpening has on surface areas while concentrating the sharpening to the edges. It's sometimes very hard to determine the extent to which to blur the edge mask. We suggest zooming in on critical areas of your image and applying the Gaussian Blur to the layer mask while looking at the actual image. Adjusting the pixel radius of the blur up or down lets you fine-tune the effect for your specific image.

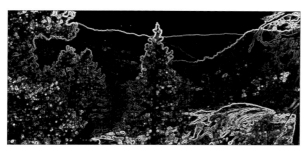

Figure 5-14 Adjusting the softness of the edge mask

Original edge mask with no blur

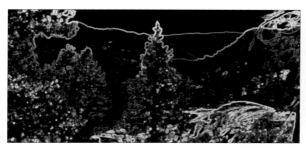

Edge mask with a 1-pixel Gaussian Blur filter

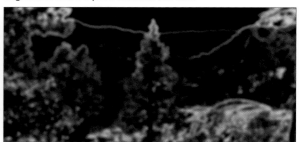

Edge mask with a 2-pixel Gaussian Blur filter

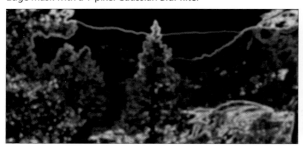

Edge mask with a 3-pixel Gaussian Blur filter

Edge mask with a 4-pixel Gaussian Blur filter

Figure 5-15 Comparing the addition of an edge mask at 400% zoom

Sharpened image without edge mask
(USM (Unsharp Mask) Amount 400, Radius .7)

Sharpened image with edge mask with a
3-pixel Gaussian Blur filter applied to the mask

Find Edges, Then Gaussian Blur…or Vice Versa?

The order of operations does matter. Figure 5-16 shows the result of changing the order in which the Gaussian Blur was applied. The first image shows the proper order of Find Edges and then Gaussian Blur. The second image shows what happens to the edges if you apply the blur before the Find Edges filter. In general we suggest using Find Edges first—particularly for higher-resolution images where you want to accurately control how the edges are tweaked.

You may also wonder whether you want to apply the edge mask as a layer mask before or after you do the image sharpening to the pixel layer. That will depend in large part on your sharpening workflow. It doesn't functionally matter whether you apply the edge mask as a layer mask before or after you apply the sharpening. If you are sharpening by eye (which, as we've stated, has risks), you may want to sharpen the layer and then apply the layer mask with blurring to suit the image. Often, tonal adjustments must be done after the edge mask is made into the layer mask.

Figure 5-16 Comparing the order of operations

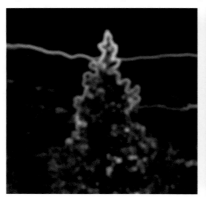

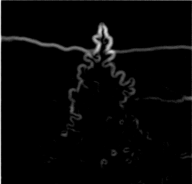

Edge mask with Find Edges, then Gaussian Blur

Edge mask with Gaussian Blur, then Find Edges

Blurring the edge mask can go only so far. Generally you must adjust the tonality of the mask to your image. You can use Levels or Curves, but we find the quick tone adjustment of Levels to be more suitable, since we are generally trying to choke (make smaller) or spread (make bigger) the edges. By lightening the tonality, more of the sharpening effect will be allowed to pass through with the increased opacity that a lighter mask gives.

Figure 5-17 shows the effect of substantially lightening the clipping point of the mask.

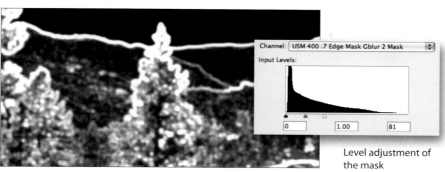

Lightened edge mask

Level adjustment of the mask

Figure 5-17 Lightening the mask to increase the sharpening effect

You can also fill with a slight opacity of white to lighten the entire mask to ensure that all of the image will get a touch of sharpening. Jeff often does this with high-resolution scans of large-format film (4" x 5" or 8" x 10" chromes, but not negatives) because he scans without any sharpening.

Figure 5-18 shows the result of taking the mask from Figure 5-17 and adding a 25% opacity fill with white.

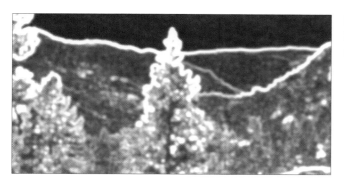

Figure 5-18 Filling the mask with a 25% opacity of white

This can be done right on the mask with the layer mask targeted while viewing the color image. You can undo the fill if you don't like the effect, or modify it by using the Fade command to cut back on the strength of the fill.

Edge masks will generally want to be sharper masks, but when you want to turn an edge mask into a surface mask, you will generally need further blurring and tone modification.

Surface Masks

While edge masks are used for sharpening the edges in an image, a surface mask can be used to apply noise reduction to the non-edges areas that we call surfaces. Surface masks are often more blurred and lighter in nature to allow noise reduction to gently hit more areas of the image prior to sharpening the result of the noise reduction. That's the order you'll want to do the effects: noise reduction before (or during, at least) the sharpening.

Figure 5-19 shows the result of taking the original edge mask from Figure 5-14 and adding an 8-pixel Gaussian Blur to make a softer surface mask.

Figure 5-19 Surface mask made from the original Find Edges result, then blurred 8 pixels

There are times when you may need to modify the tonality of a surface mask, usually by increasing the strength of the edge protection from noise reduction. Figure 5-20 shows darkening the edges to reduce the smoothing effect of the noise reduction.

Figure 5-20 Darkening the mask edges to reduce smoothing of edges

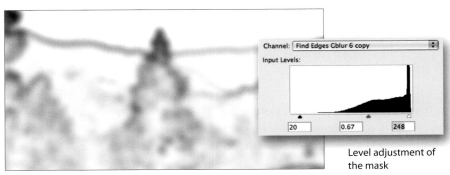

Level adjustment of the mask

Darkened surface mask

Figure 5-21 shows a contact-size image with the final Layers and Channels panel. The contact-size image was output sharpened for the book. The entire image would have reproduced as a 13" x 9" image at 300 ppi.

At the bottom of the layers stack is a layer that used Reduce Noise at an Amount of 6 and Preserve Details setting of 60%. It had a surface mask based on the Find Edges result and then blurred 8 pixels. The sharpening layers used an Unsharp Mask filter with an Amount of 400 and a Radius of .7. The edge mask was a 2-pixel blur of the original edge mask shown in Figure 5-14.

All of this is rather abstract considering that ultimately we want to create images, not a bunch of layers and masks, right? Well, the rest of this chapter is chock full of edge and surface masks, and rather than rewrite the steps each and every time, we wanted to concentrate on how to create and use layers and masks for sharpening and noise reduction. Now let's move on to capture sharpening as a process in Photoshop.

Figure 5-21
Final sharpening and noise-reduction results

Contact-size crop

Layers panel

Channels panel

Selections, Channels, and Masks

Selections, channels, and masks are all the same thing as far as Photoshop is concerned. They are simply three different roles played by the same data.

A selection is simply a temporary channel, which can be made permanent by saving it using the Save Selection command from the Select menu.

Saved Channels appear in the Channels palette. To load a channel as a selection, you can choose Load Selection from the Select menu, then choose the channel in the Load Selection dialog box. Or you can do this much more quickly by Command-clicking the channel's tile in the Channels palette.

To add a channel as a layer mask, you must first load it as a selection using either of the methods just described. Then you can add it as a layer mask by selecting the layer and either choosing one of the Layer Mask commands from the Layer menu, or clicking the Add Layer Mask button in the Layers palette.

CAPTURE SHARPENING IN PHOTOSHOP

Capture sharpening is a combination of sharpening for source and content. The goal in source optimization is to counteract the softening effects of the demosaicing process and, when present, the antialiasing filter. The goal in content sharpening is to enhance the edges while mitigating the adverse effects of film grain or camera noise.

The capture-sharpening process varies considerably depending on whether you are using Photoshop, Camera Raw, or Lightroom. With Photoshop, you need to create sharpening layers, add layer masks for edges and surfaces, and in general do a lot of image-by-image handwork. It's tedious and time consuming, although automating large chunks makes it less of a burden. We're going to keep the automation for the next chapter and concentrate here on the process of sharpening in Photoshop. Most of these examples will be for film sharpening, where the processing techniques are used to both reduce noise while adding sharpness.

If you are scanning film, you'll want to be doing your capture sharpening in Photoshop. Scanning film properly requires a large degree of attention to detail as well as reliance on the hardware you are using. Jeff and Bruce used a high-end CCD scanner rather than a drum scanner. But even with a relatively low-end flatbed scanner, you can get good results if you make sure you don't let the scanner try to do the sharpening—and sometimes it can be a real challenge to turn off that unwanted sharpening. We'll start with the relatively easy scanning of a medium-format transparency, move on to a 35mm chrome, and finish the film scans with a very difficult ISO 1600 color negative, where we had to punt Photoshop and turn to a third-party tool.

Medium-Format Transparency

When we said scanning and sharpening medium-format film was relatively easy, we meant it. The larger film sizes equate to better image detail and generally lower film grain—the two main areas where capture sharpening is directed. We'll start by scanning a 6" x 7" transparency in the scanner's software. Figure 5-22 shows the preview of the image and the Texture controls to turn off sharpening on the software.

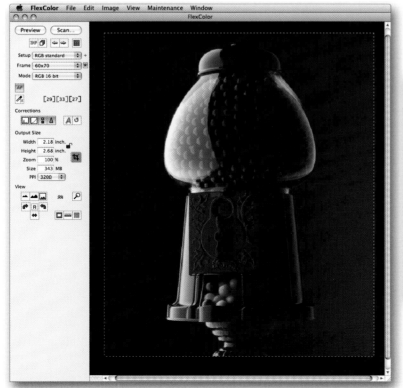

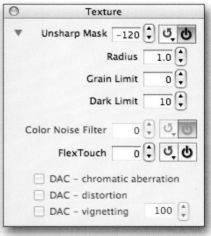

Figure 5-22
Film scanning a medium-format transparency

Texture dialog box to adjust sharpening

FlexColor dialog box

Turning Off Sharpening

As you see in Figure 5-22, the Texture dialog box controls the sharpening applied to the image during scanning. One might think that setting the sharpening to zero would turn off the sharpening, but alas, no. In order to completely eliminate any effects of sharpening, you actually have to set this to -120. If you don't know this little secret, life can be pretty irritating. For most scanners, simply turning off the sharpening is sufficient. We point this out not so much to point fun at this otherwise very good scanner software, but to clarify that one must be very careful when setting up the scanner to be sure to disable any sharpening.

Preparing for Sharpening

Upon opening the image in Photoshop, final tone and color correction was done and close-up spotting was finished. There's nothing as frustrating as setting up all your sharpening layers only to find out that what you've done is nicely sharpened a whole bunch of dust and scratches as well as your image. An edge and a surface mask were created as well. Figure 5-23 shows both masks.

Figure 5-23 Masks

 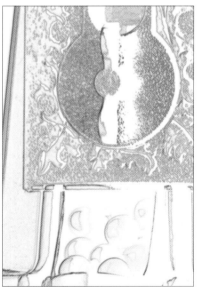

Edge mask with a 2-pixel Gaussian blur   Surface mask with a 6-pixel Gaussian blur

The low-blur edge mask allowed restricting the sharpening to the many high-frequency textural elements in the image. The softer surface mask allowed a general overall noise reduction that was already slightly edge protected by using the Reduce Noise filter.

Figure 5-24 shows a tiny contact-print-sized portion of the final image. The overall scanned image size was 22.5" x 28.25" at 300 ppi. The figure also shows the final Layers panel.

A contact-print crop of the full image with output sharpening

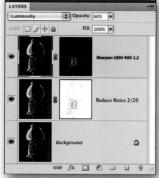

Figure 5-24 Final image and Layers panel

The Layers panel showing a Reduce Noise layer and an Unsharp Mask layer

Slight Noise Reduction and Sharpening

Since the edge mask was controlling the edge width, the Unsharp Mask filter could be used at a slightly higher radius. The Reduce Noise layer helped get rid of the film grain signature prior to the sharpening. The sharpening layer was made by creating an Option/Merged layer of the Background layer plus the Reduce Noise layer. The Blend If sharpening was a simple roll off of the lights and the darks without the need to split the sharpening haloes. As we said, noise reduction and sharpening for medium-format film scans is rather easy!

Figure 5-25 shows the original unsharpened scan as well as the noise reduction and final sharpening.

Figure 5-25 Before and after comparisons at 200% zoom

Original scan

The Reduce Noise layer

The final noise reduction and capture sharpening

35mm Transparency

Capture sharpening small-format film is a bit more difficult than medium-format. Everything done to the scan is magnified because the film is smaller, so the grain is more obvious and the images need more aggressive noise reduction and sharpening.

Moderate Noise Reduction and Sharpening

Figure 5-26 shows a scan from a 35mm transparency that requires stronger noise reduction than the previous example of a medium-format transparency. The stronger grain of 35mm requires stronger Reduce Noise settings that soften the image noticeably, so we mitigate the effect by adding a layer mask to the Reduce Noise layer that protects the edges.

Figure 5-26 Reduce Noise on a masked layer

The entire image

A 300-ppi detail

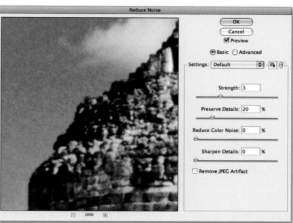

Running the Reduce Noise filter with Strength 3, Preserve Details 20, and all other settings at 0 produces the result shown below.

After Reduce Noise

This layer mask was made by creating a Luminance selection with the Noise Reduction layer targeted, then saving the selection as a channel. We then ran the Find Edges filter, applied a 5-pixel Gaussian Blur, and adjusted the white Input slider in Levels to 240.

The Reduce Noise layer after adding the layer mask

The image after adding a sharpening layer and running Unsharp Mask with Amount 200 and Radius 0.8

The addition of the edge mask to the noise-reduction layer allows for the application of enough noise reduction to reduce the grain in the sky without softening the important edges in the image too much. The addition of the sharpening layer essentially returns the image to its original sharpness, but with less grain.

High-Speed 35mm Color Negative

Where our first two examples could be handled adequately completely inside of Photoshop's toolset, this next example is simply outside of Photoshop's capabilities. The image of the Irish pub in Dublin was shot on Fuji ISO 1600 color negative film. The combination of being a negative plus the high ISO means that Photoshop's built-in tools won't make much of a dent in the excessive high-ISO grain.

Figure 5-27 shows the full frame of the image after noise reduction, sharpening, and downsampling. The film grain doesn't look very obvious in the downsampled version, but in the contact-print size (at 300 ppi), you can see all that lovely film grain busting through. If reproduced small, we really wouldn't need to do too much, but if we want to use the image near its native scan size of 13" x 20" at 300 ppi, some pretty industrial-strength noise reduction will be needed.

Resorting to a Specialized Tool

We tried a variety of special noise-reduction techniques using Reduce Noise, Surface Blur, and Despeckle, but to no avail. The high-speed film grain could not be reduced to any useful degree using just Photoshop. So, we turned to a third-party specialty plug-in called Noiseware from Imagenomic (www.imagenomic.com). Bruce and Jeff were introduced to this plug-in by our good friend and colleague Mac Holbert of Nash Editions fame. Mac prints for some of the world's top artists and photographers, and sometimes he really needs some heavy-duty noise reduction.

Figure 5-28 shows the main Noiseware Profession plug-in dialog box. The settings represent special adjustments to really go after both luminance and color noise reduction. It is hitting into the edge detail a tiny bit. You can see that the resulting layer and layer mask has a few areas painted out (black added) to reduce the effects of the noise reduction in key areas.

Figure 5-27 Original scan at full-frame and contact-print size

The entire image

A 300-ppi detail

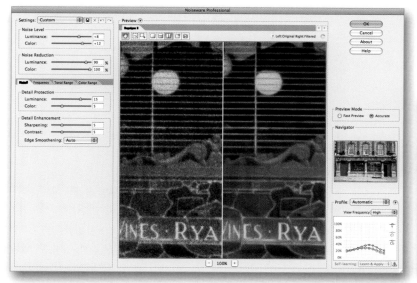

Noiseware Professional filter dialog box

Figure 5-28 Using Noiseware on a layer

Noise-reduced layer with layer mask

NOTE: A note here regarding your own personal favorite noise-reduction tool: If you already have something you like, such as Neat Image, Noise Ninja, or a variety of others, that's all fine and good. The main point we are trying to get across here is not a specific endorsement of Noiseware, but rather the fact that it's simply not worth struggling to do something in Photoshop that can't really be done. Bite the bullet and go out and get a tool that is specially designed to do serious noise reduction. This holds true both for high-speed film grain such as this example but high-ISO digital captures as well.

Sharpening the Reduced Noise

After applying noise reduction, we created a new sharpening layer by using the Option/Merged technique. This allowed us to apply sharpening on the already reduced noise image. We used Unsharp Mask with an Amount of 200 and a Radius of 1.2. We created an edge mask with a 3-pixel Gaussian blur and applied the edge mask as a layer mask. In order to allow some of the sharpening to hit all over the image, we filled the layer mask with a 33% opacity white fill. Yes, this tended to resharpen some of the reduced noise back into stronger appearance, but we could control the relative strength via the edge mask. We intentionally overreduced the grain using Noiseware with the expectation of resharpening the image.

Figure 5-29 shows the sharpening layer and the tone-modified layer mask.

Figure 5-29 Using the edge mask as a layer mask

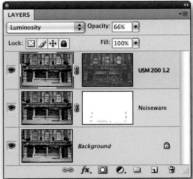

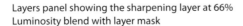

Layers panel showing the sharpening layer at 66% Luminosity blend with layer mask

Detail of the tone-modified 3-pixel blurred edge mask

The sharpening layer was set to 66% Opacity with Luminance blending. We used the typical single-layer roll off of the highlights and shadows using the Blend If slider options. The final results are shown in Figure 5-30.

Having to resort to a third-party plug-in may frustrate some Photoshop users. Yes, we agree that Photoshop could and should have the best-of-breed functionality, but we are also sensitive to the fact that one of Photoshop's greatest strengths through the years is a healthy and viable third-party development environment. If Photoshop took away all the nooks and crannies of plug-in development, we wouldn't have third parties, and the industry would be less for that.

Figure 5-30 Comparing noise-reduced and sharpened results

Noise-reduced layer

Sharpening layer

NOTE: Clearly we can't cover each and every film and scanner type in the book. The main essence of film scanning is to try to get the highest-resolution scan possible with no sharpening and in 16 bit. Optimizing the scan for tone, color correction, dust, and scratches prior to noise reduction and sharpening is imperative.

Scanning to Reduce Noise

Some scanner drivers let you scan the film multiple times to reduce scanner noise. You can often get a much cleaner scan using four passes than you can using one. Some scanner drivers let you scan as many as 16 passes, which in our view is overkill. This technique suppresses scanner noise, but doesn't address film grain. A technique that does address film grain is to scan at a higher resolution than is needed, then downsample—this mitigates both scanner noise and film grain.

Using Third-Party Raw Processing Software

Before we move on to Camera Raw and Lightroom capture sharpening, there is still another type of image sharpening that needs to be addressed in Photoshop: digital capture from cameras that aren't supported by Camera Raw and Lightroom. One such camera back is the Phase One P 65+. Additionally, when that back is mounted on the Phase One/Mamiya 645 camera using the newest lenses, you need to use the Capture One software to process out images while taking advantage of the automatic lens corrections that Capture One offers.

For this example we'll be using Capture One raw processing software to process a raw capture from a Phase One P 65+ capture. We're doing this for two reasons: For one, while Camera Raw and Lightroom can process out P 65+ raw captures, the processing isn't optimized at this point in time. We could process out the captures as digital negative (DNG) files from Capture One and then use those linear DNGs in Camera Raw and Lightroom, but there are "issues" with doing that at this time. But the main reason we want to use the Capture One software is that for the 4.x version, Phase has added automatic lens-correction processing that handles spherical aberrations, lateral chromatic aberrations, and lens distortion and vignetting. So, for the cameras and lens supported, Phase One's Capture One can output more fully optimized images. We do still like to take control of the noise reduction (if needed) and capture sharpening ourselves, however.

Using Capture One

The primary settings we want to show in Capture One are the Lens Correction adjustments. Figure 5-31 shows the main interface for Capture One 4.8 as well as details on two important panels: the Lens Corrections and the Process Recipe where Sharpening has been disabled. The Lens Correction settings are set to correct for chromatic aberration, purple fringing, sharpness falloff, and vignetting.

This is the same image we used in Chapter 2, "Why Do We Sharpen?", for the camera comparison in Figure 2-9. The capture's native size after processing is 22.4" x 26.9" at 300 ppi. There was no need for any noise reduction. The ISO for the capture was 50, the lowest on the back. There was simply no appreciable or noticeable noise in the capture. We have seen noise occur with this sensor when using longer timed exposures over 30 seconds.

Figure 5-31 Using Capture One to process raw files

The main Capture One 4.8 dialog box

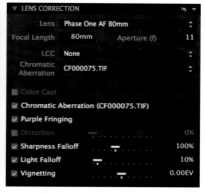

The Lens Correction panel

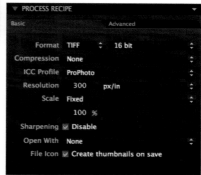

The Process Recipe panel with the layer mask targeted in the Layers palette, paint with white using a low-opacity brush

Creating the Sharpening Layers

In this simple case, we dragged the Background layer to the New Layer icon to make a copy of the layer. We applied an Unsharp Mask filter with an Amount of 400 and a Radius of .5. We set the Blend If settings to split the sharpening haloes. We also slightly modified the light halo opacity down from our normal 66% to just 50%, because we felt that, in some of the super light textural areas, we were getting just a tad too much sharpening. We could have mitigated this with the Blend If settings, but adjusting the opacity was quicker. Figure 5-32 shows the Layers panel for the darks and lights sharpening as well as the Blend If settings.

The edge mask was created using the typical Find Edges. In this case, the Gaussian Blur was 2 pixels. The actual edge width was determined more by the Unsharp Mask settings instead of the width of the edge mask. But the edge mask kept the sharpening from affecting the surface areas. Figure 5-33 shows the edge mask at a 200% zoom.

Figure 5-32 Sharpening
layers and blend settings

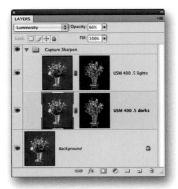

The Darks layer   The Lights layer

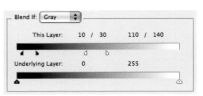

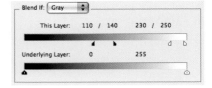

The Darks blend   The Lights blend

Figure 5-33 Edge mask
with 2-pixel radius Gaussian
Blur applied with a 15%
white fill

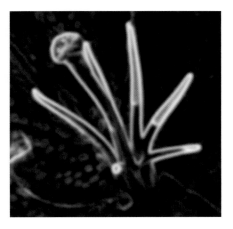

For the layer mask we filled a slight amount with white (15% opacity) to
allow some of the sharpening to be applied over the entire image. This is
really seasoning to taste, but in general we caution that it's far better to
undersharpen than to oversharpen at the capture-sharpening stage. You
can always go back and increase relative opacities or create completely new
creative sharpening to pump up the sharpening level.

Figure 5-34 shows the results from capture sharpening. The zoom view was set to 200%.

Figure 5-34 Capture sharpening at 200% zoom, before and after

Before capture sharpening

After capture sharpening

For the purposes of capture sharpening, we've covered a variety of techniques that are needed in Photoshop. In the next section, we'll cover doing capture sharpening in Camera Raw and Lightroom.

CAPTURE SHARPENING IN CAMERA RAW AND LIGHTROOM

We used to turn off sharpening in Camera Raw because the sharpening wasn't what we would call optimal. Since the advent of improved capture sharpening in Camera Raw and Lightroom, however, we rarely if ever need to resort to using Photoshop for capture sharpening. A lot of people using Camera Raw and Lightroom for capture sharpening fail to understand the relationship between the predominant edge width in the image and the radius being set for sharpening. While it's not absolutely critical that you nail the correct radius in measurements of .1, it is critical that you don't completely misconstrue and use the complete opposite. For narrow-edged images that have a lot of high-frequency textural image data, you'll want to use a radius below 1.0. For images with wider edges that have lower frequency, the radius should be above 1.0.

Determining Edge Width

Images with super high-frequency texture aren't all that hard to find. Many if not most landscape images tend to have a high preponderance of narrow edges. Most portraits of people tend toward wide edges and lower frequency. Figure 5-35 shows the super high-frequency edges while 5-38 shows low-frequency edges.

Figure 5-35 Super high-frequency edges

Super High-Frequency Edges

All of the images in the super high-frequency array of images need very small radius settings in Camera Raw or Lightroom. While not disastrous, a radius of 1.0 (the default) will be suboptimal, particularly if you push the amounts higher than the default of 25. In general you'll also want detail settings that are on the higher side.

To further drive home the point, we'll use an image of golden-colored Aspen trees as an example. Figure 5-36 shows the sharpened image with the Camera Raw and Lightroom settings that we arrived at as optimal.

The Radius setting of 0.5 is the smallest radius we can get in Camera Raw and Lightroom at this time (that's not to say it won't change in the future—we hope it gets lowered). To arrive at the radius was pretty simple. Experience has taught us that cutting the radius in half for these kinds of images is suitable. Reducing the radius allows us to increase the amount of the sharpening as well as the detail setting to further concentrate the sharpening into the high-frequency range. Remember that radius is tied to the detail settings as well as to the mask settings, so getting the radius correct is important.

Figure 5-36 Capture sharpening a super high-frequency image

Left to right: Camera Raw Detail panel, the super high-frequency image, Lightroom Detail panel

Figure 5-37 shows the preview of the Radius, Detail, and the Masking settings we determined were optimal. Note that this image has Luminance noise reduction set to 20, which allows us to push the Detail settings higher than default.

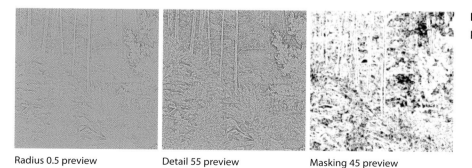

Radius 0.5 preview   Detail 55 preview   Masking 45 preview

Figure 5-37 Sharpening parameter previews

Low-Frequency Edges

We present a series of images in Figure 5-38 that we have determined are low-frequency-edged images. All of these images will need a radius setting above the 1.0 default. How much higher? That takes an image-by-image assessment, but the upper range that we've found useful is a radius of 2.0. Generally 1.2 to 1.5 is what we consider the normal setting for these sorts of images.

Figure 5-38
Low-frequency edges

We'll take an image by Martin Evening of model Courtney as our example for the edge adjustment. The primary areas of the image we need sharpened are the eyelashes, hair, and lips. We don't want to emphasize the skin texture —if anything, we'll end up wanting to minimize it. Figure 5-39 shows the final settings we arrived at for this image. We used a Radius of 1.4, which is almost 50% larger than the default 1.0. We also used a lower Detail setting and a rather high Masking setting.

We'll admit to a certain degree of local image correction and spot healing on this image—discretion precludes us from showing just how much. It suffices to say that Martin's lighting and the excellent makeup went a long way toward making the image look good, but reality always requires a special touch. Since we did some touch-up (in Camera Raw/Lightroom only, not Photoshop), we were free to punch up the strength of the capture sharpening.

Figure 5-39 Capture sharpening a low-frequency image

©2008 by Martin Evening

Left to right: Camera Raw Detail panel, the low-frequency image, Lightroom Detail panel

With Detail set to 15, we've deemphasized the high-frequency texture and suppressed the haloes. That allowed us to increase the amount to a rather high 65. We also have Masking set rather high and added a touch of noise reduction. The original image was well exposed at an ISO of 125, but we wanted to further smooth down the skin (which Luminance noise reduction will do) and could compensate with increased sharpening. Figure 5-40 shows the Radius, Detail, and Masking previews.

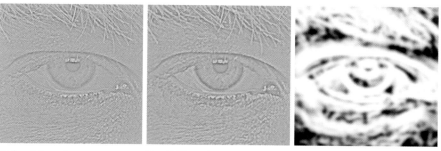

Radius 1.4 preview

Detail 15 preview

Masking 55 preview

Figure 5-40 Sharpening parameter previews

Medium-Frequency Edges

While it's fairly easy to discriminate between the two opposite extremes of edge frequencies, where it becomes more of a challenge is when the frequencies fall in the middle—what we call "medium," which we realize isn't very definitive, but there you have it. Figure 5-41 shows a range of images that we consider medium with regard to the frequency of the edges.

Figure 5-41
Medium-frequency edges

The one thing these images have in common is each image has areas of higher frequency that might benefit from a really low radius, while other areas in the images would do better with a higher radius. The only guidance we can offer is to do what looks best for each individual image. Know that the range of radius settings will probably be above 0.5 and below 1.5.

Setting the Detail will have a big impact on the way in which the higher frequency is handled. Also know that a bit of masking will almost always be needed, and most images—even well-exposed, low-ISO images—may benefit from a small amount of noise reduction. Where the real challenges lay, however, is when you have an image that has diametrically opposed sharpening requirements. When you encounter this sort of image, it's time to call in the big guns (if you want the optimal results): either Camera Raw or Lightroom *and* Photoshop.

Blending Image Frequencies with Smart Objects

When faced with an image whose sharpening needs exceed the ability for either Camera Raw or Lightroom to adequately cope, the only option is to do the capture sharpening twice and blend the result. You could simply process the image twice and bring both images into Photoshop as layers for blending using layer masks. This is a good technique, but it's not quite as flexible as we like. We like to use Camera Raw or Lightroom raw files opened in Photoshop as Smart Objects (SOs).

Setting Up Camera Raw to Create Smart Objects

To create SOs from Camera Raw, you must open an image in Camera Raw to access the Camera Raw Workflow Options dialog box. Figure 5-42 shows Camera Raw, the Workflow Options dialog box, and what happens to the Open button when you change the options.

As shown in Figure 5-42, once you select the "Open in Photoshop as Smart Objects" option, the main Open button alerts you to the change in the behavior. If you want to bypass the Smart Objects option and simply open the image directly as a raster image in Photoshop, hold down the Shift key when clicking the Open button.

Using Camera Raw Snapshots

Actually, before even opening the image in Photoshop, we suggest fine-tuning the two sets of capture sharpening you'll want to use in your SO. The reason to adjust the sharpening before opening as a SO is because once opened in Photoshop, the embedded raw file no longer has a direct relationship to the original raw file. It's very difficult to propagate any changes made in the embedded raw file inside of the Smart Object back to the original raw file.

Figure 5-43 shows the result of adjusting the sharpening for the two primary edge widths in the image. Two Snapshots are created and saved before opening the image in Photoshop.

Figure 5-42 Configuring
Camera Raw to create Smart
Objects in Photoshop

Main Camera Raw dialog box

Button to open the Workflow
Options dialog box

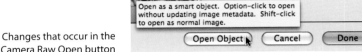

ProPhoto RGB; 16 bit; 3072 by 1907 (5.9MP); 300 ppi

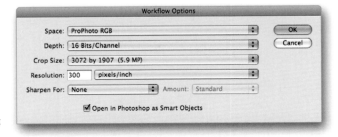

Workflow Options dialog box

Changes that occur in the
Camera Raw Open button

Image opened in Photoshop
as a Smart Object

Figure 5-43 Adjusting edge widths and saving as Snapshots

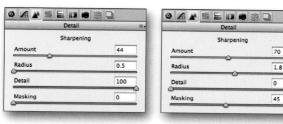

High-frequency capture
sharpening settings
(HF Sharp in Snapshots)

Low-frequency capture
sharpening settings
(LF Sharp in Snapshots)

Top of the Camera Raw Snapshots panel

Creating a Smart Object Copy Layer

Combining two or more copies of a raw Smart Object requires a slightly
different technique than simply dragging the SO to the New Layer icon in
the Layers panel. You need to use the New Smart Object via Copy command, found in the Layers > Smart Objects menu. Using this command
keeps both layers as discrete objects and allows you to alter the parametric
settings of each object separately. Figure 5-44 shows the command to create
a new Smart Object via Copy.

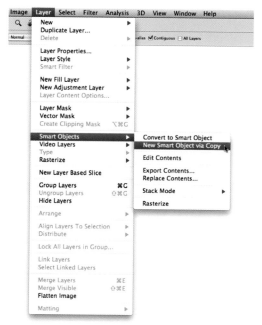

Figure 5-44
New Smart Object via
Copy command

Editing Smart Object Parameters

Once you have both SO layers in your stack, double-clicking either image icon will actually launch a special version of Camera Raw designed for Smart Objects. Instead of the Open buttons, they are changed to OK and Cancel.

Figure 5-45 shows double-clicking the top SO copy and selecting the LF Sharp Snapshot from the Snapshots panel. If you wanted to make any other changes, such as tone or color adjustments, to the image, you could do so at this time. Once you've made the Snapshot selection, clicking the OK button will update that layer's settings. From there, it's a matter of using a layer mask to blend the modified sharpening in or out by painting on the mask.

Figure 5-45 Opening and adjusting a Smart Object's settings and layer mask modifications

Double-clicking the layer icon

Selecting a different Snapshot from the Snapshots panel

Detail of the top of the Snapshots panel

Layer stack showing the bottom layer with HF Sharp settings and the top layer with LF Sharp settings with a layer mask

The final results in Figure 5-46 show the two layers and the final combination using a layer mask. Note that on the HF Sharp layer, the noise in the sky and the high-frequency texture are both enhanced. In the LF Sharp layer, a wider radius and the Detail settings reduced to zero have the effect of substantially smoothing out the image. The final result shows the higher-frequency textural enhancements while preserving the smoother areas of the sky.

Figure 5-46
Comparing the layers at 200% zoom

Layer containing the HF Sharp settings

Layer containing the LF Sharp settings

The final layer combination

Using Smart Objects with Lightroom

Both Camera Raw and Lightroom can create Smart Objects in Photoshop. Both also support the creation of Snapshots, as shown in Figure 5-47. Lightroom allows you to create the Snapshots and automatically adds them into the resulting embedded raw Smart Object inside Photoshop.

Figure 5-47 Creating Snapshots in Lightroom

Detail showing the Snapshots panel

Main Lightroom window

Editing in Photoshop from Lightroom

In the Edit In menu, rather than selecting the normal Edit in Adobe Photoshop CS4, we'll select the "Open as Smart Object in Photoshop" option. Lightroom hands off the image to Photoshop, where the embedded raw object will be on a layer, as shown back in Figure 5-42. In fact, once the Smart Object file is created in Photoshop, everything is the same as the preceding sections, including the way in which you add a copy layer and edit parameters. Since we've created Lightroom Snapshots, those same Snapshots will be available inside of the special version of Camera Raw. In fact, it is Camera Raw that will be doing the Smart Object layer parameter editing, even though you started out in Lightroom.

Figure 5-48 shows the Lightroom command in the Photo menu.

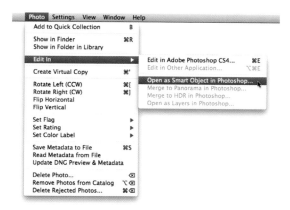

Figure 5-48 "Open as Smart Object in Photoshop" from Lightroom

Saving the Smart Object in Lightroom

Once you complete the image editing, including any creative sharpening you may want to do, saving the image from within Photoshop will make that Smart Object image file appear back in Lightroom as a rendered TIFF or PSD file (depending on your Lightroom preferences). Figure 5-49 shows the original DNG file as well as the edited TIFF file back in Lightroom.

Figure 5-49 The saved Smart Object image imported back into Lightroom

Reediting the Smart Object File

With Lightroom, the ability to keep original raw files and rendered image files (such as this Smart Object file) together greatly aids in image organization. You can still edit the Smart Object image file back inside of Photoshop by selecting the Edit in Adobe Photoshop CS4 command in Lightroom. In the dialog box that opens, shown in Figure 5-50, you can select what you want to edit in Photoshop, or you can select Edit a Copy with Lightroom Adjustments, Edit a Copy, or Edit Original. Select Edit Original to be able to open the original Smart Object image file with all your layers intact.

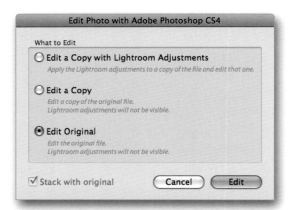

Figure 5-50
The Edit in Photoshop dialog box

Using Smart Objects for dual-edge frequency sharpening does provide a lot of flexibility to combine multiple iterations of raw files. It does, however, come at a price: file size. An image whose pixel dimensions might be 4000 x 2700 would be about a 63 MB file when saved as a flattened 16-bit TIFF. The same file with the original Smart Object dual layers and perhaps a couple more retouching layers would swell to a file over 250 MB saved to disk. If you are looking to save hard drive space, using Smart Objects isn't the way to do so.

While we do encourage people to be very conservative when saving layers files (save all the layers you may ever need to change), using Smart Objects for a large number of raw files isn't advisable. That brings us to the discussion of whether or not you should keep layered files containing all your capture sharpening saved as layers.

CONTROLLING FILE SIZE

Sharpening and noise-reduction layers and masks add significantly to the size of the file. A single sharpening layer doubles the size of the file, and each extra channel or layer mask adds one-third of the original file size. So file sizes can balloon quite quickly.

Of course, the only way to retain complete control over the sharpening is to keep the layers intact and take the hit on file size. Other sensible strategies are

- Once you've tweaked the sharpening to your satisfaction, archive the layered file and continue to work on a flattened copy.

- Once you've tweaked the sharpening to your satisfaction, simply flatten the image.

- To retain some degree of control over the sharpening, create a new layer using Option-Merge Visible, then delete the sharpening layers and masks. Note that the merged layer will be a Normal blend layer with 100% opacity, so you won't be able to reduce the sharpening. You can work around this by increasing the opacity of the sharpening layer to 100% before creating the merged layer, then you can reduce the opacity of the merged layer to the strength you prefer.

So, to the question of whether to flatten or not, our answer is yes and no. Yes, it is useful and advisable to save the layers—you can always flatten a Smart Object down to a simple pixel layer. But no, if you are sure you've optimized the image file for capture sharpening, then go ahead and merge or otherwise reduce the layer count—if you are sure you won't ever need to revisit the layers.

This is one of the reasons we greatly prefer Camera Raw and/or Lightroom for capture sharpening—the sharpening parameters are stored only in meta-data and can be changed at any time until the file is rendered into pixels.

This brings us to the close of the capture sharpening discussion. The next section starts down the road of being creative (something many people refuse to admit they love to be).

Smart Filters

Bruce and Jeff have a standing reaction to anything on which Adobe hangs the "Smart" moniker in Photoshop. The feature itself isn't necessarily smart, but it sure does take a really smart person to use the feature. Smart Filters follow along with the Photoshop legacy. If you want to use Smart Filters, you better plan on getting an advanced degree in Photoshop.

Smart Filters can be attached to any Smart Object (you see the trend here?), and to use Smart Filters you must have Smart Objects in your file. Figure 5-51 shows a Smart Filter applied to a Smart Object in the same image as our Smart Objects example image. The Smart Filter appears in the Layers panel below the Smart Object, as layer effects do. The difference is that you can double-click the filter to reaccess the filter dialog box to make changes.

Figure 5-51 Adding Smart Filters

Unsharp Mask filter being applied to a Smart Object

Layers panel showing the addition of an Unsharp Mask Smart Filter with layer mask

You can also access and modify the filter's Blending Options. However, unlike the Layers Style dialog box, the Blending Options for a Smart Filter are limited to opacity and blend mode. There are no Blend If options available. Figure 5-52 shows accessing the Blending Options dialog box for the Smart Filter.

The Smart Filter has a built-in layer mask that allows localized layer mask opacity controls. You can disable or delete the layer mask by using the context menu. Figure 5-53 shows using a layer mask and modifying the Filter Mask Display options. As we stated, you can apply a Smart Filter to any Smart Object and can convert pixel layers to Smart Objects, so just about any layer can have Smart Filters applied.

Figure 5-52 Editing the Blending Options

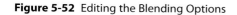

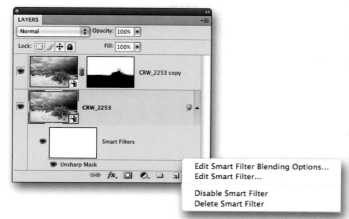

Flyout menu showing Smart Filter options

Blending Options dialog box

Figure 5-53 Working with Smart Filter masks

Smart Filter with layer mask applied

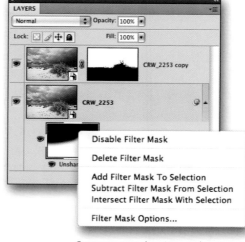

Context menu showing mask options

Filter Mask Display Options dialog box for
changing the way a mask appears

continues on next page

Smart Filters *continued*

Figure 5-54 shows the process of converting a regular layer to a Smart Object layer so you can apply a Smart Filter.

As we said, it takes a pretty smart person to use this feature. While it does have its uses (we have used Smart Filters a time or two), for the most part it's a feature in search of a problem to solve. And if you are at all concerned about file sizes, adding Smart Filters won't help you there. The file size for the final Smart Object example when including two Smart Filters grew from over 250 MB to just over 500 MB. By our calculations that's over 425 MB of "Smart" (too smart for us).

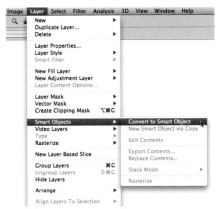

Figure 5-54 Command for converting pixel layer into a Smart Object layer

CREATIVE SHARPENING IN PHOTOSHOP

Creative sharpening is the catch-all term for localized adjustments to image detail. We include blurring and a few additional techniques as well as sharpening. Unlike the optimizations for capture and output processes, creative adjustments can't be applied automatically based on specific parameters—they require creative judgment, hence the name.

But automation plays an important role in making many of the tools we use for creative sharpening. The only part of the process that can't be automated is the actual localizing of an effect to a specific area of an image. So in this section we'll discuss building creative sharpening (and blurring) tools and applying them effectively to images in Photoshop. The first valuable lesson to learn is that you can turn any adjustment into a brush!

You can turn any adjustment into a brush using three simple steps:

- Make the adjustment on a separate layer—usually you'll create the layer using Option-Merge Visible, then apply the adjustment globally to the entire layer.

- Add a layer mask set to Hide All—that is, solid black. The easiest way to do this is to Option-click the "Add layer mask" button in the Layers palette. This hides the effect.

- Select the brush tool with the desired size, hardness, and opacity, and paint with white on the layer mask to reveal the effect.

This deceptively simple technique offers very precise control over localized sharpening. As long as the layer has a layer mask, you can paint the effect in or out depending on the color you paint onto the mask. You can start with an all-white or all-black mask, which we'll show you next.

Choosing the Type of Mask

Figure 5-55 shows an image that has a Midtone Contrast effects layer created as the top layer. To localize the effect, we'll add a layer mask. The question is whether to add a "reveal all" mask or a "hide all" mask, as shown in Figure 5-56.

Figure 5-55
Adding a layer mask

Image with Midtone Contrast layer

Layers panel showing Add layer mask button

Figure 5-56 Creating a hide all or reveal all layer mask

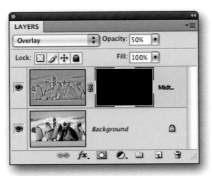 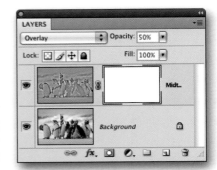

A hide all mask   A reveal all mask

Whether you add a hide all or reveal all mask is really dependent on how you want to get to where you want to end up. Either mask can produce the same results once you're done editing the final mask. The real question is which approach will get you to your final result the quickest. If the effect you want to add needs a gentle addition and will be kept in relatively smaller localized areas, we suggest creating a hide all mask. This allows a slow build-up of the effect by addition rather than subtraction. Figure 5-57 shows the addition of the effect by painting white gently into the hide all mask.

Figure 5-57 Painting an effect into a layer mask

Brushing in white with the mask targeted

Resulting layer mask with white added to the mask

One word of caution when painting into layer masks: Make very sure you have actually targeted the layer mask and not the pixel layer *before* starting to paint. We can't tell how many times we've failed to make sure and ended up painting into the pixels instead of the mask. Since Photoshop can't know in advance what your true intentions are, it's really up to you to make sure you do the right thing. Figure 5-58 shows using the other alternative approach of painting out an effect.

Figure 5-58 Painting out an effect on a layer mask

Brushing in black with the mask targeted

Resulting layer mask with black added to the mask

Sharpening Brush Techniques

You don't have to do everything with the brush, though it's often easiest. The goal of brushing is to localize the effect and to obtain the desired relative strength of the effect within the brushed area. In addition to black and white brush strokes, you have two other important controls over the effect:

- You can increase or reduce the layer opacity as a master control over the strength of the effect.

- You can make tonal edits to the layer mask using Levels or Curves to adjust the way the effect is applied locally.

As you work the mask, regardless of what flavor you started with, you can toggle back and forth between white or black (the foreground and background colors) by pressing the X key.

We tend to paint on masks with a rather low opacity or flow. You are not restricted to using only a paintbrush to modify the layer mask; you can use any selection tool and fill with black or white. You can also run filters over the layer mask such as a Gaussian Blur to soften the mask.

Most of the techniques we'll be covering in this section are designed to be used locally and often in very low doses, as some are "industrial strength." Use these techniques with a degree of subtlety.

Depth-of-Field Brush

You can't really counteract insufficient depth of field (DOF) any more than you can make out-of-focus elements in focus. But you can produce a reasonable illusion by using the following technique, which combines Unsharp Mask and Overlay/High Pass sharpening (discussed in Chapter 4).

We start the process by making a sharpening layer set to Overlay blend with a 50% opacity and the Blend If options set to roll off highlights and shadow. We'll run an Unsharp Mask at an Amount of 200% and a Radius of 2.5 followed by a High Pass filter at a radius of 30 pixels.

Figure 5-59 shows the creation of the sharpening layer, the application of the filters, and the addition of a layer mask set to hide all. The last figure shows the final painted layer mask.

Figure 5-59
Building a depth-of-field sharpening layer

Creating a sharpening layer at the top of the layer stack

Creating a hide all layer mask for the DOF layer after the filters have been run

Blend If slider settings

The final layer mask showing the areas sharpened in white

The effect is something between conventional sharpening and a midtone contrast boost. It's often quite difficult to see the effect while you're painting it in, but turning the layer on and off makes it quite obvious. This doesn't take the place of proper focusing but, in a pinch, can increase the apparent sharpness of areas within an image. Figure 5-60 shows the before and after with detail crops.

Figure 5-60 Depth-of-field sharpening layer, before and after

Contact-print-size crop before DOF brush

Before detail at 300% zoom view

Contact-print-size crop after DOF brush

After detail at 300% zoom view

Haze-Cutting Brush

The haze-cutting brush is a variant of the depth-of-field brush that's useful for bringing distant elements in landscapes closer. It uses the same techniques as the DOF brush, but incorporates a cooling step after creating the sharpening layer. While we used the same numbers for the Unsharp Mask and High Pass filters in this example as we did in the previous example, feel free to play with different amounts and different blends. This is, after all, a creative process. Once you get a formula you like, create an action so you can achieve the same effects repeatedly. We'll cover creating actions in the next chapter.

Figure 5-61 shows the addition of a sharpening layer and layer mask to concentrate the effect to the horizon to alleviate the aerial haze in downtown San Francisco. After the sharpening we created a Color Fill layer set to a Color blend mode and opacity of 33%. The exact opacity will vary, since the amount of color needed to kill a colorcast will vary. The main idea to grasp is to select a color that is the opposite color of the haze.

Figure 5-61 Building a haze-cutting layer

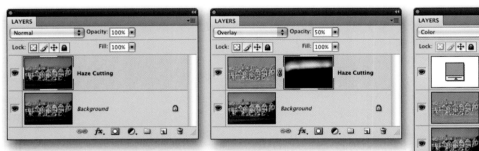

Creating a sharpening layer at the top of the layer stack

Creating the layer mask for the haze-cutting layer

Adding a Color Fill layer

Creating a Clipping Mask

Once you've added the Color Fill layer, you'll see that the color goes over the entire image. We want to localize the cooling color just to the areas where we painted in the layer mask. To accomplish this, we'll create a Clipping Mask so the Color Fill layer will be applied only in the areas where we painted in white on the sharpening layer's mask. In this way, the one layer mask controls both layers' local opacities. It's a useful two-for-one deal and allows for adding or subtracting both effects at the same time. You'll note, however, that the Color Fill layer retains its own discrete layer mask in the event you need to edit the local opacity of just the Color Fill layer.

Figure 5-62 shows selecting the Layer > Create Clipping Mask command as well as the resulting layer stack with the Color Fill layer clipped to the Haze Cutting layer mask.

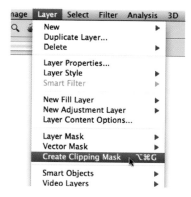

Selecting the Create Clipping Mask command in the Layer menu

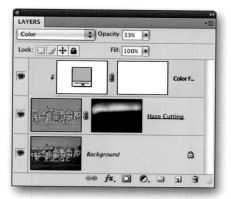

The resulting layer stack with the Color Fill layer clipped to the Haze Cutting layer mask

Figure 5-62
Creating a clipping mask

The final result both clears the warm smog haze from the skyline and pops out the detail of the distant buildings. Figure 5-63 shows the results of applying the haze-cutting effect.

Figure 5-63 Haze-cutting sharpening layer, before (top) and after (bottom)

Effects Layers

The previous examples of creative sharpening relied primarily upon hand brushing the effects in or out. Now we're going to switch direction and deal with blurring layers instead of sharpening, and concentrate on different approaches to localize the results. Layer masks will still be involved, but sometimes you need a more precise application instead of freehand brush strokes.

Lens Blur Layer

We've often stated that sometimes the best way to make something look sharper is to soften everything else in the image. The Lens Blur filter is a perfect tool for this. Gaussian Blur works fine for mechanical blurs, but if you want the blur effect to look photographic, Lens Blur looks far more authentic. Figure 5-64 shows the image we'll be working on in this example, before any sharpening.

Figure 5-64 Lens Blur example image, before

This image of an old automobile was actually shot in Ushuaia, Argentina (even though it looks like it could be Colorado). The intent was to isolate the car from the background. While it was shot at 70mm wide open at F4, the foreground and background intrude.

To make the car stand out, we duplicated the Background layer and created a path outline of the car. The hard outline was then softened by creating a selection from the path with a 2-pixel feather and saved as a channel. The channel was further modified so that the resulting blur would better blend into the foreground and background. The next step was to turn the channel into a layer mask on the Lens Blur layer. Figure 5-65 shows the path, the channel, and the resulting layer mask.

Figure 5-65 Creating the
Lens Blur layer mask

Car outline path

Channel with additional brush work

Applied as layer mask on the Lens Blur layer

The key to using the filter to increase the apparent lens bokeh (the out-of-focus areas) is to select the Layer Mask option in the Lens Blur Depth Map.

To be accurate, we could have used a channel instead of a layer mask as the source for the Depth Map option. However, we find it easier to visualize what the final result will be when we use the layer mask as a guide to what will and won't be blurred. Figure 5-66 shows the technique we use of temporarily inverting the layer mask to aid in determining the visible area needed in the layer mask.

Figure 5-66 Adjusting the
Lens Blur layer mask

Layer mask temporarily inverted

Image with inverted layer mask

Once the layer mask is in place, we apply the Lens Blur filter to the layer. Figure 5-67 shows the Lens Blur filter dialog box and the Depth Map option selected.

Figure 5-67 Adjusting the Lens Blur filter settings and options

Detail of the Depth Map's Source option

Lens Blur filter dialog box

The final result is shown in Figure 5-68. If you compare Figure 5-68 with the before image in Figure 5-64, we think you'll see that the car itself has increased in apparent sharpness. We haven't done anything to the sharpness of the car except make everything else appear less sharp. Pretty sneaky, huh?

Figure 5-68 Lens Blur example image, after

Box Blur Filter

The Lens Blur filter can do a convincing imitation of lens bokeh, but it can be very slow. We often use an alternative filter when we don't need to apply Lens Blur's special options. Our alternative is the Box Blur filter. The algorithm for Box Blur is very similar to Lens Blur in that it uses a shape to modify the blurring. Where Lens Blur uses multi-sided shapes (as in a lens aperture), Box Blur uses a simple square box.

Progressive Sharpening Layer

We could use the depth-of-field effect in an attempt to recover a certain degree of focus, but the effect is limited. The concept in this next example is to build up sharpening step-by-step; each new step will use the previous step's result and apply increasing degrees and levels of sharpening. Be warned, however: Any areas of your image that are already sharp will probably break and result in being substantially oversharpened.

Figure 5-69 shows the full frame of the image we'll be using in this example as well as the sharpening layer set to Luminosity blend mode. At this point, the opacity is left at 100% to be able to judge the effects as they build up.

Figure 5-69 Progressive sharpening example image, before

Progessive Sharpen layer set to Luminosity blend mode

Image at full frame

NOTE: While we'll show you the progression that we used for this image, note that all of this process is subject to modification and adaptation based on the demands of your image. You should remain flexible and be willing to try variations upon this basic theme.

Figure 5-70 shows the Unsharp Mask filter dialog box for the first sharpening round. Immediately after the application at full strength, we selected Fade Unsharp Mask and reduced the opacity to 20%. This resulted in a substantial reduction in the strength from the 500% and Radius .3 of the first filter application.

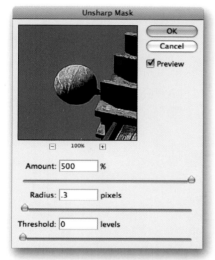

Unsharp Mask filter set to 500% and Radius .3

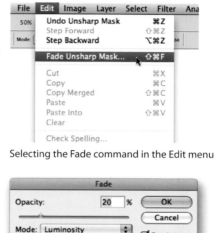

Selecting the Fade command in the Edit menu

Fade dialog box showing a 20% opacity

Figure 5-70
First application of Unsharp Mask

At this point we barely scratched the surface, so to speak. To build up the effect, we kept applying additional Unsharp Mask applications at gradually reducing amounts and increasing radii. The following applications were used:

1. Amount 500%, Radius .3, faded to 20% opacity (the first step shown)

2. Amount 300%, Radius .6, faded to 20% opacity

3. Amount 200%, Radius 1.0, faded to 20% opacity

4. Amount 100%, Radius 5.0, faded to 20% opacity

5. Amount 50%, Radius 10, faded to 20% opacity

6. Amount 25%, Radius 25, faded to 20% opacity

As you might expect, the buildup of sharpening can be substantial. Each subsequent step builds on the previous step, producing an end result you can't duplicate with any single application of the filter.

Figure 5-71 shows a 100% zoom view of the image before and after the complete sequence of applications.

Figure 5-71 Comparison of before and after

Image at 100% zoom before

Image at 100% zoom after

We warned you, right? At the full 100% opacity, you really wouldn't want your image to look like this. Reducing the opacity of the sharpening layer and adding a layer mask to get rid of the vastly oversharpened areas, however, produces a very useful result, as shown in Figure 5-72.

Figure 5-72 Adjusting the progressive sharpening strength

Layers panel showing the opacity reduced to 33% and an addition of a layer mask

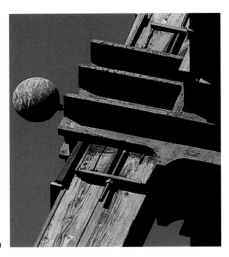

Image at 100% zoom after reduction

Remedy for Oversharpening

Since we've shown how to oversharpen your images, we thought it was only fair to also show you how to address oversharpening when it occurs. As with any remedy, the ideal is to not need it in the first place! But if you are handed an oversharpened and brittle mess, there are a couple things that will help mitigate the disaster.

Figure 5-73 shows the full frame of the example image as well as a 100% zoom view.

Figure 5-73 Oversharpening example image

Full-frame image   100% zoom view

There's no Un-Unsharp Mask filter, but there is a Gaussian Blur filter. We created a blur layer at 100% opacity set to a Darken blend mode, which will apply the .2-radius Gaussian Blur to darken the lighter areas. We applied the .2-radius five times in a row—no fade, just ran it five times. Figure 5-74 shows the result of five applications.

continues on next page

Figure 5-74 Oversharpening, reduced

Layer panel showing the blur layer
set to Darken blend   100% zoom view after five Gaussian Blur applications

Remedy for Oversharpening *continued*

The blurring set to Darken has reduced the amount of overlightening of the high-frequency texture that has occurred as a result of the oversharpening. It's not a perfect fix, but it does help restore a better tonal balance to the texture. To go further will require handwork up close. Figure 5-75 shows working up close with the Clone Stamp tool set to a Darken blend mode. The cloning is reducing the white halo between the sky and the shoes.

Figure 5-75 Handwork with the Clone Stamp tool

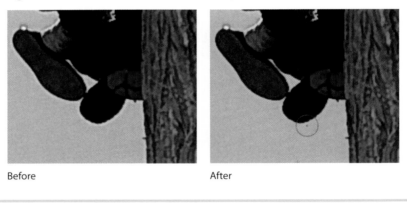

Before   After

The next two examples aren't strictly sharpening nor blur layers, but they are effects layers that will impact the detail in your images.

Image Sculpting

This technique was taught to us by R. Mac Holbert (the R stands for Roy) of Nash Editions, where he has deployed this on thousands of images (often without his clients even knowing it). It's an extension of the basic concept of midtone contrast, but rather than using the image to modify itself, it's up to the user to paint in the midtone contrast effect.

We're going to break form here a bit and show the before, middle, and final results up front. Then we'll show you how we did it. Figure 5-76 shows the example image. This image was a three-image stitch done in Photoshop CS4.

Figure 5-76 Sculpting example image

Before

After midtone contrast

After sculpting effects

We added a Reduce Noise layer with surface mask as well as a sharpening layer with edge mask. Since we did the stitch in Photoshop, we couldn't do our normal sharpening in Camera Raw because the sharpening might get altered or distorted by the stitching process. We also added a Midtone Contrast layer with a 75-pixel High Pass filter set to 25% opacity. We used the Blend If slider to concentrate the effect on the midtones. Once we reached this stage, we added a new layer filled with 50% gray also set to Overlay blend mode. The opacity was 66%, and we rolled off the highlights and shadows with the Blend If sliders. Figure 5-77 shows these steps.

Figure 5-77 Adding the Sculpting layer

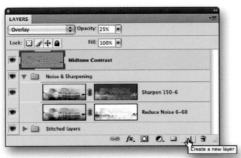

Adding a new layer

Filling with 50% gray

Setting the blend mode to Overlay at 66%

At this point, we painted in with white to lighten and black to darken specific areas of the image. Some of the work was done with a selection outlining the iceberg, and a lot of the work was done by hand. We also used a Color Range selection for a portion of the tone work.

Figure 5-78 shows preliminary painting through a selection, close-in freehand detail, and the final Sculpting layer.

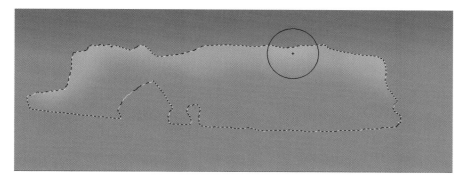

Figure 5-78 Painting on the Sculpting layer

Preliminary painting through a selection

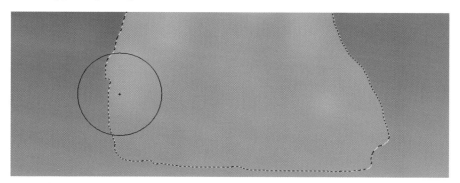

Close-in freehand painting

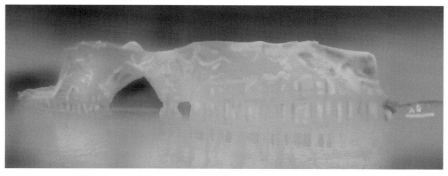

Final Sculpting layer

If you flip back and forth between Figures 5-76 and 5-78, you can see the areas where we lightened and darkened to bring out the contrast in the image. Since this is an interactive process—meaning, you can toggle the foreground and background color to change the effect you're painting with—this is a process that can't easily be duplicated with traditional tone adjustments alone. We freely admit this isn't so much a sharpening technique as it is an image-enhancement technique, but it does achieve more enhancement than a simple Midtone Contrast layer ever could.

The next example is also a departure in that instead of sharpening or blurring the image, we'll actually endeavor to *add* grain for effect.

Adding Film Grain

It may seem counterintuitive, but sometimes adding grain will actually help a digital image look a lot less digital. Extensive noise reduction or sharpening and adding blur effects will often make an image look smeared or impressionistic. Retouching can also tend to leave telltale signs of manipulation. Since we work in high bit depth (approximately 16-bit/channel in Pro Photo RGB), we rarely ever face posterization or banding, but this technique will also help mitigate that.

For this example, we're going to use an image that has had some Box Blur effects applied, which tend to overly soften the image detail. Figure 5-79 shows the full-frame image and the Layers panel with the Grain layer added at a 66% luminosity blend.

The process will attempt to replicate the natural grain found in film scans. If you remember the discussion about scanner noise in Chapter 2, the Blue channel always had the most noise and the Red channel the least. This process applies an unequal amount of noise across the three channels and then tops it off with a small dose of Gaussian Blur to soften the noise that Photoshop produces. Figure 5-80 shows targeting the Green channel, adding noise, and then adding blur.

Figure 5-79 Example image for "grain" addition

Layers panel

Full-frame image

Figure 5-80 Adding film grain

Targeting the Green channel

Adding 8% noise with uniform distribution with the Add Noise filter

Applying a .3 Gaussian Blur filter

Then we repeated the exact same process with the Blue and Red channels, but slightly changed the amounts; the Blue noise amount was 10% and the Red amount was 6%. The same .3 Gaussian Blur was used. Figure 5-81 shows the before and after.

Figure 5-81 Film grain,
before and after

Before adding film grain at
200% zoom view

After adding film grain at 200%
zoom view

We will admit that the effect of the added film grain is very subtle. While
we've zoomed into 200% to have the grain appear in the book, it's very
unlikely you could ever see the grain with any sort of downsampling. As
we've discovered, downsampling is a great noise terminator. But if you need
to upsample or are going to reproduce an image near its maximum size for
the file's resolution, then adding a touch of film grain at the end will give
digital files a more realistic "tooth" or texture. And, hey, unlike real noise,
all you need to do to get rid of it is turn off the layer.

CREATIVE SHARPENING IN CAMERA RAW AND LIGHTROOM

We would love to be able to write as lengthy of a volume on creative sharpening in Camera Raw and Lightroom as the earlier section on creative sharpening in Photoshop, but, alas, the Sharpening slider in the Adjustment Brush of Camera Raw and Lightroom is a bit lacking. Well, a *lot* lacking—which we hope will change along with the other major modifications expected with new versions. But there is one local control you can use with the Adjustment Brush in both Camera Raw and Lightroom that is worth using and is *very* difficult to do in Photoshop: negative Clarity.

Clarity produces an increase in the midtone contrast in an image. We can readily duplicate this effect in Photoshop with our local area contrast effect with Unsharp Mask or using Overlay/High Pass filter on a layer. But doing negative Clarity in Photoshop isn't so easy. You can accomplish a similar sort of contrast reduction by using a Shadows/Highlights adjustment in Photoshop, but the usability of that tool doesn't lend itself to painted-in effects.

We're going to presume that you are familiar with the basic functionality of the Adjustment Brush in Camera Raw 5.x and/or Lightroom 2.x. Figure 5-82 shows both Camera Raw and Lightroom with the Adjustment Brush tool selected. You'll see a face there in dire need of some attention. Rather than abuse an attractive model, we decided to use Jeff's face. He was cheaper, as well.

Figure 5-82 Adjustment Brush in Camera Raw (left) and Lightroom (right)

We find constantly twiddling with the sliders a bit annoying, so we suggest you do as we do and save any commonly used combination of local adjustment settings as Local Correction Settings. You can select the same saved settings from either the Adjustment Brush or the Gradation Filter in both Camera Raw and Lightroom, though note that the settings don't interchange between Camera Raw and Lightroom (which we think would be a useful capability). Figure 5-83 shows saving a Local Correction Setting in Camera Raw.

Figure 5-83 Saving a Local Correction Setting in Camera Raw

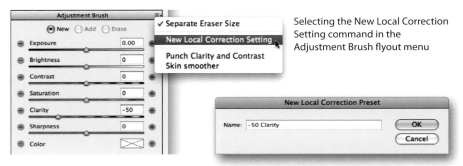

Selecting the New Local Correction Setting command in the Adjustment Brush flyout menu

New Local Correction Preset dialog

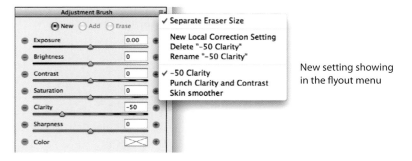

New setting showing in the flyout menu

When you save the setting, it shows up not only in the Adjustment Brush but also in the Graduated Filter panel. Figure 5-84 shows the newly saved setting in the Graduated Filter flyout menu.

Figure 5-84 The Graduated Filter panel flyout menu showing the saved settings

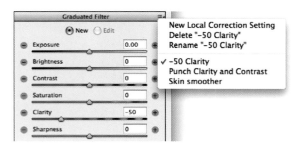

Lightroom has the same capability to save Local Correction Settings. The option is in the Effect drop-down menu, as shown in Figure 5-85.

Figure 5-85 Saving a Local Correction Setting in Lightroom

Selecting New Local Correction Setting command in the Effect drop-down menu

New Preset dialog box in Lightroom

As far as the actual effect, you simply paint it in as you would any other local adjustment in Camera Raw or Lightroom. If a single application isn't enough, you can create an additional pin (adjustment set) and keep adding to the effect. Though as with any local adjustment, one can go too far. Figure 5-86 shows the before and after on Jeff's face.

It might be said Jeff went a bit too far on his own face, but it's his prerogative to do so. Our thanks (and apologies) to Martin Evening for the use of his portrait of Jeff.

Figure 5-86 Negative Clarity before and after

Jeff's face before, at 100% zoom view (left)

Jeff's face after, at 100% zoom view (right)

As far as additional local smoothing or sharpening in Camera Raw and Lightroom, we seriously suggest deferring any substantial local adjustments of those sorts to Photoshop. The current toolset is too limited and Photoshop is too powerful to be flailing away in Camera Raw or Lightroom. Since Camera Raw is actually designed to open raw files in Photoshop, that's not much of a deferral. In the case of Lightroom, however, that limitation does require roundtripping an image from Lightroom to Photoshop and back—which just happens to be the last topic in the creative sharpening discussion.

Lightroom to Photoshop to Lightroom for Creative Sharpening (and Other Things)

While there is an advantage to keeping many of the edits to your images as parametric metadata-based edits, sooner or later you are going to need real pixel editing. Lightroom can send your raw image to Photoshop for pixel-based editing. When you save the file, it automatically imports that edited image back into the Lightroom catalog. You can even have Lightroom take the original image and the rendered pixel image stacked together.

Most people who use Lightroom are probably quite familiar with the process of going from Lightroom to Photoshop and back, but we wanted an excuse to put a photograph of Max the Perfect Dog into the book (Max was the Schewe family dog who, alas, is no longer with us). Figure 5-87 shows a raw capture of Max in the Develop module of Lightroom. You can use keyboard commands, Command-E (Mac) or Control-E (Windows), to open the image in Photoshop or use the Photo > Edit In > Edit in Adobe Photoshop CS4 menu command as shown.

Lightroom sends the image to Photoshop based on the preferences you've set in Lightroom. Lightroom 2 and Photoshop CS4 communicate using BridgeTalk, a scripting language for use between various Creative Suite applications. If you are using an earlier version of Photoshop or another application, the directions and preferences will differ. Figure 5-88 shows the Lightroom Preferences dialog box for External Editing.

We set up Lightroom to use the TIFF file format in ProPhoto RGB and 16 bits without compression. The Resolution setting is simply a metadata tag and won't alter the pixel density of the image. You can change this at any time in Photoshop, or later when printing or exporting from Lightroom.

Figure 5-87 Going from Lightroom to Photoshop

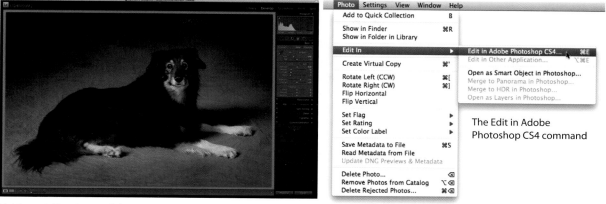

Lightroom's Develop module

The Edit in Adobe
Photoshop CS4 command

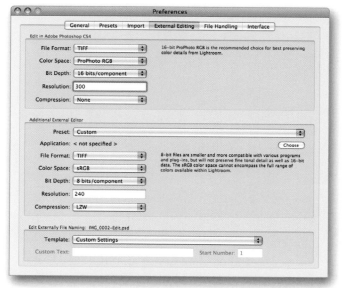

Figure 5-88
Lightroom's External
Editing preferences

Photoshop opens the image file, and then you can do whatever you need. In this example, we threw in a bunch of the creative sharpening techniques we've previously discussed, including sculpting, progressive sharpening, box blur, midtone contrast, and adding a grain layer.

NOTE: TIFF vs. PSD files? Just as Bruce and Jeff advocate for a nonproprietary raw file format such as Adobe's DNG, they also feel strongly about using a nonproprietary rendered file format as well. The TIFF (Tagged Image File Format) file type was originally created by a consortium of companies including Aldus, the primary developer, as well as Kodak and Microsoft. Adobe inherited the copyright ownership to TIFF in its purchase of Aldus in 1994. While many people presume the Photoshop PSD file format is a native of Photoshop, it ceased being the native file format when the Creative Suite was introduced. With the exception of certain Creative Suite functionality, everything you can do with a PSD file, you can also do with a TIFF file. However, TIFF is a publicly documented file format while the PSD format is not. For this reason, Bruce and Jeff have adopted using primarily TIFF files in their archives of rendered image files.

Figure 5-89 shows the image of Max open in Photoshop with the final layer stack.

Figure 5-89 "Creative" work in Photoshop

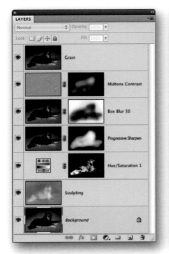

The final layer stack of creative sharpening and other edits

Max's image opened in Photoshop

While we try to do as much as we can in parametric edits to metadata, we've found that some work in Camera Raw and Lightroom is incredibly difficult and tedious but very simple and fast in Photoshop. Spot healing is great on a raw file but doesn't hold a candle to the regular Healing Brush in Photoshop for retouching. In this situation, we wanted to get the image of Max further enhanced than we could possibly do in Lightroom, but we wanted the image back in Lightroom for printing and for other purposes.

Figure 5-90 shows the saved TIFF image back in Lightroom. The figure also shows the command to edit the TIFF file back in Photoshop.

Figure 5-90 Max's retouched image back in Lightroom

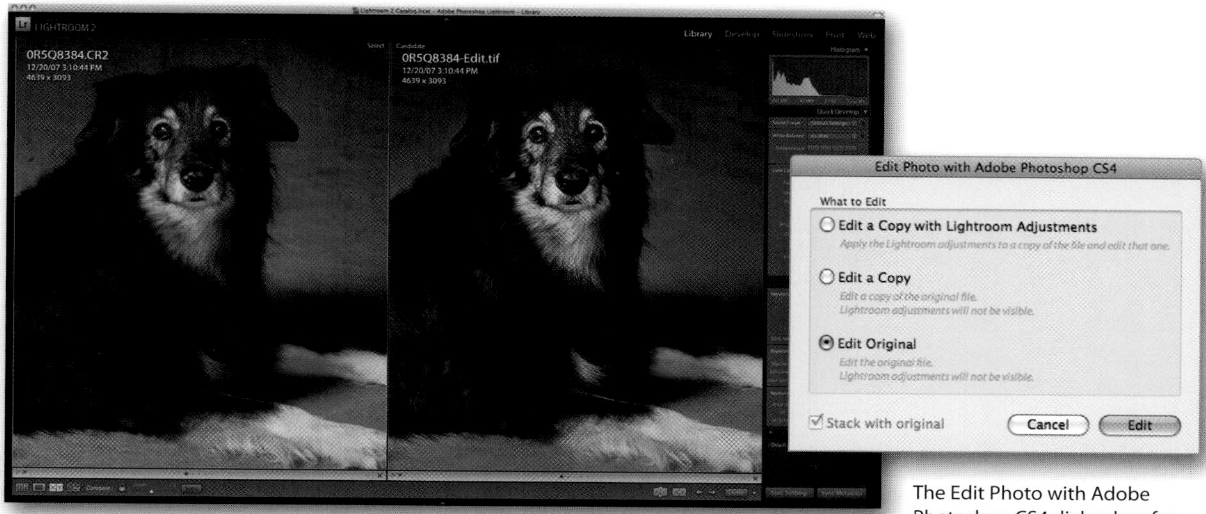

The Compare module in Lightroom showing the raw and the TIFF file

The Edit Photo with Adobe Photoshop CS4 dialog box for editing the TIFF file again

Back in Lightroom, you can always choose to reedit the rendered pixel file. As long as you saved out the TIFF file with all the layers, channels, and paths from Photoshop, you can always get back to those layers for further edits. The major caveat is you must use the Edit Original option and forgo any subsequent tone and color corrections from within Lightroom. You can choose to edit a copy, but this will spawn off yet another rendered file, which is what we are trying to avoid.

Creative Sharpening Rules

Very few rules apply to creative sharpening, which in part is why we call it creative sharpening! The big ones are:

- Always perform creative sharpening or smoothing at the image's native resolution. Remember, the goal is to create a use-neutral master image that you can repurpose through different kinds of output sharpening at different sizes.
- Don't overdo things. While judging final sharpness from the computer display is quite unreliable, if things look overdone at the creative phase, it's likely that they'll look that way in the final output too.

Ultimately, control of detail is just as important a creative function as control of tone or color, even if it tends to get much less attention. So absorb these techniques and let your creativity flow!

OUTPUT SHARPENING IN PHOTOSHOP

Where optimizing for capture and creative sharpening require human skill, sharpening for output is essentially a deterministic process, since any given print process always turns pixels into marks on paper the same way, no matter the input. Creativity at this stage is not only unnecessary, but should be actively discouraged.

In the previous workflow phases, we tried to avoid obvious sharpening haloes. When we sharpen for print, haloes are not only desirable, but necessary. The trick is to keep them small enough that they don't appear as discrete features on the print when viewed at reasonable viewing distances.

The rule of thumb that has served Bruce well is to keep the sharpening haloes no smaller than 1/100th of an inch and no larger than 1/50th of an inch, with the smaller number being preferred for small (up to 11" x 14") prints, dropping to the larger number as dictated by the resolution of the image and the size of the print.

The first and most important rule in output sharpening is that it *must* be done at the final output resolution, after any required resampling. There are no exceptions to this rule.

Do the Math

With the goal of the sharpening haloes in mind, remember that all you can do is sharpen the pixels themselves. The amount of sharpening required is a function of the size of the pixels, which in turn is a function of the resolution you're sending to the output process.

For example, this book is printed using a 150-lines-per-inch (lpi) screen, and most of the images are printed at 300 pixels per inch (ppi). Simple arithmetic dictates that a halo of 1/100th of an inch is 3 pixels wide, so that was the goal when we sharpened images for this print process.

For larger prints at lower resolutions, the same-sized halo will obviously have smaller pixel dimensions. At 180 ppi, which we regard as the lower limit for inkjet printing, a 1/100th-inch halo is 1.8 pixels wide, and a 1/50th-inch halo is 3.6 pixels wide, so again a 3-pixel halo is a reasonable aim point.

For halftone sharpening, we use plain old Unsharp Mask on a layer set to Luminosity blending at 66% opacity. In practice, it's rare that we'll adjust the layer opacity of the output sharpening layer, but it's always nice to know that we can!

We set the Blend If sliders to the values shown in Figure 5-91. There's really no point in applying sharpening to pixels lighter than level 250 (which in halftone terms is a 1% dot), and feathering off the sharpening in the deep shadows below level 10 (which is a 99% dot).

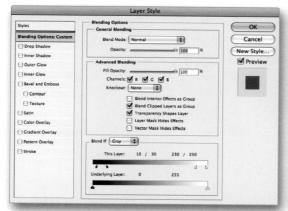

Figure 5-91 Halftone sharpening at 300-ppi output for 150-line screen

Create an Option-Merge Visible layer with the Layer Style options at left, then apply Unsharp Mask with the settings at right.

Halftone Sharpening

The very simple sharpening shown in Figure 5-91 works very well for 300-ppi, 150-lpi halftone printing on coated paper. For uncoated papers, we increase the Amount setting in Unsharp Mask to 158. Bruce arrived at these numbers empirically, which is to say, by trial and error, but they have now been through extensive testing on tens of thousands of images, and we stand by them.

Figure 5-92 shows an image before and after output sharpening for this book's halftone process. For lower screen frequencies, use a smaller Radius value and a higher Amount; for higher screen frequencies, use a larger Radius and a lower Amount, always with the goal of keeping the sharpening haloes around 1/100th of an inch.

Figure 5-92 Before and after output sharpening

Before output sharpening

After output sharpening

These actual pixels from the edge of the flower pistil show a 1.5-pixel light contour and a 1.5-pixel dark contour, for a total of a 3-pixel halo.

Detail area before sharpening at 3200% zoom view

Detail area after sharpening at 3200% zoom view

Inkjet Sharpening

Inkjet printers use error-diffusion screening rather than halftone dots, which produces a rather different effect that in turn requires a rather different type of sharpening. You can use the same Blend If settings in the Layer Style dialog box as for halftone sharpening, but we use a combination of Unsharp Mask and Overlay/High Pass sharpening.

For a 300-ppi inkjet print on glossy or semigloss paper, we create the sharpening layer but leave it with Normal blending for the Unsharp Mask step, which is Unsharp Mask with Amount 320, Radius 0.6, and Threshold 4. Then we immediately choose Edit > Fade with 70% opacity and Luminosity blend mode. Next set the layer to Overlay blending with an opacity of 50% and run the High Pass filter with a Radius of 2 pixels.

Obviously we can't show you inkjet screening in this book. The results of the inkjet sharpening are very similar in pixel terms to those of the halftone output sharpening, but the haloes are just slightly more intense (even though they're the same size as for halftone sharpening). The tighter dither of the inkjet screen can render the contrast a bit more precisely than halftone output can, so the higher contrast is effective.

Figure 5-93 shows a detail from the image in Figure 5-92, comparing halftone sharpening and inkjet sharpening.

Figure 5-93 Halftone and inkjet sharpening at 300 ppi

Halftone sharpening at 400% view

Inkjet sharpening at 400% view

Continuous-Tone Sharpening

For continuous-tone printers such as the Durst Lambda or the Fuji Frontier, we use the same sharpening technique as for inkjet, but with slightly different values (which again were the product of much trial and error). For 300-ppi output, use Unsharp Mask with Amount 350, Radius 0.6, and Threshold 4, faded to 70% opacity with Luminosity blend mode, then set the layer to Overlay at 50% opacity and run the High Pass filter with a Radius of 1.5 pixels.

For lower resolutions, use smaller Radius settings and higher Amount settings; for higher resolutions, use larger Radius settings and lower Amount settings, always keeping in mind the final size of the sharpening haloes.

Sharpening for Computer Display

It may seem obvious, but we suppose we need to say it anyway: When sharpening for output that is intended to be seen on a display or video screen, it's a very good idea to sharpen it to look good on that final screen. How you do that, however, is not so obvious or straightforward. Assuming you are starting with rather high-resolution images, simply downsampling using Photoshop's Image Size tool, shown in Figure 5-94, will certainly get your images smaller, but perhaps at a cost of detail.

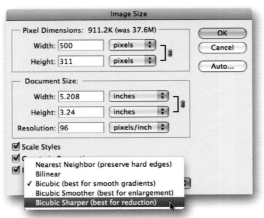

Figure 5-94 Photoshop's Image Size dialog box

Taking an image from 3252 x 2023 pixels to 500 x 311 pixels means that a whole bunch of image pixels need to just go away in the interpolation. Which pixels go and which stay is up to the algorithm, and you have very little control over the results other than choosing the downsampling algorithm in the Image Size dialog box. Generally, going down in size means using Bicubic Sharper, while upsampling uses Bicubic Smoother; plain old Bicubic is sort of the middle ground. However, if you do the downsampling in one big jump, you're stuck with just the one algorithm, which is one of the reasons we suggest downsampling in steps. Figure 5-95 shows an alternative downsampling approach.

Figure 5-95 Step interpolation using multiple algorithms

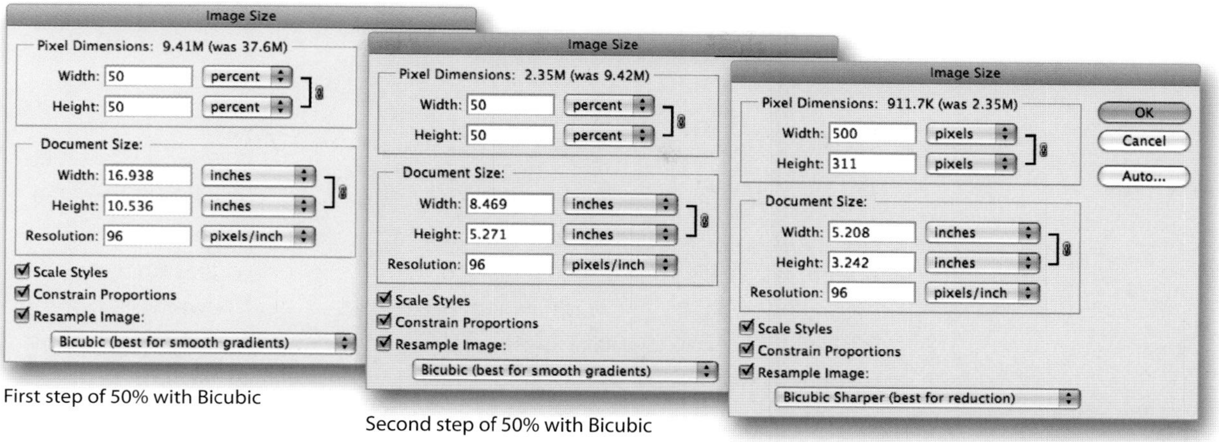

First step of 50% with Bicubic

Second step of 50% with Bicubic

Final step to a specific pixel size using Bicubic Sharper

We don't suggest using multiple steps of Bicubic Sharper; the results would be way oversharpened. Using the two downsampling steps using Bicubic plus the last step of Bicubic Sharper has the benefit of using both algorithms. You end up with the sample number of pixels as you would with a single big downsample, but experience has shown us that fine texture is held better doing it in steps.

Smart Sharpen for Display Sharpening

While we tend not to use Smart Sharpen for general sharpening tasks, we find it an excellent sharpening tool for display purposes. We like to see the image in the dialog box at 100% and look at the image preview at 200% to judge what is happening to the pixels. Figure 5-96 shows the settings we used for this image.

You'll see that the amounts of sharpening we've done is rather slight. On top of that, we used the Fade command to set the blend to Luminosity and faded to 75%. Since this was a disposable image intended for the Web, we didn't bother creating a separate sharpening layer. The sharpening halo, with Smart Sharpen set to a 0.6 radius, is just over 1 pixel. Depending on the edge frequency in the image, you can tweak this up or down a few fractions, because while other output sharpening is not edge-width-dependent, sharpening for display is.

Figure 5-96
Using Smart Sharpen for
display sharpening

Smart Sharpen settings

Image at 200% zoom view

Figure 5-97 shows a comparison of three approaches to the downsampling and sharpening. We'll warn you that here in halftone, it's not as easy to see what we see on our display. We've presented these images at a screen zoom of 300% to show the relatively subtle differences in techniques.

Figure 5-97 Comparing
downsampling techniques

Result of a single downsample
using Bicubic Sharper

Result of a single downsample
using Bicubic

Result of a three-step downsample with Smart Sharpen

Magic Numbers

The numbers we've quoted for the sharpening settings for different output processes may seem like voodoo, but they're the product of exhaustive testing, by both Bruce and Jeff. That said, it's entirely possible that you can come up with numbers that you prefer to ours.

We recommend you take heed of this key piece of advice: The only way to evaluate print sharpening is to sharpen the image, make a print, and examine it carefully. Looking at image pixels on the screen can give you a gross picture of the size of the sharpening haloes, but subtle differences like the ones shown in Figure 5-93 can be evaluated only in the print itself.

OUTPUT SHARPENING IN CAMERA RAW

As we indicated in Chapter 3, we don't think output sharpening for Camera Raw is quite finished. Yes, you can set your images to a specific megapixel size and use the batch save function to quickly process a lot of images for both capture *and* output sharpening, but only if you pull out your calculator. Since output sharpening must be applied only at the final output size and pixel density, you'll need to do some figuring to do it in the current version of Camera Raw.

Figure 5-98 shows setting up Camera Raw's Workflow Options for the pixel size of the processed image.

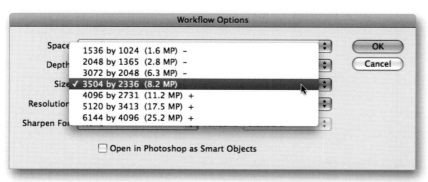

Figure 5-98 Selecting a pixel size in the Workflow Options dialog box

Pixel Dimension drop-down menu

Resolution numerical entry field

As you see in Figure 5-98, you can select only from a fixed set of interpolation sizes and are limited to specifying the pixels per inch. You have no direct control over image dimensions—which, if you are outputting for print, is rather important. So, we weren't kidding when we said to keep a calculator handy, because unless you can do the math in your head, you'll need it to figure out print sizes. Figure 5-99 shows how to determine the final print size.

Figure 5-99 Calculating image print size

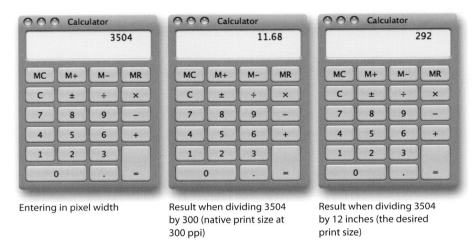

Entering in pixel width

Result when dividing 3504 by 300 (native print size at 300 ppi)

Result when dividing 3504 by 12 inches (the desired print size)

If you want your 3504-pixels-wide raw image processed out for a 12" print width, you need to enter 292 as the resolution—not the sort of elegant solution to output sharpening we would like to see from Camera Raw. If you can properly set up Camera Raw's resolution to achieve your desired print size, Camera Raw is capable of optimal output sharpening.

Figure 5-100 shows Camera Raw's output sharpening drop-down menu options. Note that normally you wouldn't see both drop downs; this was done to save space.

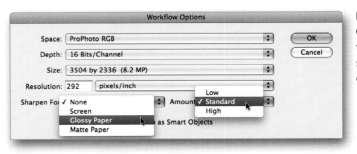

Figure 5-100 Camera Raw's two output sharpening drop-down menus

We have a high degree of confidence (and a bit of inside information) that the current usability limitations won't last long. It's our expectation that future versions of Camera Raw will address this limitation, and that image sizing and output sharpening in Camera Raw will be equal to that in Lightroom.

OUTPUT SHARPENING IN LIGHTROOM

We kept the best for last. As you know, Bruce, Jeff, and the other members of PixelGenius (PG) are rather proud of the output sharpening found in Lightroom. While Bruce never actually got to use it, he knew it was going to happen. Bruce was incredibly proud that Adobe (and the Camera Raw/Lightroom team members) had wanted to use PhotoKit Sharpener's inkjet output sharpening right in Lightroom. We (Bruce, Jeff, and PG) would like to particularly thank Thomas Knoll for being so persistent and making it happen.

Truth be told, Jeff really no longer does output sharpening in Photoshop for anything except images intended for halftone reproduction. Lightroom deals only with inkjet/contone sharpening and sharpening for the screen. In this section, we'll primarily discuss output sharpening in the Lightroom Print module, as that's where Jeff does the majority of his output sharpening.

Output Sharpening in the Print Module

One of the highly desirable aspects of output sharpening in the Lightroom Print module is that it happens on the fly. Since Lightroom sets the image dimension based on the print cell size, you don't need to make different sized images for different sized prints. Believe us, that is a really big thing. As long as the native resolution of the image is between 180 and 480 ppi, Lightroom will resize without resampling and then sharpen the print as it sends the image to the printer. The only thing you need to worry about is properly setting the media type (and the sharpening strength).

Figure 5-101 shows the main Print module interface as well as details of the Guides options and the image size and output resolution readouts that appear on the print preview.

Figure 5-101 Lightroom's Print module

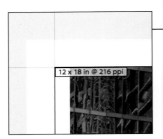

The image size and output resolution readout

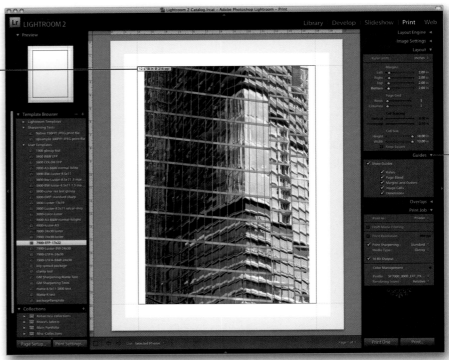

Main Print module window

The Guides display options

Determining the Size and Resolution

Lightroom does not have (nor does it need) a function for actually changing the size and resolution of the original file, only the print or an export. However, when printing, it's useful and sometimes important to know the exact size that a specific image will print and the native resolution of the image at that size. In the Guides panel, if you select the Dimensions option, the actual dimensions will appear in the upper-left corner of the print preview. If you don't select the Print Resolution checkbox (force an interpolation), the readout also shows the image resolution. This image would print at 12" x 18" at 216 ppi as the readout shown in Figure 5-101 shows. This is in the range of the suggested 180- to 480-ppi resolutions for printing to inkjet.

Figure 5-102 shows the Print Job panel and the output sharpening options.

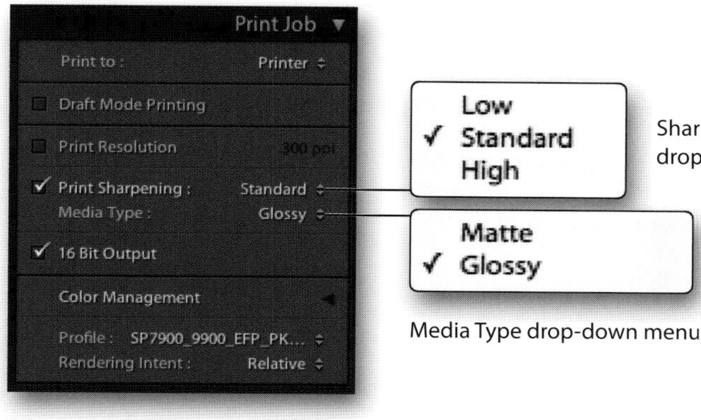

Sharpening strength drop-down menu options

Media Type drop-down menu options

Print Job panel with output sharpening active

Figure 5-102 Lightroom's Print Job panel

Print Sharpening Options

When you have output sharpening active, you'll have the option to select the strength and the media type on which you'll be printing. There is an inside joke at PixelGenius that John Paul Caponigro, a well known fine-art photographer and print maker, always complained the PhotoKit Sharpener was a bit too strong on his output. On the other hand, Mac Holbert (now a principal of PixelGenius) always thought it was too weak, while Bruce always thought it was just right. So Jeff always thinks of the options in Lightroom as Low for JP, High for Mac, and Standard for Bruce. Jeff almost always uses Standard. Since the output sharpening is tied to the capture sharpening in the Detail panel, you may need to test where your images fall when properly capture sharpened.

As for the media type, the primary distinguishing factor for Glossy or Matte is whether the paper you are printing on has a strong coating on which the ink will sit or it's at all absorbed into the paper. Watercolor paper absorbs a lot of ink and is therefore considered matte. A photo paper that has a sheen or a gloss on the surface would, naturally, be glossy. The sharpening differs between the two media types in an attempt to achieve the same apparent sharpness in the print.

Upsampled Print Output

In the previous edition of *Real World Image Sharpening with Adobe Photoshop CS2*, Bruce stated that he didn't see any point in up- or downsampling images for print. This is what Bruce wrote in 2006:

> *Some pundits recommend resampling images to reach print resolution. I cheerfully downsample images, particularly for halftone printing where it's certain that any additional resolution beyond 2.5 times the screen frequency will simply be discarded. But I tend to avoid upsampling unless there's really no choice. I've made a good many satisfying 20-inch prints from an 8-megapixel camera by sending the printer 180 real pixels per inch. I've yet to see a benefit to forcing Photoshop to make up more pixels by upsampling.*

Fast-forward to mid-2009 and Jeff has some new ideas. While he certainly agrees with Bruce that it's silly to contemplate downsampling your images solely for the purpose of hitting some magic number, with the advent of Lightroom's excellent output sharpening, he needed to slightly alter Bruce's position.

With Lightroom 2.3 and above (there was an important "fix" in Lightroom 2.3), you can see a benefit with some images whose edge frequency is high when making prints where the final resolution is on the low side of the acceptable range. If the final output resolution is below 300 ppi and the image has high-frequency image data (or strong high-contrast diagonal lines), adding about 50% to the native resolution will produce a better and smoother result on most media.

If the image is already at about 300 ppi or above, there really isn't any benefit. The primary reason for this is Lightroom has an adaptive upsampling routine that combines the Bicubic and Bicubic Smoother algorithms, and adaptive upsamples the image prior to output sharpening at the final size and resolution.

Figure 5-103
Upsampling the image resolution to 300 ppi in the Print Resolution field

Figure 5-103 shows taking our example image and entering 300 ppi. This will take the native resolution as reported by Lightroom (see Figure 5-101) and upsample to 300 ppi, and then perform the final output sharpening for the print. Does it help? For this image, yes it does. Proving it in the scope of this book is sort of difficult, so you'll have to take our word for some of it and use your imagination for the rest of the proof.

In order to actually "see" Lightroom's output sharpening applied after the adaptive upsample, we needed to use Lightroom's ability to print to a file. Figure 5-104 shows taking the native resolution of 150 ppi up to 300 ppi. We changed the print dimensions so we would end up with even multipliers to aid in making screenshots. The differences between 150 ppi and 219 ppi were negligible. The final print dimensions (including the white borders) were 24" x 30" at either 150 ppi or 300 ppi after the upsampling.

Figure 5-104 Using Lightroom's Print to: JPEG File option

File resolution before upsampling

File resolution after upsampling

Simulation of print with borders

This is the part you'll have to trust us on: If you look at both images printed out from an Epson Stylus Pro 7900 (Jeff's printer of choice) on Epson's Exhibition Fiber Paper (EFP), you can see a difference between the 150-ppi and the 300-ppi prints. The print at 300 ppi shows less stair-stepping on the diagonals and better overall high-frequency image area. While we can't show you the prints in the book, and it would be useless to try to scan the prints and then reproduce them in halftone, we will make both images available for download from the *Real World Image Sharpening* website at www.peachpit.com/RWIS.

We can give you some hint of what we are seeing by looking at two screenshots from the resulting JPEG print files. We've set the screen zoom to be effectively 400%, although that required downsampling the 300 ppi using the Nearest Neighbor option in Photoshop's Image Size command. Why the resample? Because the 300-ppi image was literally two times the pixel density as the 150-ppi image, the actual screen zooms in Photoshop were out of scale. Trust us, this works but you can download the files yourselves. Figure 5-105 shows the two resolutions.

Figure 5-105 Comparing Lightroom's upsampling and output sharpening

150-ppi native resolution at 400% zoom view

300-ppi upsampled resolution at 400% zoom view

What you see in Figure 5-105 is a magnified view of what Jeff sees when looking at the two prints. The 150-ppi print has the jaggies on the strong diagonal lines and a reduction of high-frequency texture compared to the 300-ppi print.

Does this mean every image should just be resampled to 300 ppi for printing? No. You really won't see much difference on watercolor paper really, just glossy media types. You also won't see much difference for images without high-frequency texture. If your images are already over 300 ppi, upsampling won't gain you anything. You also certainly would *never* want to throw pixels away by downsampling unless you have in excess of 480 ppi (the upper limit). Lightroom will even make sure you don't. If you try to enter in more than 480 in the Print Resolution field, you'll get the warning shown in Figure 5-106.

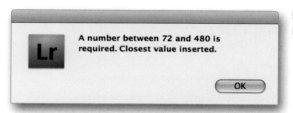

Figure 5-106 Lightroom Print Resolution warning dialog box

Output Sharpening with Export

Lightroom also provides the opportunity for output sharpening when exporting. The Lightroom Export dialog box shown in Figure 5-107 shows where it's activated. The fact that Lightroom provides better size and resolution controls means exporting makes sense from Lightroom while saving out of Camera Raw at this point doesn't. We'll cover how to use Export for batch processing in the next chapter.

Figure 5-107 Lightroom's
output sharpening in Export

Main Export dialog box

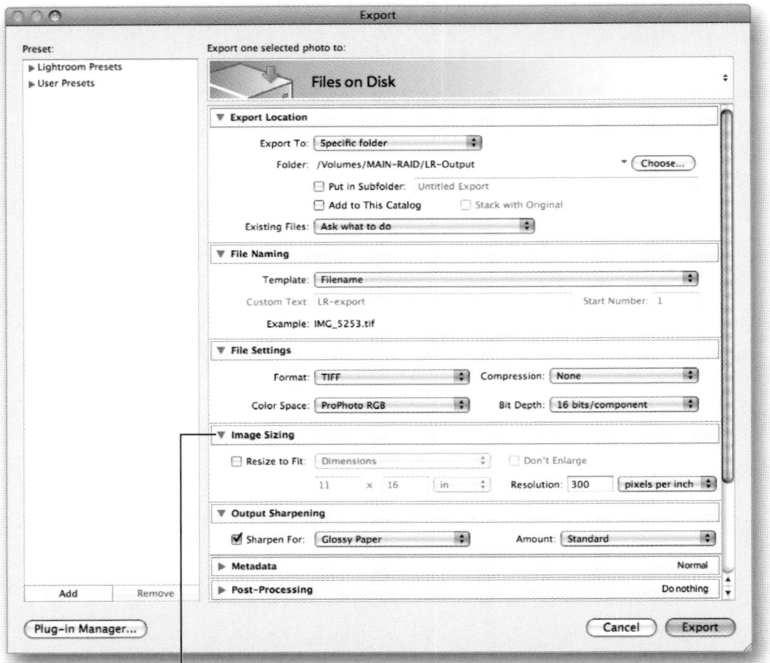

Detail of the Export Output
Sharpening options (note
second drop-down added
for clarity)

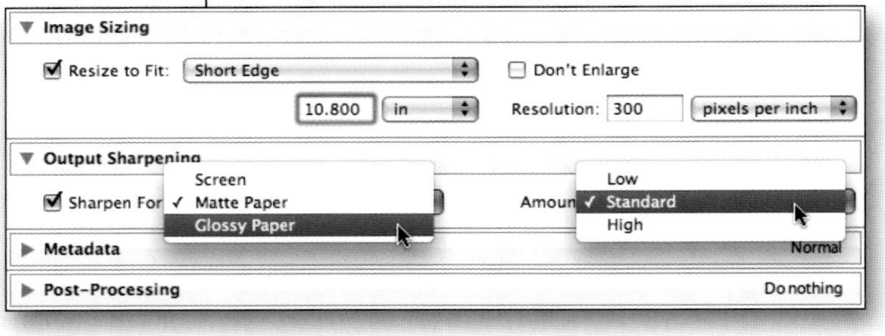

THE POWER OF THE WORKFLOW

The biggest advantage of the sharpening techniques we've described in this chapter is that images receive optimal sharpening. That in itself is no small thing, but an equally significant advantage is that images receive optimal *use-neutral* sharpening, so you can easily repurpose them for different outputs and sizes.

Decoupling the image source and image content concerns from the demands of the output process makes sense from both a quality and a productivity standpoint. It's conceivable that in the future, savvy printer vendors will build optimal output sharpening into commercial software or hardware RIPs (raster image processors) and printer drivers so that we can deliver images without having to worry about output size and resolution.

Looking even further forward, it's at least conceptually possible that display profiles could contain sharpness parameters that controlled antialiasing to the display, ironing out differences in sharpness the way they do color differences today. But in the here and now, it's fair to say that detail control is a subject that has received far less attention than tone and color control.

In the next, final chapter, we'll demonstrate how to harness the tools and techniques in an efficient sharpening workflow that incorporates actions, presets, and automated batch processing.

CHAPTER SIX

Putting the Tools to Work

Building a Sharpening Workflow—Efficiently

In the last couple of chapters, we covered a large body of sharpening and noise-reduction tools and techniques. In this chapter, we'll show you how to combine them to make a complete but efficient sharpening workflow. The primary goal of the sharpening workflow is, of course, optimally sharpened images, but other benefits accrue too:

- Images that have been optimized for source and content become "use-neutral" master images that can easily be repurposed for multiple outputs.

- Much of the workflow can be automated (the creative localized sharpening application cannot). An automated sharpening workflow can help you make hundreds of images good, so that you can reserve the manual work for the smaller number that need to be made great.

Regardless of the optimization, the steps involved are often repetitive, tedious, and error prone if you aren't paying close attention. For these reasons (and that, fundamentally, we're lazy), we try to improve our efficiency through automation. But simply automating without a structure in place would be pointless. That's why we need to know when to sharpen and how so we automate the process efficiently.

When Do We Sharpen?

As detailed in Chapter 3, "Sharpening Strategies," the sharpening workflow uses three sharpening phases, one of which, creative localized sharpening, is optional.

- Optimization for source and content can be achieved in a single operation we call capture sharpening. We recommend carrying out this phase as soon as basic spotting and retouching, and all major corrections for tone and color have been done. Large moves in tone or color can increase noise, and distort or even wipe out sharpening, so the image should be close to final tonality before the initial sharpening.

- Optional creative sharpening can be done at any time after the initial optimizations for source and content have been carried out, but should be done at the image's native resolution prior to any resampling for output.

- Sharpening for output should be done after any resampling to final output resolution. We do output sharpening as the last step prior to the color space conversion to output space.

Each of these phases can be partially or completely automated. With capture sharpening, a specific source and edge frequency can be turned into a single action that returns layers for post-application modifications. In the case of creative sharpening, the steps required for creating the effect can be recorded—even the selection of a brush and a layer mask can be automated. You will, however, need to manually paint in the effect. Output sharpening for a specific device, media, and resolution can easily be turned into a time-saving action, too. These actions can be applied to a variety of files without constantly producing errors, but it requires some practice and expertise. We can offer the expertise, but the practice is up to you.

AUTOMATION IN PHOTOSHOP

Our general rule of thumb is that if you find yourself using the exact same series of steps more than three or four times on a regular basis, you would benefit by recording an action to make your life easier (and, at least, spend less time at the keyboard). The more complicated and tedious the steps, the stronger the argument for automation. Many of the tools and techniques we've discussed are prime candidates for automation. Before we get into lengthy and complicated action writing, we need to cover some of the fundamentals.

Action Basics

Recording an action to accomplish a series of steps and arrive at a final goal may seem a bit geeky and certainly needs to be done with a clear head (and not under the pressure of short deadlines), but it's really not too difficult. The key is to start simple and then grow your ambition.

Creating an Action Set

The Actions panel of Adobe Photoshop CS4 contains a set of actions called Default Actions. They were written to provide some useful examples and to have something populating the panel. However, you should start off by creating your own set of actions. Figure 6-1 shows clicking the "Create new set" button and naming the new set "Sharpening."

Figure 6-1 Creating a new action set

Click the "Create new set" button on the Actions panel.

Name it "Sharpening" in the New Set dialog box.

Once you've named and created the set, actions that you create will be added to that set. We'll walk you through the process of recording the exact series of steps required for making a sharpening layer, one of the most basic components you'll need to create in order to automate sharpening. As we said in Chapter 4, "Sharpening Tools," there are two ways of creating a sharpening layer: duplicating the Background layer or using the Option/Merged procedure. This action will use the Option/Merged procedure.

Recording an Action

You must have an image open in order to record this action. It is useful if the image is something other than a simple Background layer image. Since this sharpening layer will often need to be produced after basic spotting and retouching as well as major tone and color corrections, the image you use to record the action should already contain those layers (even if you simply make them up for the purpose of the recording).

Figure 6-2 shows the beginning of the action-recording process.

Figure 6-2 Recording a new action

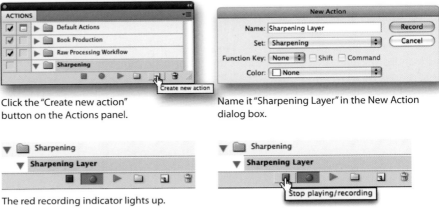

Click the "Create new action" button on the Actions panel.

Name it "Sharpening Layer" in the New Action dialog box.

The red recording indicator lights up.

"Stop playing/recording" button

At this point, Photoshop is recording. Before you actually start recording steps, relax, think your way through the process, and don't rush. Photoshop will wait patiently as you plan and execute each step. Remember, you can always stop at any step in the process and start again. You can also simply trash an aborted recording and start again from the top.

We find it useful to do some practice runs and, if need be, take notes (particularly of specific settings) while rehearsing. While the Actions panel does not offer an excellent editing environment, you can go back in and edit steps, reorder them (take great care with that), and drag individual steps to the trash.

We'll go through the next steps, shown in Figure 6-3, rather quickly—they should be familiar from Chapter 5, "Industrial-Strength Sharpening Techniques."

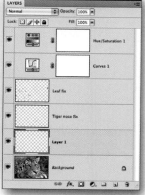

Figure 6-3 Recording the Sharpening Layer action

1. Start from the middle of the layers stack.

2. Click the Background layer to record that step.

3. Add a new layer above the Background layer.

4. Use the Merge Visible command with the Option key (Mac) or Alt key (Windows) pressed.

5. The Option/Merged layer is still targeted.

6. Choose Layer > Arrange > Bring to Front.

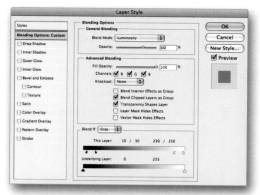

7. Rename the layer "Presharpen."

8. Change the Layer Style blending options.

9. Stop the recording.

To record this action, we included an additional step not previously mentioned to make the action run whether or not the image has layers. After selecting the Background layer, we added a new blank layer. If we didn't, running the action on an image without any layers would fail, since the command to Merge Visible cannot run on a simple Background layered image.

Figure 6-4 shows the final recorded action steps.

Testing an Action

Once you record an action, you should test it on a wide variety of images with different layers and layer types to be assured that the action is error proof. There's nothing worse than starting a batch operation on a bunch of images only to find out later

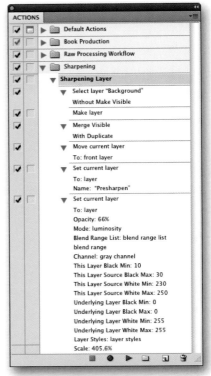

Figure 6-4 The recorded action steps for the Sharpening Layer action

that the action has kindly stopped and given you a warning or otherwise halted the whole process. Actions, like any sort of computer programming, are logical steps written in code that either work or don't work. While it may seem at times like Photoshop conspires to thwart your efforts, we can assure you there is no conspiracy going on, just a rather limited (yet valuable) tool that takes you at your literal word. If you say, "do this, then do this," that is exactly what the action will do, time and time again. So it behooves you to be sure that what the action does is what you want to do.

To test a recorded action, you can run it either by clicking the Play button or using the keyboard shortcut of pressing Command (Mac) or Control (Windows) while clicking the actual action name.

The Actions Panel Flyout Menu

There are some important options in the main Actions panel flyout menu, shown in Figure 6-5 along with the Action Options and Playback Options dialog boxes. At the top of the flyout are commands that duplicate the functions of the panel buttons.

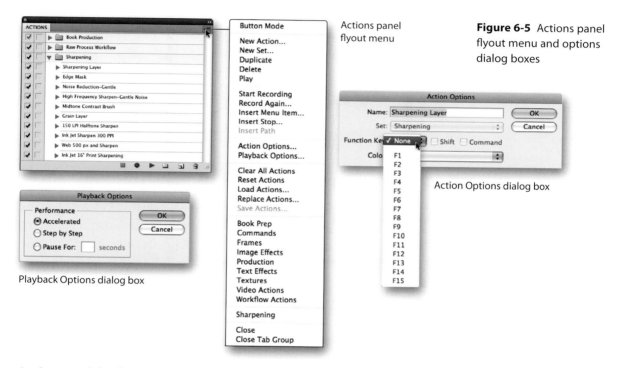

Figure 6-5 Actions panel flyout menu and options dialog boxes

Actions panel flyout menu

Action Options dialog box

Playback Options dialog box

At the top of the flyout menu is an option called Button Mode. You are welcome to try this out, but since we tend to have many, many actions installed, making each and every action into its own button doesn't work for us, but it may for you.

The two options dialog boxes are important to set up correctly:

- **Action Options** allow you to rename actions (which you can also do by double-clicking the action name) as well as assign Function keys to play actions at the press of a button.

- **Playback Options** are for accelerated or step-by-step operations. You can also program in a pause for a specific set of seconds. For action troubleshooting, it's often useful to take the playback off of accelerated to allow you time to watch what the action is doing. Normally you want the accelerated options selected—unless you charge by the hour and want to pad your invoice.

From the flyout menu you can choose Insert Menu Item, which is a useful function when recording actions that call up menu items and dialog boxes. You can also record an Insert Stop command to allow you to include messages or instructions, but this isn't useful for batching.

> **TIP:** When you run an action on an open image in accelerated mode, it will run as fast as Photoshop can, given the fact that certain interface items tend to slow things down. Photoshop doesn't try to update most windows and icons, but if you want to run an action as fast as possible, try putting Photoshop into the background as a process (activate a different application of the main Finder). You'll see the speed jump up considerably. This is important when running a Photoshop batch operation as well.

Editing Actions

Once you record an action, you can do limited editing of it. Double-clicking the action step will prompt whatever dialog box was recorded to reopen for modifications of the settings. This can be frustrating because the exact same conditions that existed when the action was recorded must also exist to edit the step.

In Figure 6-6, the last step of our recorded Sharpening Layer action was used to record the Layer Style options and Blend If settings. If you double-click the step on an image that has no layers, you'll get the dreaded "command not currently available" warning. All that means is you must remember to re-create the conditions that allow that action step to be rerecorded in order to edit that step.

Figure 6-6 Rerecording action steps

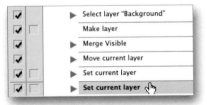

Double-clicking an action step to rerecord   Warning if conditions don't allow editing

When you record the settings of a filter or some other command such as a tone adjustment, the parameters are hard-coded into the action. You can double-click them to rerecord the parameters, or you can toggle the option to force the dialog box for the filter or adjustment to appear for manual entry. Figure 6-7 shows toggling the dialog box by clicking in the dialog box column. You can also decide to temporarily disable any steps in a recorded action. The action will bypass those steps and either stop or continue running as though those steps were never recorded.

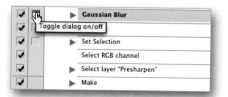

Button to toggle the step's dialog box on or off   Button to toggle the item's activated status

Figure 6-7 Toggling dialog boxes and steps

In the event you accidentally record a step or record an undo and a new step, you can always choose to eliminate steps from a recorded action. Figure 6-8 shows the easy way of dragging the step to the trash.

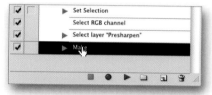

Click on a step.   Drag the step to the trash.

Figure 6-8 Trashing an action step

One of the action-editing steps we often use is to copy individual action steps from one action to another. In the event we forget a step, we can grab the step from an action that has the step we need. Figure 6-9 shows taking the important step of adding a layer from the Sharpening Layer action we previously recorded, and adding it to an action recorded subsequently.

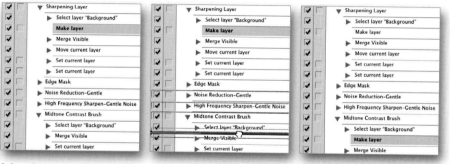

Select the step to copy.   Drag the step while holding the Option/Alt key.   The copied step in the second action

Figure 6-9 Copying a step from one action to another

If you just drag a step from one action to another, the step will only move. If you hold down the Option (Mac) or Alt (Windows) key while dragging, the step will be copied, not moved. We already mentioned that adding the new layer step was important for making an error-proof action, but when we recorded the Midtone Contrast Brush action, we missed that step, so we needed to add it after the fact.

Saving Your Action Set

Once you create a series of actions, it's important to save them as a set. You can't save individual actions, only sets. It's critical to save sets because until saved they exist only virtually in Photoshop's preferences. If you quit and restart Photoshop "normally" you won't have a problem, but if you crash, whatever you've done in an action set will be lost unless you save it. We can't tell you the number of times that we have personally been burnt by this, and it hurts! Hours spent recording and troubleshooting some complicated actions can be completely lost.

Figure 6-10 shows the Save Actions command from the Actions panel flyout menu and the Save dialog box.

Figure 6-10 Saving your action set

Save Actions command in the flyout menu

Save dialog box showing where the set will be saved

Where you save your action set isn't particularly important unless you want the set to show as an Actions panel flyout menu option. If you do, you must save the set in the root Photoshop CS4 application folder, in the Presets folder under Actions. It's the same location for Mac and Windows.

We could continue going through the tools and techniques that we've outlined in Chapters 4 and 5, but space limitations preclude us from doing so. In lieu of extended examples, we've taken the actual actions written for the book and made them available on the *Real World Image Sharpening* page on the Peachpit website, www.peachpit.com/RWIS. The actions are shown in Figure 6-11.

Figure 6-11 The saved action set available for download

Batch Processing Using Photoshop

The Batch command (which you access by choosing File > Automate in Photoshop or Tools > Photoshop > Batch in Adobe Bridge) is one of Photoshop's most powerful and scary features, but conceptually it's very simple. You point it at a batch of images, it runs an action on them, and then it does one of the following:

- Saves new files

- Delivers open images in Photoshop

- Saves and closes, overwriting the source files or creating new ones

The devil, however, is in the details, and some of the details in the Batch dialog box are distinctly counterintuitive if not obtuse. Figure 6-12 shows the Batch dialog box before customizing any of the settings.

Figure 6-12 The Photoshop
Batch dialog box

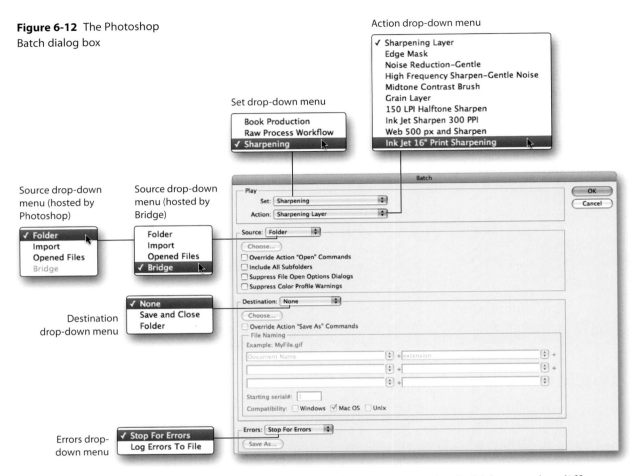

The dialog box is split into four sections, each of which controls a different aspect of the batch process's behavior:

- **Play** lets you choose an action from an action set that will be applied to all the images. Be sure this is the action you really want!

- **Source** lets you designate the source of the images on which the batch will be executed. It also lets you choose some very important options whose functionality will become apparent later. You can run a batch:

  - On a designated folder that you choose in the Batch dialog box by clicking the Choose button

  - On opened files

  - On images imported through the Photoshop File menu's Import command

• When Batch is called from Bridge's Tools > Photoshop menu, on the images that are currently selected in Bridge

For processing raw images, the source will invariably be a folder or the selected images in Bridge.

• **Destination** lets you control what happens to the processed images. None delivers them as open images in Photoshop or as images saved by steps in the action. Save and Close saves and closes the processed images. Folder lets you designate a folder in which to save the processed images. It also includes the renaming features offered by Batch Rename.

Unless you are experienced at batch processing, you should choose either None or, much more commonly, Folder. Save and Close often ends up being a "hurt-me" button because its normal behavior is to overwrite the source image. So avoid Save and Close unless you are really, really sure!

• **Errors** lets you choose, when an error is encountered, whether to stop the entire batch or log the errors to a file. We usually stop the batch when debugging an action used in Batch, and log errors to a file when actually running a batch in a production situation.

The difficulties that users typically encounter in running Batch are in the way the selections in the Source and Destination sections interact with the action applied by the batch operation. Here are The Rules. (Note: These are *our* rules and we swear by them. They don't represent the only possible approach, but by the time you're sufficiently skilled and knowledgeable to violate them with impunity, you'll have long outgrown the need for this book.)

NOTE: The Batch function can be launched by either Bridge or Photoshop. However, the only way you can select images to run a Batch from Bridge is if Bridge has launched the Batch operation. The Batch operation from Photoshop is limited to running on folders, imported images, or open files. While Bridge can communicate to Photoshop via scripts, there's no way for Photoshop to query Bridge to discover selected images. As a result, we suggest always starting from Bridge when calling the Batch function if you need to run a Batch on specific images rather than on an entire folder of images.

The Rules for Opening Files in a Batch Operation

To make sure that raw files get opened and processed the way you want them in a batch operation, you need to record an Open step in the action that will be applied in Batch. When you record the open step, make sure that Adobe Camera Raw's Settings menu is set to Image Settings, so that it applies the custom-tailored Camera Raw settings you've made for each image. You'll also want to make sure that Camera Raw's workflow settings—Space, Bit Depth, Size, and Resolution—are manually set to produce the results you want.

Now comes one of the counterintuitive bits. If you record an Open step in the action, you must select Override Action "Open" Commands. When you select this option, you'll get a warning as shown in Figure 6-13. If you don't, the batch will simply keep opening the image you used to record the Open step in the action. Override Action "Open" Commands doesn't override everything in the recorded Open command; it just overrides the specific choice of file to open, while ensuring that the Selected Image and workflow settings get honored.

If you aren't processing raw files, however, the Open step is optional and likely not a good idea unless you encounter a situation that requires it.

Figure 6-13 The Override Action "Open" Commands conundrum

The Rules for Saving Files in a Batch Operation

To make sure that the processed files get saved in the format you want with the options you want, you need to record an actual Save step in the action that will be applied in Batch. This Save step dictates the file format (.tif, .jpg, .psd) and options that go with that format—TIFF compression options, JPEG quality settings, and so on.

Now comes the second counterintuitive bit. You must select Override Action "Save As" Commands; otherwise, the files don't get saved where you want them, saved with the names you want, or possibly saved at all! Selecting this option will give you the warning shown in Figure 6-14.

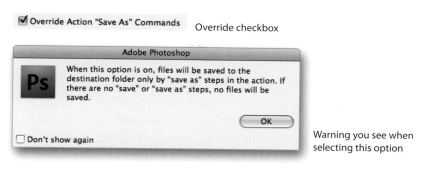

Override checkbox

Warning you see when
selecting this option

Figure 6-14 The Override
Action "Save As" Commands
conundrum

Also, the file format and file format parameters recorded in the action's
Save step are applied when saving the file, but the name and destination are
overridden by the options you specified in the Batch Choose Destination
dialog box.

Yes, recording or not recording an Open and Save As step is confusing to
say the least. You also need to decide whether the remaining checkboxes in
the Source dialog box are selected or unselected. The option to Include All
Subfolders is straightforward; selecting this option will burrow down and
process all images in the enclosing folder. However, the subfolder structure
will be lost. So be careful when selecting this. The Suppress File Open
Options Dialog is something you can pretty much always leave selected
unless your open command requires some sort of user input such as selecting which page in a PDF to open or how to rasterize an EPS file. The
Suppress Color Profile Warnings is another one you probably always want
to select unless you like seeing color management warnings.

Playing by the Rules

If you follow these relatively simple rules we've provided, your batch operations won't fall prey to any of these ills, and they'll execute smoothly with
no surprises. If you fail to do so, it's very likely that your computer will
labor mightily and then deliver either results that are something other than
you desired or, even more frustrating, no results at all—or, heaven forbid,
your original files ruined! The best way to learn batch processing is to do so
when you are not already under an incredible time crunch. Batching is
meant to save time, not ruin images.

SAVING IMAGES WITH IMAGE PROCESSOR

If the discussion of batching with actions has left you just a bit queasy from geekiness, you'll be happy to know there is a simpler and easier method of selecting a bunch of images in Bridge and getting processed files out the backside. It's called Image Processor and it offers a quick (and arguably much easier although less powerful) method of saving up to three versions of the selected images—a JPEG, a TIFF, and a Photoshop file, with each format in a separate subfolder. You can set different sizes for each format and, optionally, run an action and include a copyright notice.

Figure 6-15 shows the Image Processor dialog box.

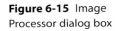

Figure 6-15 Image Processor dialog box

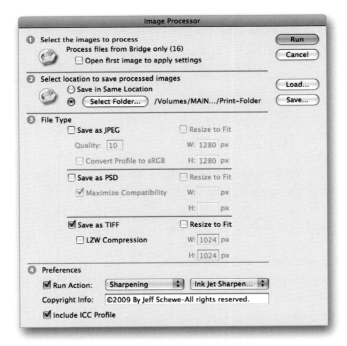

These are the Image Processor options:

- **"Open first image to apply settings"** is primarily useful for processing unedited raw images that require approximately the same treatment. When you run Image Processor, the first raw image opens in Camera Raw. The settings you make there are applied to all the other images.

These settings are used only by Image Processor—they aren't written to the image's metadata.

- **"Select location to save processed images"** lets you save the images in either the same folder or one that you designate here. In either case, if you've chosen multiple file formats, a subfolder is created for each file format.

- **File Type** lets you save any combination of JPEG, PSD, and TIFF, with the option to resize the image in any of the chosen formats.

- **Preferences** lets you choose an action that runs on all the processed images. It should be noted that the action will run when the image is first opened, which means you could also run an action that includes separate save steps. The Copyright Info allows you to include copyright information if you haven't done so already, and gives you a choice to include the ICC (International Color Consortium) profile in the images.

One nifty feature of Image Processor is that it takes care of flattening and downsampling to 8-bit/channel automatically for the JPEGs while saving the PSDs and TIFFs as layered 16-bit/channel images if an action you choose to run creates layers. So it's by far the quickest and easiest way to save a high-resolution TIFF and low-resolution JPEG version of the same image—something many of us need to do often.

Whether you go the full-blown action and Photoshop batch operations route or use the simpler Image Processor (hey, we use it all the time because of expedience), you still need to learn how to create sharpening, noise reduction, and mask-making actions simply to make your life quicker and easier. The other thing we love about actions is they never have a hangover or headache, and they'll produce the exact same results on Friday at the end of a busy workweek as they do first thing Monday morning! Consistency is almost as important as saving time.

EFFICIENT CAPTURE SHARPENING IN CAMERA RAW

While there isn't an automated way of applying capture sharpening in Camera Raw, there are more efficient methods than simply opening an image at 100% in Camera Raw and fiddling with the sliders until you get the image looking sharp. That works, don't get us wrong, but doing it image-by-image is a slow and tedious process. If you need to edit a ton of images, make picks, and deliver good-quality processed raws with capture sharpening, you can do so more quickly if you make and use Camera Raw presets.

Creating Camera Raw Sharpening Presets

If you remember back to Figures 5-35 and 5-38 from Chapter 5, we showed you examples of high-frequency and low-frequency edge widths. It's really not all that hard to train yourself to be able to determine the most predominate edge width right from within Bridge, so that makes it a perfect place to apply presets—but only if you've already taken the time to create them.

Figure 6-16 shows the image we'll use to set up a new preset. The figure includes the optimized sharpening settings in the Detail panel of Camera Raw.

Figure 6-16 Adjusting Detail panel parameters

Camera Raw dialog box

Detail panel with settings adjusted

Once you have the settings adjusted, you'll navigate to the Presets panel to create a new preset. Figure 6-17 shows the Presets panel as well as the New Preset dialog box you get when you click the New Preset button.

Figure 6-17 Creating a new preset

Presets panel in Camera Raw

New Preset button

New Preset dialog box with name entered

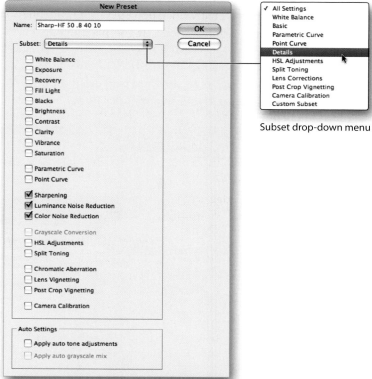

Subset drop-down menu

In the New Preset dialog box, it's useful to give the preset a descriptive name that will make sense to you in what might be a lengthy drop-down menu down the road. We like to include the specific parameters and some sort of name start that provides for alphanumeric order. You can't change the preset order, and currently you can't even rename them in Camera Raw—you can only delete or re-create them. We used the name Sharp-HF to indicate it's a high-frequency image sharpening preset, and the settings we used were 50, .8, 40, and 10 as shown in Figure 6-16.

It's also important to understand the impact of saving presets as subsets. In this case we've selected only the Details subset, which includes Sharpening,

Luminance Noise Reduction, and Color Noise Reduction. We specifically selected that subset from the drop-down menu, as shown in Figure 6-17, because we want to be able to apply this subset over other presets without overwriting those image settings. As a result we can apply a White Balance subset, a curve, and some split toning for effect, and still be able to use the sharpening preset to only modify the Detail settings.

We wish we could further break down the parameter settings for Sharpening in presets, but alas, not at this time (it's something we're hoping for in the future). Once you've created and saved your preset, it will show up in the Presets panel in Camera Raw as well as in Bridge. Figure 6-18 shows the new preset in the Presets panel and the same preset in the Bridge Develop Settings flyout menu under Edit.

Figure 6-18
The saved preset

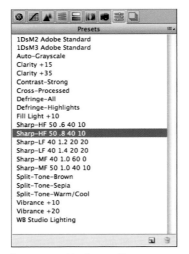

Presets panel in Camera Raw   Develop Settings flyout menu in Bridge

One of the things we like to do is use the Context Menu directly on thumbnails in Bridge. The Context Menu provides a variety of useful things to do to images, including the same Develop Settings flyout as in the Edit menu.

Controlling Camera Raw's Preferences

As useful as presets in Camera Raw may be, it still takes some sort of decision on your part when to apply the preset, and of course you need to have already made the preset. Instead, you can have Camera Raw automatically apply a given set of parameters every time Camera Raw first sees an image. This is called the Camera Raw *Default*, and it differs from presets in two ways. First, the default settings in Camera Raw preferences can be dependent on the camera's serial number, not just model. So, if you have two cameras of the same model, you can tweak the defaults of each camera based on its serial number stored in metadata. Second, you can have Camera Raw apply different default settings based on the metadata of your camera's ISO setting.

Figure 6-19 shows the three ways to access Camera Raw's preferences.

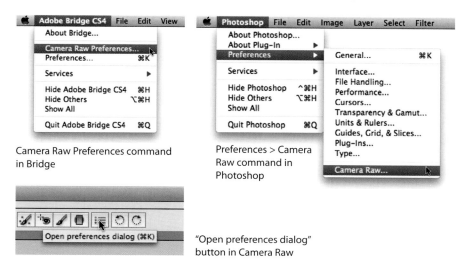

Camera Raw Preferences command in Bridge

Preferences > Camera Raw command in Photoshop

"Open preferences dialog" button in Camera Raw

Figure 6-19 Accessing Camera Raw's preferences

Once the Camera Raw preferences dialog box, shown in Figure 6-20, opens, you'll see a variety of options. There are a couple of rather important settings you need to consider.

Figure 6-20 Camera Raw
Preferences dialog box

In previous versions of Camera Raw, it was often advocated to turn off image sharpening when processing out of Camera Raw. We now no longer believe this is the case; in fact, we like the new sharpening. But if you really don't want Camera Raw to sharpen your images, you can change the option in the "Apply Sharpening to" drop-down menu.

In the Default Image Settings section, you can choose to make the defaults specific to camera serial number and ISO setting. We think each is an important consideration and well worth the time and effort to arrive at camera- and ISO-specific defaults.

When you alter the defaults, be aware that any settings you change from the standard Adobe-provided default will be captured as part of the new default. While you may want to tweak the Luminance Noise Reduction settings for your camera's ISO 400 setting, if you've adjusted any other parameter, that parameter will be part of the new default; so an adjustment for exposure or brightness will also be caught as well as the ISO setting.

The ideal situation is to open an image that has no actual image settings applied yet, and set only the parameters you want to change. For the camera serial number, it may be the calibration settings or perhaps an exposure bump if that one camera's meter is off. In the case of the ISO settings, we suggest modifying only the Luminance and perhaps to back down on the Color settings. Zoom in 200% to 400% and really evaluate the noise signature, and try to arrive at an optimal.

Figure 6-21 shows the Camera Raw flyout menu option to Save New Camera Raw Defaults as well as the command to set them back (in case you change your mind).

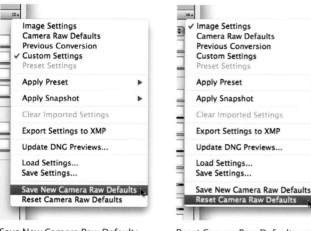

Figure 6-21
Camera Raw flyout menu options for Camera Raw defaults

Save New Camera Raw Defaults command

Reset Camera Raw Defaults command

While Camera Raw and Lightroom can't easily exchange presets (because the formats differ), what a lot of users don't realize is they do share the same Camera Raw defaults. That means if you make changes to Camera Raw's Adobe-provided defaults, Lightroom picks up those same changed defaults. This has gotten Jeff a couple of times when working with new cameras.

Figure 6-22 shows the Lightroom command to change the defaults as well as the dialog box that gives you the option to update or restore the defaults.

Figure 6-22 Changing the Camera Raw defaults in Lightroom

Develop > Set Default Settings command

Set Default Develop Settings dialog box

While you can move presets from computer to computer by placing them in the correct locations for Camera Raw and Lightroom, respectively, there is no easy way to move the default settings. You can take the same image you used to create the new defaults, copy that image to a different computer, and use that image to change the defaults. Not elegant, but it works.

An Efficient Sharpening Workflow for Lightroom

Since Lightroom contains an entire workflow (well, except for creative sharpening), simply setting up Lightroom's Develop module is just the tip of a pretty big iceberg (almost 90% of an iceberg is actually invisible and underwater). You also have the ability to import images with presets as well as using output sharpening for prints and upon export. Lightroom is a rich sharpening ecosphere even without the creative sharpening.

Creating Sharpening Presets in the Develop Module

The place to create capture sharpening presets is the Develop module. You need to zoom to 100% (1:1 in Lightroom) in order to see the sharpening and the previews in Lightroom. Figure 6-23 shows an image zoomed to 1:1 with sharpening adjusted for a high-frequency image. It's only happenstance that the settings are pretty similar to the settings arrived at for the seal image in Camera Raw.

The settings here really pop this high-frequency image detail. Normally, since the ISO was set to 200, we would probably tweak the noise settings. Ideally we should have already altered the Camera Raw/Lightroom shared defaults. Unfortunately, we don't always practice what we preach.

Once you arrive at the preferred settings, you'll use the Create New Preset button on the Presets panel, as shown in Figure 6-24.

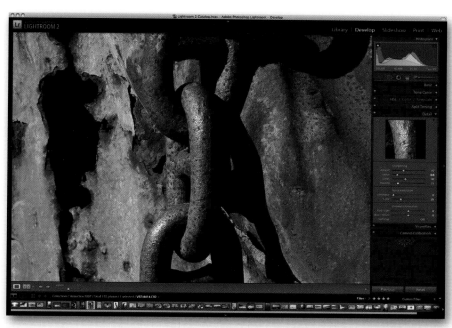

Develop with image at 1:1

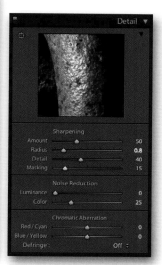

Figure 6-23 Adjusting sharpening settings in Develop

Close-up of the Detail panel

Figure 6-24 Creating a Develop preset

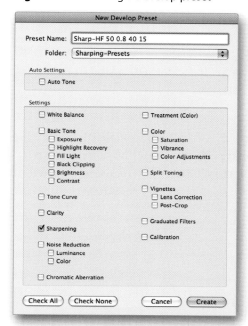

New Develop Preset dialog box

Create New Preset button

Presets panel showing the new preset

Once you create the new preset, you may need to modify or rename it. Unlike Camera Raw, Lightroom allows you to use a context menu to modify the name or update the settings. You can also export or import the settings in the event you need to move to different computers. Figure 6-25 shows the context menu items when you Control-click (Mac) or right-click (Windows) a preset.

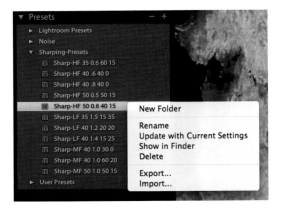

Figure 6-25 Context menu for modifying a preset

Once you have the preset saved, it becomes available in a variety of time-saving locations. For example, you can access the Develop settings in the Library module's Quick Develop panel, shown in Figure 6-26, as well as in the Lightroom Import dialog box. Both areas offer a great degree of power and flexibility aiding in creating an efficient workflow.

As with Camera Raw presets, you can apply multiple presets from Quick Develop that include subsets. You can apply tone and color settings, and then select sharpening settings to apply on top. As long as you keep the subsettings separate, they won't overlap and compete—although Quick Develop will display only the last settings. If the subsettings do compete, the last setting wins.

While you can apply multiple settings in Develop and in Quick Develop, you can apply only a single Develop setting when importing images. Figure 6-27 shows the Import Photos dialog box in Lightroom with the Sharp-HF 40 .6 40 0 settings selected as the Develop presets.

Figure 6-26 Applying a Develop preset from the Quick Develop panel in the Library module

Figure 6-27 Applying a Develop preset in the Import Photos dialog box

While the application of presets at import is slightly limited (you can't apply some presets to certain images and different presets to other images), you can at least start down the road of being as efficient as possible when working in Lightroom. That's not to say that applying a preset somehow locks you into a specific set of parameters. The advantage of parametric editing is you can always go back later and make adjustments.

Figure 6-28 shows working on a single image from the previous import and zooming into the image to fine-tune the sharpening settings.

Figure 6-28 Fine-tuning the sharpening settings in Develop

The coin image needed a slight modification from the applied preset. Rather than keeping the Radius at .8, we reduced it to .7. We also increased the Detail setting to 60 to increase the high-frequency texture. We kept Masking the same but increased the Luminance settings. This was done in part to compensate for the rather high Detail settings.

Whether you use Lightroom presets in the Develop module, in the Library via Quick Develop, or when first importing into Lightroom, the key point to remember is that you need to have already created the presets. Not unlike sitting down to record actions for Photoshop, the process of creating presets needs time set aside outside the hubbub of a busy deadline. The upside to presets (as opposed to images processed by actions) is that any Develop preset you apply in Lightroom can also be unapplied.

We wish we could include a whole section on Lightroom's creative sharpening but, as we've indicated, we still consider that functionality under development. We advocate the trip from Lightroom into Photoshop and then back for Lightroom's organizational capabilities and, more importantly, the ability to make printing much easier.

Creating and Using Templates in Print

The Print module has become the primary place for both output sharpening for inkjet and photo lab prints, as well as harnessing Lightroom's capabilities for making and using templates to increase efficiency and reduce user error. Quick, everyone who has ever sent a job off to a printer with the wrong paper orientation, raise your hands. That's everybody, correct? This, as well as other potential spots for user error, can be eliminated. Yes, you do still need to load the correct paper size and type in the printer—there's not much Lightroom can do about that. But in the Print module, selecting the correct printer, printer profile, image orientation, output sharpening, and image size is distilled down to a simple click of a button—once you've made your templates.

Figure 6-29 shows an image in the Print module. On the right side are the primary module settings, and on the left are the Templates storage and the Collections access.

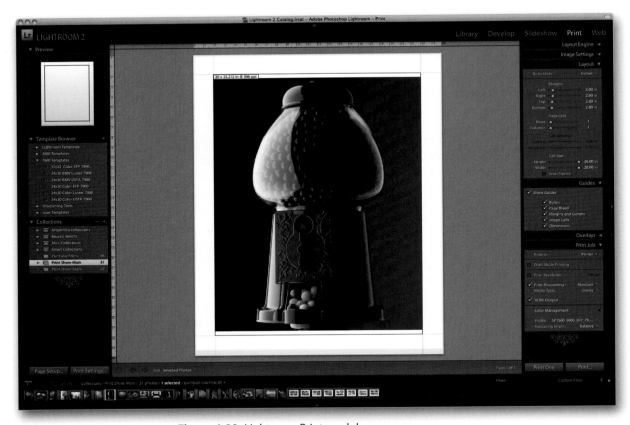

Figure 6-29 Lightroom Print module

The image shown in this Print module is one of the images in Jeff's main retrospective print show. At the bottom of the Print module is the filmstrip (very small) showing the other 30 images in the show. On the left is Lightroom's Collections panel (more about that in a moment).

The Right-Side Print Module Panels

The main emphasis when using Lightroom's Print module is to make printing simple, efficient, and painless. One of the most irritating aspects of printing is when your page setup doesn't match your image orientation. Accidentally printing a vertical image on horizontal paper sucks! Lightroom can easily handle that with the Rotate to Fit option shown in Figure 6-30.

At the top right in the Print module is the Layout Engine. As you can see in the figure, we're going to concentrate on dealing with a single image, not contact sheets or picture packages of multiple images.

Figure 6-30 Print module's Layout Engine and Image Settings panels

The Image Settings panel holds the most important productivity enhancement. When you select the Rotate to Fit option, Lightroom will automatically rotate a landscape image to fit a portrait paper setting (or vice versa). So you never need to change your paper orientation settings in the print driver, nor physically rotate an image, as you would in Photoshop. If you do a lot of printing, this is a simple and yet critical enhancement for workflow.

The next panel down is the main Layout panel, where you determine the page margins and the image cell size settings. While the overall page dimensions are set by the printer's page setup, the Layout panel determines how big the image will be and with what margin size. Figure 6-31 shows the margins set to 2 inches and the cell size set to a maximum of 26" x 20". This reflects the page size of 30" x 24" minus the margins. The actual size of the image will end up being 20" x 25.21" because the 20" dimension tops out due to the image's proportions.

Figure 6-31 Print Module's Layout panel

We've already covered selecting output sharpening in Chapter 5, but the Print Job panel is also where Lightroom handles color management duties. This is another area of potential user error, and simplifying the selection and use of output profiles makes Lightroom more efficient.

Figure 6-32 shows the Print Job panel as well as the drop-down menu options for the Profile and Rendering Intent menus.

Figure 6-32 Print Job panel

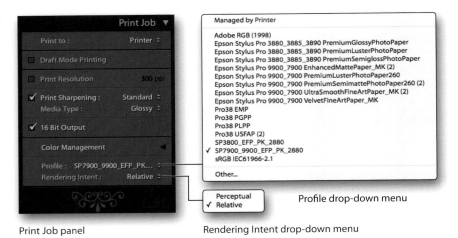

Print Job panel

Rendering Intent drop-down menu

Profile drop-down menu

Once you set Print Resolution and Print Sharpening, the primary settings you'll want to set and ultimately capture in a saved template are the Color Management settings. In the Profile menu (see Figure 6-32), you choose the profile you want to print with. You'll notice this is a short and abbreviated list; we have a lot more profiles loaded. If you click the Other option in the Profile drop-down, you can choose which profiles you want shown in the display. Figure 6-33 shows the dialog box that allows you to select visible profiles. Figure 6-32 also shows the Rendering Intent menu. Which is the best one? Unfortunately the only way to know is to use soft proofing (which Lightroom doesn't yet have) and see which intent works best with *your* image. For critical final color, we use Photoshop for soft proofing, which we combine with creative sharpening duties.

Figure 6-33 shows the list of installed output profiles. The only profiles that will appear are RGB printer-type profiles and optionally Display Profiles (which we translate to mean RGB color spaces such as Adobe RGB). The profiles selected are for the Epson 3800 printer and constitute the three papers Jeff commonly uses for that printer: Enhanced Matte (EMP), Premium Glossy (PGPP), and Premium Luster (PLPP).

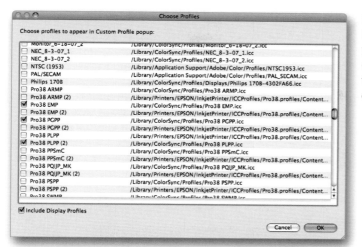

Figure 6-33
Dialog box you get from choosing Other from the Profile drop-down menu

The Left-Side Print Module Panels

The real joy in using Lightroom manifests itself with the capability to capture both the Page Setup and the Print Settings for your paper size, media type, and print driver. Figure 6-34 shows the Mac version of the Lightroom buttons and the Page Setup and Print dialog boxes for Mac.

Figure 6-34 Page Setup and Print Settings for Mac

Page Setup and Print Settings buttons

Page Setup dialog box

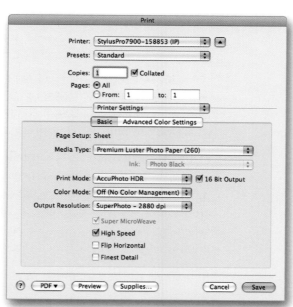

Print dialog box

The key thing to note on the Print dialog box is that on the bottom, the button says Save, not Print. This is because what you are doing is actually setting up Lightroom's print template to capture the page and print settings. Figure 6-35 shows a Windows Vista version of the Print Properties dialog box.

Since Windows print properties can set both page setup and print driver settings, Lightroom has a Print Settings button only on the Windows version (shown in Figure 6-35).

Figure 6-35
Print properties for Vista

We really must stress the potential for a greatly enhanced print workflow when capturing all the layout, print job, page setup, and print driver settings to store in a Lightroom print template. Figure 6-36 shows creating a new template.

One of the real time-savers Jeff has found is when you create a collection in your main Lightroom catalog, that collection will be available not only in Library but in the other modules, such as Slideshow, Web, and Print. This greatly facilitates the assembly of print shows and organized collections of images intended for printing.

Figure 6-37 shows the Collections panel in the Print module as well as the filmstrip at the bottom of the module.

Clicking the Create New Preset button

New Template dialog box

Figure 6-36
Lightroom Print Module
Template Browser panel

The saved template highlighted

Context menu for renaming
or updating the template

Collections panel
showing Jeff's
collections

Figure 6-37
Lightroom Print Module Collections panel

Film strip showing a single image selected

Film strip showing all 31 images selected

If it hasn't dawned on you yet, perhaps Figure 6-37 will help drive home the point. In Photoshop, to make a print you need to open the image, make sure it's the right size for the print, correctly set the page setup and the print driver, navigate through a myriad of dialog boxes for color management, and finally hit the Print button—and hope you set everything correctly. If you want to make one print from each of 31 prepared print files in Photoshop, you would need to do the exact same series of steps correctly, 31 times. In Lightroom, you would create one Print module template, select the 31 images, and click Print. Then all you need to do is make sure the printer is on and loaded with paper. Which seems the most efficient to you?

Consider also that with Lightroom, you don't need to spawn off a new file interaction each and every time you want to make a different sized print, and that output sharpening is automatically applied at the right output resolution for whatever size and media you are printing to. That's one of the reasons we really love Lightroom for printing.

Figure 6-38 shows the real payoff: the Print One button in Lightroom.

Figure 6-38 Lightroom Print buttons

To be clear, you can still use the old-fashioned Print button if you have a burning desire to see more dialog boxes (the main Print dialog box will come up). But if you've got everything set correctly, all you need to do is click the Print One button. That bypasses any other dialog boxes and sends the image to the printer. If you have one image selected, only that one image goes. If you have multiple images selected, they all get sent to the printer. Cool, huh? Makes using Lightroom just as a print utility program almost worthwhile.

The last part of the efficient Lightroom sharpening workflow deals with output sharpening when exporting images.

Image Sizing and Output Sharpening in Export

While we tend to keep images inside Lightroom and roundtrip to Photoshop only for creative sharpening or soft proofing for print, there are of course times when we need to produce consumable files for outside of Lightroom. Producing images for this book is a prime example, since we need to do output sharpening for CMYK output. When you need to get images out, use the Export dialog box, as shown in Figure 6-39.

Figure 6-39 Lightroom Export dialog box

The left side has the ever-present presets, which we'll address in a moment. On the right are a series of drop-down menus highlighting the main Export functions such as Export Location and File Naming. We want to concentrate on the Output Sharpening and the Image Sizing sections. Figure 6-40 shows the main Image Sizing portion as well as a drop-down units menu.

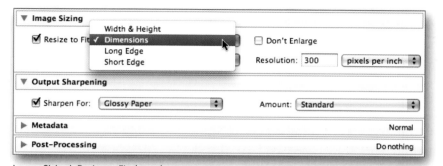

Image Sizing's Resize to Fit drop-down menu

Figure 6-40
Image Sizing panel

Units drop-down menu

Since output sharpening really can't be done until the image is at the final dimensions and pixel resolution, exporting the files from Lightroom means properly setting the Image Sizing panel settings. You can set the panel to Width & Height, which allows explicit sizing, but if your images vary in orientation or proportions, that is less useful than the other options. We find it easier to determine the Long Edge or Short Edge dimension, then set the Resolution settings. Figure 6-41 shows changing from Dimensions to Long Edge.

Figure 6-41 Changing Resize to Fit options

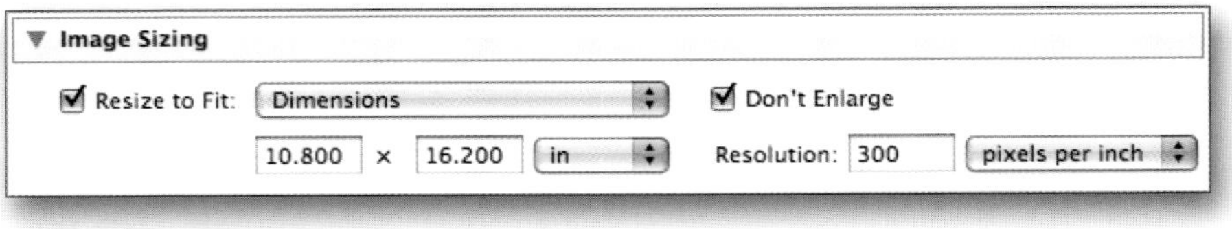

Resize to Fit using Dimensions

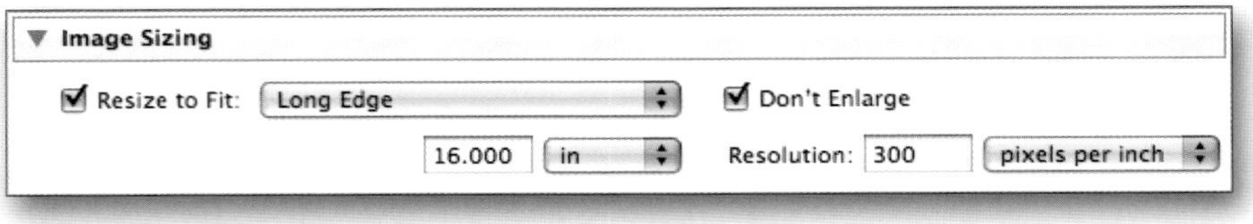

Resize to Fit using Long Edge

Here the Long Edge option is set to 16 inches at 300 ppi, which means that any images will end up 16" by whatever their cropped proportions dictate. Vertical, horizontal, and square images will all respect the Long Edge image settings.

After setting the final dimensions and resolution, then we can set the output sharpening. If we were going to output images for halftone reproduction, of course we can't do the sharpening in Lightroom, since only print and screen sharpening are offered. In that case, simply deselect the Sharpen For options. Figure 6-42 shows the Output Sharpening options.

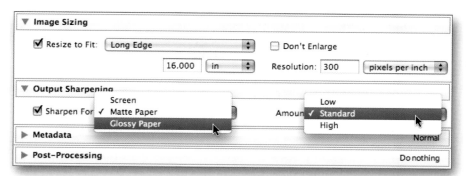

Figure 6-42 Output Sharpening drop-down menus (both are shown for clarity)

In this case, we want to select the Glossy Paper option for the output type and we tend to prefer the Standard Amount setting. If we were saving for Web output, we would use the Screen option instead of either of the paper settings. In testing we've determined that whether you are printing from an inkjet-type printer or a continuous-tone printer, such as might be used at a photo lab, the same respective media settings will work well. However, you may want to test which sharpening amount to use, as the machine settings on continuous-tone printers can have an impact on both the resolution and apparent sharpening.

Output Presets in Export

As might be expected, if you often have to export the same type of files, you would want to take advantage of Lightroom's capability to create Export presets. The whole purpose of drilling down on Lightroom's preset and template capability is to encourage their use. Creating and then getting used to *using* presets can greatly improve your workflow efficiency (and gives hope for having a life outside of digital imaging).

Figure 6-43 shows the New Preset dialog box in the Export module and the resulting preset saved in the User Presets menu.

Figure 6-43 Creating Export presets

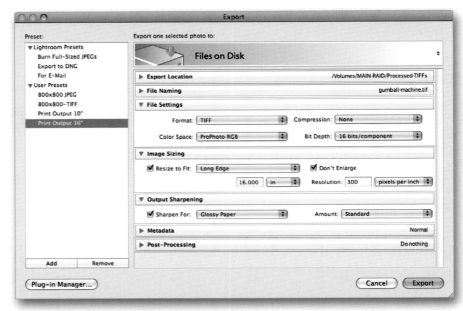

New Preset dialog box

Preset displayed in the User Presets menu in Export

Post-Processing from Export

Normally Lightroom can't take advantage of any actions or recorded macros. There are presets, templates, and defaults you can use, but you need to actively command their use. However, from Export you can use Lightroom to command Photoshop to process exported files using Export actions (which are really just Photoshop droplets).

Figure 6-44 shows the Post-Processing After Export drop-down menu.

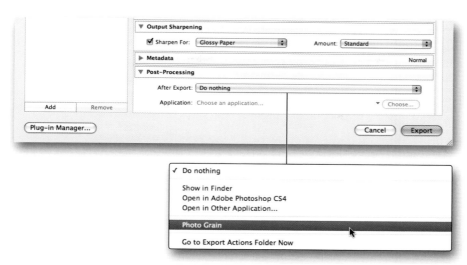

Figure 6-44 After Export drop-down menu in Post-Processing

As you can see, you have the choice to do nothing, show or open the resulting image, or actually use a Photoshop droplet that is appearing in the menu because we previously created and saved a droplet from Photoshop. Figure 6-45 shows the Photoshop Create Droplet dialog box, which is accessed from File > Automate > Create Droplet.

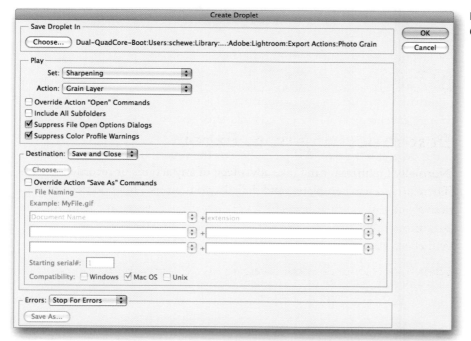

Figure 6-45 Photoshop's Create Droplet dialog box

If it looks like the Photoshop Batch dialog box, that's because that is what a droplet actually is: a saved Batch process in executable form. In this case we've created a droplet using the Grain Layer action from the Sharpening set (which you can download). We've saved the droplet to the location that Lightroom needs to be able to "discover" it from, and once saved it will show up in the After Export menu. Figure 6-46 shows that actual saved droplet.

The exact location to save droplets in for Mac is User/Library/Application Support/Adobe/Lightroom/Export Actions. The easy way to navigate to the folder is select the Go to Export Actions Folder Now command in the After Export drop-down menu.

For Windows users, well, the location is a bit more complicated:

Figure 6-46 The Photo Grain droplet

- Vista: User\Username\AppData\Roaming\Adobe\Lightroom\Export Actions

- XP: Documents and Settings\Username\Application Data\Adobe\Lightroom\Export Actions

Or just use the Go to Export Actions Folder Now command!

There are some caveats to using Photoshop droplets (either in Photoshop or Lightroom), the first being that the actual action that is embedded into the droplet executable is no longer editable once you've created the droplet. If you want to alter or edit the action, you'll need to save out a new droplet. If the droplet has a Save As step as part of the action, be very, very careful that the destination is known and understood. Once you save the action as a droplet, you can't really tell where files will be saved. If the file is saved in the same location as the original, you risk overwriting that file, which could be a disaster. We seriously suggest keeping Save As steps out of any actions you save as droplets to eventually be run from Lightroom. Be safe, not sorry, when it comes to automation—which is actually a good rule to follow with any sort of automation you may deploy, be it in Photoshop, Camera Raw, or Lightroom. It's better to know *exactly* what will be the final output than guess—particularly when it involves original images and unattended automated processes. Seriously, we don't want to automate you out of all your priceless original images!

SWEATING THE DETAILS

We admit that this chapter's drill-down on automation in Photoshop and the creation of presets in Camera Raw and Lightroom may seem like a whole bunch of work. It is, but the work done setting up an efficient sharpening workflow offers a return on investment that makes the sweat equity worthwhile.

The way we handle image detail is every bit as important to the final appearance of our images as is the way we handle tone and color. Yet detail control has, thus far in the short history of digital imaging, received far less attention than those other, admittedly crucial, aspects of imaging.

For years, we, like most practitioners, did sharpening as an *ad hoc*, seat-of-the-pants procedure until the realization slowly dawned on us that by flailing around trying different sharpening tricks, we often created extra work and produced results that, while acceptable, weren't nearly as good as they should be.

In evangelizing the workflow approach to sharpening that we've taken throughout this book, our goal has been to educate and inform, but also to move the discussion forward. We don't claim to have all the answers, but we hope you've found the ones we do have useful.

INDEX